The Legion of Christ
A History

ÁNGELES CONDE — DAVID MURRAY

The Legion of Christ
A History

Circle Press
NORTH HAVEN
2004

Spanish Original: *Fundación. Historia y actualidad de la Legión de Cristo* (2004)

Historical advisors:
    Salvatore Bonventre
    Javier García LC

The Legion of Christ: A History
Ángeles Conde – David Murray
© 2004 Circle Media, Inc.
Translated by J. Luxbacher and D. Koonce
English edition slightly adapted with authors' permission
Cover Design by A. Assad
Text Layout by A. W. Bennett, Inc.
Cover Photo: Tingüindín train station

Published by Circle Press, 432 Washington Avenue,
North Haven CT 06473
Circle Press is a division of Circle Media, Inc.

Printed in the United States of America
ISBN 0-9743661-2-9

Contents

Foreword   vii

Acknowledgments   xi

1. The Call   1
2. Childhood Influences   11
3. Called to Found   39
4. Church Bells Ring in Orizaba   51
5. Montezuma Seminary (1938-1940)   71
6. The Founding (1940-1941)   85
7. The Early Years (1941-1946)   101
8. God in a Hurry (1946)   111
9. A Latin American Breeze in Comillas (1946-1947)   137
10. Born Into the Church (1948)   157
11. God Draws Up the Route (1949-1955)   179
12. The Great Blessing (1956-1959)   195
13. At the Church's Pace (1959-1979)   221
14. Yesterday's Seed, Today's Harvest   267
15. "Cast Out in the Deep"   299

Chronology   309

Source Notes and Bibliography   313

Foreword

The Legion of Christ was founded in 1941, and since then, no one had ever put an account of its history into print. In January 2002, Ángeles Conde and David Murray undertook the challenge. The Legion agreed to help them track down sources and gain access to historical documents. Their task would not be easy.

As the congregation and its various apostolic works have grown and developed over the years, there has been increasing interest to hear about the path along which God has led us. Although a number of Legionaries had been conscientiously collecting documents, testimonies, and information dealing with important dates and events of the congregation throughout their lives, the actual writing of a history remained on the "to do" list. Our founder, Father Marcial Maciel, has never slowed down long enough to sit down and write it out—and he shows no signs of slowing down any time soon. A few years ago I found a small note that he had written and left lying on his desk. I think it speaks for itself:

Lord, I do not want to spend even one minute reaping the harvest, let me keep sowing. There will be others, let them reap the harvest; allow me the privilege of continuing to sow. There will be others, let them write the history; allow me the privilege of continuing to bring history about according to your plan. There will be others, let them look back and tell the story; allow me the privilege of not looking back at what has been accomplished. Allow me the privilege of continuing to sow up to the very end.

Those others have come, and it is time to remember and recount the history.

The authors of this book have carried out earnest, painstaking investigation, gathering testimonies of our founder and many other protagonists and eyewitnesses. The Legion of Christ has contributed to the effort by dedicating several people to the work of research. Oral history has been an extremely important element of this undertaking, as it is with any other work of recent history. The authors used already-existent sources as much as possible, complementing them with interviews and crosschecking them with ample written documentation. Finally, they put all the sufficiently documented data into order. We are indebted to Ángeles Conde for giving the history its final form: warm, easy-to-read, and reader-friendly.

The history of the Legion of Christ points back to God's initiative. As a branch growing out from the fruitful trunk of the Church, the Legion is written within the story of salvation history. God is the real protagonist, but he has desired to act through human beings who are free either to cooperate with his work, or to end up getting in its way. In the pages that follow, it is easy to discover this constant interplay between the human and the divine, thanks to the authors' spiritual sensitivity and historical acumen. Father Maciel has always wanted to avoid "getting in the way," and God has been able to "make use" of him to bring about his eternal design throughout the adventure of founding a new congregation. In this sense, the words of Eduardo Cardinal Pironio, then Prefect of the Congregation for Religious and Secular Institutes, to Father Maciel in the basilica of Our Lady of Guadalupe in Rome on 30 June 1983, are eloquent: "I would like to thank you for having been a faithful instrument, self-sacrificing, in some moments even crucified, but always a fruitful, paschal instrument in the Church in the work of transmitting this gift."

After working and living next to the founder of the Legionaries of Christ for the past 17 years, I have learned that one of the things he detests most is the option of facing life constantly worrying about "what others might think." His life option has been to live in the sight of God and be true to his conscience. Unpretentious, and without pious sighs or pompous show, he starts to feel uncomfortable whenever anybody starts referring to the Legion of Christ or the Regnum Christi Movement as *his* doing. He attributes any merit to the Holy Spirit and he recognizes himself plain and simple as "just an instrument."

It goes without saying that it would be impossible to write about the history of the founding of a new order within the Church without studying the history of the founder, the one chosen by God to "get the ball rolling." The authors of this book were aware of the fact, and since this is the first study on the founding of the Legion of Christ written on the basis of primary historical sources, they decided to cover the life of Father Maciel right alongside and together with the history of the work he founded. The truth is that it would have been futile to go about this project in any other way.

Throughout the length of these pages the human and divine are interwoven, for there is always a more than merely "natural" framework as the Church's history unfolds. Neither falling into pietisms nor ignoring the demands of historical objectivity, this book narrates the sequence of events in a way that allows readers to catch a glimpse of the sacred dimension common to all historical happenings within the Church. The authors have tried to present the transcendent significance of objective facts. A Christian vision will be our guide, therefore, and help us discover the narration's unsuspected depth. It is, at the same time, a simple, human story.

The subject at hand is not the happy result of some wisely-crafted human project; it is a walk of faith. God indicated what steps were to be taken at every turn. He placed the right people in the right places at the right time. He always reserved for himself the right to keep the "next step" up his sleeve. God's designs for this quickly driven history include continuous surprises and startling events, yet one cannot help but admire that the same unchanging principles appear over and over again. They are sound, refreshing principles that bear God's signature and continue to manifest themselves today. Hence this book will not only offer a look at the path that the Legion of Christ has walked from the founding of the congregation to the present date, but also key principles of the Legion's spirituality and apostolic charism.

It is worth adding that the Legion of Christ and Regnum Christi would never have been possible without the lives of so many men and women who believed without seeing, who placed their trust in God and who knew how to respond honorably in hours of difficulty: ecclesiastics, friends, benefactors, Legionaries, Regnum Christi members, parents . . . In a particular way, perhaps, we should perhaps mention the Popes who have always shown us special fatherly closeness and support. All of them, over the course of the Legion's short history, have instilled a good dose of faith, hope and love in the establishment of the Legion of Christ. Without a doubt they would deserve many more pages than those proffered in this present volume. In any case, their names and their good deeds are already indelibly written in salvation history and in the hearts of all of those who have benefited from their generous self-giving.

There is still a long road ahead, a lot of ground to be covered by historians and by the Legionaries of Christ. Those of us who feel most intimately bound to the Legion of Christ would like to express our sincere gratitude for this book, the first milestone on the road of future studies and research.

Evaristo Sada, L.C.
General Secretary of
the Legion of Christ

Acknowledgments

When anyone comes into contact with the Legionaries of Christ for the first time the instant, albeit unvoiced, question is always: "Who are these people?" It is a question that we have set out to answer in this book.

"The Legion of Christ: A History" makes ample use of the writings of Father Maciel's and audio recordings spanning many years. Whenever possible, we have corroborated our data with sources external to the Legion.

We would like to thank the Legionaries of Christ for their help in our task. Without their support our work would simply have been impossible.

A special word of thanks to the many people who, in so many ways, have contributed to this book: those who have allowed us to publish their writings or quote their testimonies, those who gave their time to answering our many questions, those who provided much-appreciated advice, and those who offered their encouragement and moral support as we researched, compiled and wrote.

We hope the reader will find an answer to our question in the pages that follow.

I didn't ask you for it . . . nor did you consult me.
But that is how you wanted it . . .
And you created me because you wanted to. I didn't ask.
Nevertheless, you wanted it that way,
and that's why you had me born into a Christian family,
allowed me to come to know your Son
and take part in his life through baptism.

I didn't choose it; I didn't ask.
You didn't consult me. You decided.
And that has been your way of acting all through my life.

You chose the road for me without asking my point of view . . .
You gave me an inscrutable mission,
one that infinitely surpassed my strength and my smallness.
I have the consolation of knowing that I wasn't the one
who chose my path: you chose it for me.
You chose my mission.
I don't know how much road lies before me,
but I am aware of your infinite love for me,
and how the heart of such a good God
has been an ocean of love for this small, flawed, miserable creature,
whose only greatness lies in your loving gaze.

Marcial Maciel LC, 10 March 1998

The Call

January 3, 1936. It was a chilly Friday night.

Marcial, a 15-year-old with 25 pesos in his pocket, had dreams of becoming a priest. He was lying under the open sky on a cold wooden bench at the train station of Tingüindín, a two-hour drive from his hometown Cotija de la Paz. He had thought of sleeping in a hotel, but he still needed to pay his fare to Mexico City and buy a ticket to Puebla, where the Carmelite Fathers were waiting to receive him into their seminary. Being away from home for the first time, he also wanted to have some money to spare for any unexpected expenses. "Better to sleep outside," he concluded, and bundled himself up in the well-worn brown overcoat that his brother José had lent him just before saying good-bye to his family that afternoon.

Shivering a bit on the hard planks of his makeshift bed, perhaps young Marcial said a few prayers. It had been a long, tiring, emotion-laden day, and it was time to get some sleep. He tried to clear his mind of all the thoughts, sentiments and impressions that were darting through his head. It had been quite a day. His suitcase had been prepared long in advance, and this morning he had only needed to slip in some last-minute items.

The list with everything he would need for the seminary had been sent to him months earlier, and he had been purchasing everything out of his own pocket: six pairs of socks, six handkerchiefs, one blanket, four sheets . . . He had worked hard over the past year to pull it off. After school, he made the rounds of the town and its outlying areas, collecting eggs and then selling them to Mr. Francisco Gallegos, who let him make a profit of five centavos on every hundred. He had also delivered blocks of wax, and for this, too, he received a few pennies each.

The waiting-year stipulated by his father was over, and the Carmelites had written to say they were expecting him on January 6. At two o'clock that afternoon, as Francisco Maciel was leaving to check up on Los Tazumbos, one of his ranches, Marcial approached his father. "Dad," he said, "the year is up; I'm off."[1]

His father gazed at him. Yes, a year ago Marcial had told him he wanted to be a priest, but he had not taken his son too seriously. Not wanting to see him go, he had explained that he didn't have the money to pay the seminary's monthly fee—and that Marcial should ask them for a discount. When the Carmelite Fathers agreed to cut the sum in half to 15 pesos, he had once again insisted that he could not afford it. Marcial wrote the Carmelites another letter, and they responded offering him a full scholarship. That was when his father had asked him to wait another year to think it over well.

"Dad, the year is up." He looked at his father with serene blue eyes waiting for his answer.

"He just looked at me," Father Marcial says, recalling that moment. "He gave me his blessing, cried a little, and walked away."[2]

His father would cry again nine years later at his son's first Mass in his hometown of Cotija, this time with tears of happiness. By then, Marcial would have already been at death's door more than once, been thrown into jail, been expelled from three seminaries, and established a new congregation . . .

The bus for Tingüindín left Cotija at 4 p.m. each afternoon, and Marcial found that he only had two hours to say goodbye to his mother, brothers and sisters, and go to the local parish where the Blessed Sacrament was exposed for First Friday devotions, entrusting his life and his future to Christ once again. He then ran to catch the bus, suitcase in hand. His mother Maura (more commonly called *Mamá Maurita*) had hugged

---

[1] cf. Marcial Maciel LC (January 1992)
[2] *ibid*

him and given him her blessing. From the very first she had approved of, encouraged and defended his vocation. Although no written records describe what took place at their farewell, it is not difficult to imagine that she shed a few tears as he departed.

Looking up at the stars from the dark shadows of that cold winter night, before fatigue got the better of him, maybe Marcial's eyes were also filled with tears, thinking of his mother. The train, they had told him, would arrive before dawn, and daybreak was now only a few hours away. So it was for real, after all! Just a few short hours more, and he would be on his way to the seminary to give his life for Christ. He had been waiting for this moment for over a year and a half . . .

I want to be a priest!

In May 1934, Marcial had just come back to Cotija after spending a few days of vacation in Mexico's capital. His mother had insisted that, while there, he drop in on his uncle, Bishop Rafael Guízar y Valencia.[3] Although he was the bishop of Veracruz, Bishop Rafael was living in Mexico City due to the religious persecution underway in his own diocese.

Since it was the month dedicated to the Blessed Virgin Mary, Marcial had gone to pray an afternoon rosary in Cotija's parish church. He was walking home as usual along Javier Mina Street that evening, carefree and alone, when he ran across two nuns—Sister Crucita and Sister Angelita, who stopped to speak with him, wondering why they had not seen him recently.[4]

"Marcial! Where've you been?"

---

[3] Details about Bishop Rafael Guízar Valencia and the seminary of Veracruz can be found in two works by Celestino Barradas: *Seminario, trayectoria de un siglo y realidad presente*, Mexico, "Ut Unum Sint" Jalapa Seminary, 1966, pp. 109–161, *Seminario, trayectoria y presencia, 1864–1999*, Jalapa, Ediciones San José, 2000, pp. 104–135. Renowned for his life of holiness, Bishop Rafael Guízar y Valencia was beatified by Pope John Paul II in Rome on 29 January 1995.

[4] Sister Crucita (a diminutive form of the Spanish word *cruz*, "cross") González Mendoza was a Sister of Guadalupe from Cotija. Angelita Pulido was a postulant.

"I was in Mexico City."

"Oh, in Mexico City . . . who'd you see?"

"My uncle Rafael."

"Then why didn't you stay at the seminary with him?"

"What for?"

"To be a priest."

"You mean I could become a priest?"

"Yes, of course you can be a priest!"[5]

The two women continued on their way. But Marcial did not: he retraced his steps, murmuring: "So I could be priest . . . I could be a priest . . . " He knelt down before the Blessed Sacrament and prayed. "I spoke to Jesus and I spoke to Mary. I listened to what they said to my heart and resolved to always follow God's will."[6] The adolescent felt "an incredible force that left no room for doubt"[7] that he was being called to love and serve God, dedicating himself to the spiritual good of all men and women. "I received this call from God with a real flood of joy. Kneeling, with my forehead pressed to the ground, I gave thanks, blessed and kissed the loving hand that reached out to me to offer me this incredible gift."[8]

That very night he told his mother he wanted be a priest. Mamá Maurita was overjoyed, but advised not to mention it to his father or brothers just yet. "Speak with your confessor and your spiritual director," she said, "and I'll let you know when you can tell dad."[9]

As a girl Mamá Maurita had wanted to become a Teresian nun, but her father, Doctor Santos Degollado, had opposed her decision and directed her towards married life. When she was 16, she agreed to marry Francisco Maciel (fifteen years her elder) in obedience to her father, something customary then. In fact, she had been told by her confessor "Your dad's will is, for

---

[5] cf. Marcial Maciel LC (January 1992)

[6] Marcial Maciel LC (1980s)

[7] Marcial Maciel LC, *Letter to the Legionaries of Christ and consecrated members of Regnum Christi* (Chicago, 20 December 1982–Rome, 29 May 1988)

[8] *ibid*

[9] Marcial Maciel LC (1980s)

now, God's will for you," and her uncle, the holy bishop Rafael Guízar, had also encouraged her to follow that path. It had not been a mistake: with her husband she had succeeded in forming a happy Christian home and raising a large family (11 of her children survived birth). Now, however, one of her sons felt a priestly vocation, and she knew that this was something holy, something inviolable. If his spiritual director, Father Raúl Manzo, thought that it might truly be God calling him, she would support his vocation—and take care of any possible difficulties at home.

Marcial began to write letters asking various seminaries and religious congregations to accept him. He wrote to the diocesan seminary at Zamora, and to orders such as the Salesians and the Carmelites. He didn't have the foggiest idea of differences between diocesan seminaries and novitiates of religious congregations. He was simply interested in becoming a priest, and it didn't matter to him where or with whom. Weeks and months went by. An elder brother had discovered his plans, and had been intercepting the mail. If letters were delivered, they never got to Marcial. One, however, finally slipped past his brother's checkpoint: the Carmelites in Puebla said they would be willing to accept him.

That was when Marcial's father told him to wait a year and to seriously think it over. So Marcial had waited, but never wavered inside. "Fortunately, I never had any doubts. They just never entered my head."[10] He had made his decision, and until he left for the seminary, the dream of becoming a priest absorbed his attention and colored all of his activities, by day and night. Even though the call had caught him by surprise and promised to alter all his plans for the future, his life-style did not change during the months that followed.

Mr. Francisco Maciel possessed several thousand heads of cattle and horses between his ranches, and at the time, a good horse and a well-stocked library constituted the pride of any Cotija resident. "Horses were his weakness,"[11] recalls Marcial.

---

[10] Marcial Maciel LC (1999)
[11] Marcial Maciel LC (28 November 2002)

Each year, if they wanted, Francisco Maciel allowed his children to trade in their horses. The last horse Marcial had was named *El Alazán,* and he didn't want to exchange it for another. It was his—and it wasn't going to be easy for him to leave it behind. When Father Maciel recounts his vocation, he always mentions that his two most costly sacrifices were to leave behind his family and his horse.

He spent that year in Cotija between school, home, the outdoors, the parish, and lively town fairs and fiestas. As he had done ever since he was a child, Marcial dedicated a large part of his leisure time to serving the poor, following his mother's example. Each day after lunch, he tried to go to a nearby chapel called *the Sanctuary* in the Gualajarita neighborhood, in order to spend some time alone with Christ. He usually had the chapel all to himself, and he liked being able to speak with Jesus Christ in the intimate silence of the Eucharist: one-on-one, heart-to-heart. Kneeling only inches from the altar, he spoke to "his Friend and Lord," asking Christ to help him get the permissions he needed to go to the seminary.[12]

Another of his favorite pastimes would also help him prepare for his future mission. When he was smaller, he had discovered a vantage point that was ideal for thinking and dreaming. He climbed a hill known as the *cerro Calabazo* (pumpkin hill) and sat down on his rock. From that simple lookout post, he had a commanding view of the whole Cotija valley. Looking to the left he would see the red-tiled roofs and the parish bell tower nestled in folds of the green slopes. Straight ahead, far off in the distance, his gaze would fade into the last blue silhouette of the mountain range. He asked himself about the countries and the people that lay beyond, behind the mountains; other worlds he knew nothing about. *Where were their lives leading them?* he would wonder. To his right, the cemetery spread out below him at the foot of the hill. At times Marcial would leave his rocky perch, preferring to walk amidst the tombstones, many of them already forgotten, overgrown, their en-

---

[12] Marcial Maciel LC (1999)

gravings blurred. Their titles no longer made any difference: all the honors, the dignities and the riches were dust, ash and nothingness. Time, fleeting and implacable, had erased their memory. A deep nostalgia for eternity engulfed him. Wasn't there anything that doesn't pass away, that resists the ravages of time? Something worth struggling through life for? *God*, he found himself concluding: *God alone*.[13]

"My life and my existence were engraved there when I was 11 or 12," says Father Maciel. It was there that he found "an absolutely sure handhold":

> There have been strong tremors, there have been hurricanes, there have been tidal waves; death will come, and I will be reduced to dust, ash, to naught . . . but I will always be caught up in God, and I'll always be with him—in time and in eternity.[14]

He was a boy with deep thoughts, but above all one profoundly familiar with prayer, especially after hearing God's call. In moments of solitude and on his knees before Jesus, he delved into what being a priest would mean for him:

> I grasped that if I really wanted to be a priest, I'd have to resemble Christ the priest. That's how I'd summarize the fundamental conclusion I arrived at during that time of waiting: "Christ suffered and died to redeem me, so I have to suffer and die to help redeem others with Christ. I'll be a worthy, useful priest to the plain and simple degree that I identify myself with Christ crucified: Christ, sorrowful and suffering; Christ, who accepted death to redeem humanity, out of love.[15]

He concluded that God called him to the priesthood to love, laying down his life like Christ. Indeed, God would guide the train of his entire life along those two inseparable, parallel tracks: the track of love, the track of suffering.

---

[13] cf. Marcial Maciel LC (3 March 1965)
[14] Marcial Maciel LC (3 March 1965)
[15] Marcial Maciel LC (1980s)

The train!

It was three o'clock in the morning, and Marcial sprang into consciousness. There was no mistaking the muffled, rhythmic sound of the train in the distance. He saw the gigantic black form thundering towards Tingüindín, and soon there was a sharp screech of metal on metal and one last hiss as the train ground to a halt. Marcial pulled on his coat and hoisted up his suitcase. The bell rang, and Marcial, excited and fully awake, quickly climbed the steps onto the train. It was all set: he was on his way.

At noon, after nine monotonous hours, the train finally pulled into Yurécuaro station. Twenty hours had already passed since leaving home, and a hungry Marcial took advantage of the chance to eat lunch. There was no rush: the Guadalajara-Mexico Express would not be leaving until 8 or 9 that evening. Marcial slept on the train that night, but not much. There were too many thoughts going through his head: he missed his family; he wondered what seminary life would be like; he thought about the mysteriousness of being called by God; and maybe he tried imagining himself celebrating Mass or preaching in the missions. "I am going to be a priest!" he repeated to himself, and this thought was enough to fill him with enthusiasm.

He arrived in Mexico City on 5 January 1936.

"18 Otoño Street, please," he said to the taxi driver, giving him Bishop Rafael Guízar's address,"—in Atzcapotzalco."

The bishop of Veracruz was happy to see him.

"What are you up to, boy?"

"Well, uncle, I'm going to Puebla. I'm going to join the Carmelites—and my mother told me I should stop by and say hello."

"Never mind the Carmelites. You'll stay here and try to discover God's will."

"No, uncle, I can't . . . my dad didn't say I could."

"I'll write your dad."[16]

There was no way he could say "no" to a bishop, especially considering the bishop was his uncle, and widely consid-

---

[16] cf. Marcial Maciel LC (January 1992)

ered a living saint. So Marcial stayed in Mexico—and the good Carmelites were left waiting for him in Puebla.

Only seven years had passed since Mexico's federal government and the Catholic Church had reached an agreement signaling the end of the Cristero War and religious persecution in Mexico, but persecution against the Church continued unabated in the states of Veracruz and Tabasco. Bishop Guízar had therefore decided to run a clandestine seminary[17] from Mexico City, under the direction of Father Jerónimo Ugalde.[18]

On January 6, the day after Marcial's arrival, Father Ugalde came looking for the "bishop's nephew".

"Get your bags," he said, "and let's get to the seminary."

"He didn't ask me if I wanted to or not. And so, well—off I went to the seminary."[19]

Many years later Father Maciel would pray aloud, speaking to God about his priestly vocation. "I didn't ask, and you didn't consult me," he said.

> I didn't choose it; I didn't ask. You didn't consult me. You decided. And that has been your way of acting all through my life . . . . I cannot doubt your fidelity and love. The task and road that you chose for me have been costly: undoubtedly. But how beautiful they've also been, how full of mystery![20]

Marcial placed his trust in God, and his daily prayer was simple: "Let me be faithful to the end."[21] He was just a brand-new, 15-year-old minor seminarian: there was no way he could foresee the mission God would give him before a few short months had passed.

---

[17] It was clandestine because the Mexican State still prohibited the Church from running seminaries.

[18] Father Jerónimo Ugalde was the acting superior of the minor seminary at the time, but was not officially the rector, a position that the bishop of Veracruz reserved for himself throughout his entire life.

[19] Marcial Maciel LC (4 September 2002)

[20] Marcial Maciel LC (10 March 1998)

[21] *ibid*

II

Childhood Influences

Young Marcial manifested profound determination to follow his vocation, and his life would have a deep effect on many people. In the face of difficulties and setbacks, his love for Christ seemed only to grow stronger. Can Marcial's lifework be traced to the innocent remarks of two country nuns?

Before returning to Marcial's formation at the minor seminary in Veracruz, it is important to take a look his childhood, in an attempt to discern what moved him to feel such an ardent desire to give Christ his life.

Cotija de la Paz

Marcial was born on 10 March 1920 in Cotija de la Paz, Michoacán. It was an excellent place to grow up: a good Christian family, and a cultured, prosperous community with long-standing customs and religious traditions.

Cotija de la Paz is a small, out-of-the-way town that is really not "on the way" to anywhere; until a few years ago, it was only serviced by one road. It was hard, therefore, to end up there by chance or accident. Travelers who wanted to reach Cotija just couldn't miss it. From Guadalajara they traveled to Zamora, and from there on, the route to Cotija was straightforward, leading through gentle mountains, winding hills, and lush fields. Crops of corn, wheat, sugarcane, beans, chickpeas, strawberries, onions, potatoes and alfalfa stretch out on both sides of the road. There are many springs, water is plentiful and the earth is rich and red. It is a fertile region.

During the 1800s and until about 1950, the town was composed of a core group of Creole families, descendents of the first settlers of the Cotija valley. Since Cotija remained on the sidelines when the federal government drew up Michoacán's transportation and communication networks, most of the children and grandchildren of these original families have since gone to live in the big cities, especially Guadalajara and Mexico City.

The red-tile-roofed, adobe houses are brightly whitewashed, and their stout wooden doors are always open to passers-by. At the center of the town stands the parish church.[1] "It's not a very big town; peaceful, picturesque," remembers Marcial's sister, Olivia. With a touch of nostalgia, she adds, "we loved it."[2]

At the beginning of the 20th century, the atmosphere in Cotija reflected an elevated level of cultural, human, and social education, and these values were also carefully cultivated and safeguarded at the Maciel household. Describing the spirit that reigned at home as she was growing up, Maura, another of Marcial's sisters, explained:

> Each of my brothers was like a father, friend, and mentor; someone who looked after me, loved me, educated me, and formed me in all the different areas, and who was concerned about me—from how I could keep myself entertained, to how to acquire all the things I needed. If mom wasn't around, they'd even comb my hair or prepare me something to eat. . . . We were very close . . . . Pepe would play the mandolin, someone else would be playing the guitar, another singing, and another reciting something.
>
> I remember once learning entire chapters of Hamlet simply by ear, because Pancho played the part of Prince Hamlet. He'd be practicing, and I'd be learning it at the same time. I'd say to him: "Lend me the book!" He'd say, "No. No, it's no good for you to read the book,

---

[1] More information on Cotija's history can be found in the following books: Heriberto Moreno García, *Cotija* (Monografías Municipales del Estado de Michoacán), Morelia, Government of Michoacán State, 1980, pp. 246 ff; Father José Romero Vargas, *Cotija, cuna de trotamundos* (vol. I), Mexico City, Progreso, 1973 and *Cotija, durante las revoluciones* (vol. II), Mexico City, Amic Editor, 1978.
[2] Olivia Maciel (27 August 2001)

because you won't understand it. It's better to listen. Or, if you want to learn a part, I'll recite it to you out loud."

When they went out and bought books, they'd always make sure to bring books for us, and not just for them . . . . They had some deep intellectual discussions. . . . They debated a lot, and dad, who was a great conversationalist, showed interest in all the current ideas: he knew a lot. So, it was a very pleasant life.

They sang: Francisco, my brother, sang beautifully; mom sang; Pepe doesn't have much of a voice . . . but Pepe and his guitar still can't be parted.[3]

It is said that in the olden days notes from a piano or violin often drifted out from the ancestral homes and into the streets. The sounds of pianos and violins are less frequent now, but another, more native type of harmony can be heard on the streets and in Cotija's air: a intermittent symphony of braying, chirping, barking, crowing and lowing. Bell towers exchange notes of clanging revelry, and a rooster, apparently disoriented by all the commotion, cock-a-doodle-doos all day long.

In Cotija, as in many other villages in Michoacán, time is in no hurry. It follows the rhythm of the seasons, harvests, popular festivals, and liturgical feasts. Cotija de la Paz—"Cotija of Peace"—is a fitting name.

The Faith in Cotija

In the Cotija of yesteryear, faith was born and nourished at home. It was cultivated in the parish and it ripened within one's conscience. It was outwardly expressed in both the trivial and the most important social occurrences. There were many deeply rooted traditions: Sunday Mass, regular catechism lessons for the children, First Friday confession and

---

[3] Maura Maciel (30 August 2001). Maura is the youngest daughter of Francisco and Maurita Maciel. In the time period that she mentions here, Marcial had already gone to the seminary. Father Maciel also remembers the atmosphere that characterized their daily home life: songs, music and interesting conversations with his father, especially at lunch and dinnertime.

communion, novenas, religious processions and festivities on liturgical solemnities or on the feast days of patron saints. Nor was it uncommon to pray the daily rosary together as a family: sometimes at home, and sometimes kneeling together—parents and children—at church in the evening. A confusing murmur of voices would echo in the evening shadows as some families recited a Hail Mary while others prayed the Our Father or the Litanies. The Maciel children liked praying in the church, because after they had finished, their parents bought them peanuts and candies and allowed them to play and run for a while in the town square before returning home ("So that we'd sleep well,"[4] explains Olivia).

Mr. Francisco Maciel Farías and Mamá Maurita, Mrs. Maura Degollado Guízar,[5] had formed a large family. Of their 11 children, seven are still alive:[6] José, Olivia, Teresa, Maura, Blanca, Javier the younger, and Marcial. Francisco, the oldest son, died in 1973. Alfonso, who came between José and Marcial, died of typhoid fever in 1940 at the age of 22. Two other boys, Reinaldo and Javier, died due to illnesses when they were five and six.

Mamá Maurita guided Marcial and his brothers and sisters, encouraging them to live their faith with their whole heart. It meant spontaneous, cordial dialogs with Jesus or Mary, and small gestures of love, just like the ones they would offer to their parents or friends. She worked constantly and gently, and had a knack for educating.

There were rosebushes, gardenias, jasmines, and lilies in the Maciels' garden,[7] and Mamá Maurita would tell them, "The one who's best behaved gets to take the first rose to the Blessed Sacrament, and the runner-up will take the second rose to the Blessed Virgin Mary." They would run to the rose bushes, and

---

[4] Olivia Maciel (27 August 2001)

[5] In Mexico, children receive two surnames: their father's principal surname, and their mother's. Marcial, for example, would be known as Marcial Maciel Degollado.

[6] At the time of printing (2004)

[7] cf. Marcial Maciel LC (September 1986)

say: "Mom, the first bud is opening up. It'll be open tomorrow!"
They monitored the progress of each budding rose. As soon as
it blossomed, they would drag her out to the garden. "Look at
this one, mom! Who wins?" Mamá Maurita would clip the stem
and give it to the lucky "this week's best-behaved."[8]

Marcial will have won his share of opportunities, even
though it was a challenge for him to stay in line. He was lively
and restless at home, and had the reputation of being mischie-
vous. He simply liked to take to the streets, visit people's
homes, make new friends, discover things and carry out all the
"brilliant ideas" he came up with. Olivia was the next oldest,
and she was the one Marcial played with most when they were
little. "We were always up to some shenanigan or another,"
recalls an amused Olivia. "There were these rocking chairs,
and we had a great time rocking until the chairs would fall over
backwards, with us on the floor . . . Don't get the idea that we
were quiet little things—we weren't sedate. Poor mom!"[9]

Even today Cotija's hustle and bustle comes to a halt at
noon—on the street, in the fields, and in many of the shops and
stands—when the parish bells announce that it's time to pray
the "Angelus."[10] In the Maciel home, the whole family and all
of the employees gathered to offer this prayer to Mary. After
lunch, Mamá Maurita generally took her children to the image
of the Sacred Heart that dominated her bedroom, and prayed
with them for a short while. She would read to them and explain a few pages of a book by Saint Enrique de Ossò (founder
of the Teresian sisters who had educated her in Zamora) entitled: *Fifteen Minutes of Prayer*. She would teach them how to
chat with Jesus, one-to-one, as friends with their friend. "It
wasn't the reciting of prayers: it was dialog."[11]

---

[8] cf. Marcial Maciel LC (25 August 2001)
[9] Olivia Maciel (27 August 2001)
[10] The residents of Cotija would also stop all their activities and spend a moment
in silence when the bell rang in the evening to announce the parish priest was
giving Eucharistic benediction.
[11] Marcial Maciel LC (7 October 1999)

Charity in Cotija

For the Maciels, being Christian above all meant loving one's neighbor. Francisco Maciel had several ranches, and he always ensured that his employees and their families had everything they needed. He lent them farm tools and plots of land, provided them with seed, and split the harvest with them. "He'd give them one or two or three milk cows so that they'd always have food for their families, and they got to keep the calves"[12] remembers Father Maciel. If some week there were no returns on their work, he would give his employees whatever they needed to support their families. Mamá Maurita dedicated herself to taking care of their employees' health and piety, teaching them the catechism, speaking to them about God, and inviting them to Mass on Sundays. The Maciel household was a school of faith, Christianity and peace. It was a "Christian community."[13]

Francisco Maciel was a disciplined, hardworking man whose honesty had weathered many a trial. He had a firm, enterprising character, and finished whatever job he started. He did everything he could to educate his children in the school of hard work. All his boys were to learn a practical profession, like how to be a plumber, electrician or tailor. He thought that some day his business luck might change, and his sons would have to earn their daily bread: that had been his own personal experience. He had started out with nothing (his grandparents had not recovered their mines in Río de las Huertas after the Mexican war of independence). His first job had been as a baker's apprentice, and he had worked as a clerk at a sugar factory before purchasing and managing numerous ranches. For his trade Marcial chose carpentry, learning the basics in Cotija's carpentry shop. He made his own school desk, which he proudly brought with him to María Neri's school one day.

At home, Francisco Maciel had laid down a rule: absolutely forbidden to speak badly of anyone, be he or she a

---

[12] cf. Marcial Maciel LC (11 October 1999)
[13] *ibid*

family member, neighbor or stranger. Christian love begins with speaking well of others.[14] But it was Mamá Maurita, above all, who taught them and gave them an example of what it meant to truly love God, doing good to everyone, especially to those most in need. She kept a ready supply of food on hand so as to be able to take care of their needs. "Oh, there were some real line-ups at the front door of our house!" exclaimed Olivia. "Whoever needed medicine, whoever needed food or clothes . . . everyone who came was offered a helping hand and left the house consoled. Mom was a great listener."[15]

Marcial remembers the lineup of sick and poor who would come to ask his mother for help.

> [She] had something for everyone. She always had a good word for everyone. She provided them all with medicine. . . . They came when their husband or child had died. . . . She'd console them, sit with them, speak to them about God, about patient acceptance, about heaven, and so on. There was a continuous mission going on here.[16]

One of Marcial's sisters, Maura, saw in Mamá Maurita a genuine teacher who taught by example more than by words.

> I believe that the lives we lived, the experiences we had at her side, her standards of judgment, and her way of facing life's many difficulties and situations were our genuine teachers, because mom—yes, she gave us kitchen recipes or told us how to do certain practical things, but when it came to the formation of our hearts and our consciences, I think she led and formed and educated us by her example. She wasn't a person who . . . would lecture a lot, or use arguments. . . . We had some-

---

[14] The opposite of the Spanish *maledicencia* (speaking badly of others: "backbiting", "slander-mongering", "badmouthing", etc.) is the Spanish term used here: *benedicencia* (creating esteem or actively speaking well of others).
[15] Olivia Maciel (27 August 2001)
[16] Marcial Maciel LC (7 October 1999)

thing a lot more powerful, the witness of her own life: how to authentically live married life, motherhood, detachment, helpfulness and mutual forgiveness . . . that was the basic rule."[17]

"Maurita helped those who were sick," added Rosita Silva, a neighbor from Cotija who knew her from her childhood.

There were so many needy people in Cotija. She'd give them corn, beans . . . Someone told her that they wouldn't let me work because I was poorly dressed. She said that if necessary, she'd go down on her knees so that they wouldn't take away my job—and they didn't fire me. I truly loved her like a mother. . . . Before she died, she left me money to buy a sweater.

She had "her" poor, there in Cotija, but she didn't talk about it. She gave, without anyone being any the wiser. . . . So much misery in the villages, so many needy people. She always took her children along. All her children are just as spontaneous. They see someone in need, and they help. . . . She was never in on tasteless things. She never spoke [ill] about people, ever. She said that appearances often deceive because even if you do happen to see something, you shouldn't say things about people. . . . She never said "no" when there was anything she could do.[18]

Marcial's mother gave the best of her time to her husband, her family, the poor, the bedridden and the dying, and she also ensured that her children learned to give of themselves in the same way. She assigned a different poor person of the neighborhood to each of them, and it was up to them to visit, help, and look after their material needs—bringing them clothing, food and medicine—as well as their spiritual ones: helping them to live in peace and harmony with others, and bringing them closer to God.

---

[17] Maurita Maciel (1 September 2001)
[18] Rosa Silva (17 July 1982)

Marcial enthusiastically imitated Mamá Maurita's example. In the afternoon, after school was out at María Neri's place, he liked to walk around the outskirts of town to visit his friends among the poor, especially in a neighborhood called "la Rinconada," a ramshackle collection of adobe or wooden lean-to's with rudely-nailed boards, straw roofs, earthen floors where the children slept, and a bed for the couple. Outside each dwelling there was a fire where the people would prepare their food, a metal hot-plate for making tortillas, and a pen where they would keep—at best—a pig or a few chickens. Marcial would constantly be on the lookout for things to bring them and they too shared whatever they had.

> I spent a lot of time after playing and classes going to visit my folk. There were lots of dads and moms whose children I godfathered, and they all received me warmly:
> "Marcial! Güerito! Wouldn't you like a taco? A corn tortilla with salt?[19]
> "Well—all right. Okay."[20]

A child couldn't do much for them on a material level, and Father Maciel remembers that it was mainly a matter of giving them love along with any help he could offer.

> If I didn't have anything on hand, at least I served them, smiling, respecting them—the poorest, the most destitute.
> My principle was to consider them kings, treating them with that type of respect and charity—incidentally, I used the same principle at the apostolic school[21] ... with all of the apostolic boys: that is why I ad-

---

[19] In Mexico, *Güero* or its diminutive *Güerito* are commonly used to designate people with blond hair or fair complexion.

[20] Marcial Maciel LC (10 March 1993)

[21] Legion of Christ minor seminaries are called "apostolic schools". Minor seminarians are commonly referred to as "apostolic boys" or simply "apostolics".

dressed them all with the "usted"-form,[22] and always treated them as people deserving deep esteem and respect.[23]

He had seen his mother treat everyone humanely, with dignity, gentleness and respect. She, in turn, had inherited her exquisite manners and politeness from the Degollado Guízar family line. Her tactful expressions and signs of courtesy were directed to everyone, impartially: friends, neighbors, servants and the poor who would knock on the door each day asking for help.

Father Maciel calls her "a living gospel," and says that she taught them how to live. She also taught them how to face death with a Christian attitude by taking them along to visit the dying, if the disease was not contagious. Once one of Marcial's teachers fell gravely ill, and Mamá Maurita took her children along to visit. She had them kneel around the bed and entrust the teacher's soul to God. After the teacher died, Mamá Maurita helped them meditate on the meaning of life and death, of time and eternity, and on the vanity of all worldly things.[24] It was not an isolated instance. She taught them how to help the moribund prepare for a good Christian death, with their souls in the peace and in the grace of God.

Were these experiences too powerful for such little children? They were Christian experiences. They were experiences of a life that hits most people hard: rich and poor alike, regardless of how good or hard-bitten or worldly they might be. That is what was in store for the people of Cotija, at least, when war hit the area. It was home to good, honest, clear-eyed, simple people, who struggled forward and sought to live a serene Christian life even when peace was absent.

Marcial was six years old, almost seven, when the soldiers arrived. Of the night the fighting started at the beginining of

---

[22] "Usted" is the polite form of addressing people in Spanish, usually reserved for adults. Friends address each other with the familiar "tú"-form. Perhaps in no other context than the apostolic school are adolescents referred to as "usted", as a sign of respect.

[23] Marcial Maciel LC (10 August 2001)

[24] Marcial Maciel LC (7 October 1999)

1927, Marcial clearly remembers the "big tigers" in a silent-screen movie they were watching in the Figueroa hotel, which opens onto the town square. All of a sudden they heard shouts and gunshots in the street, and the fighting drew nearer. Father Maciel recalls:

> Just after the movie started, we started to hear shots and the volley of bullets. The army colonel of the zone was in the theater along with a number of the soldiers. When they heard the firing, they left and began shooting back at the Cristeros. The Cristeros were out to kill them, and they, to kill the Cristeros.[25]

With shouts and shoves, the whole group of grown-ups, young people and children rushed through the overturned chairs towards the hotel's exit. They wanted to leave, some to take refuge in their homes, others to join the Cristeros.

The Mexican Catholics' armed uprising to defend the Faith erupted in Cotija that night, just as it would in many other settlements of Michoacán and the Mexican Republic during those months. The Cristero War had begun.

"There were many victims" continues Father Maciel, "children, women, men and, of course, soldiers."[26]

The two older Maciel brothers—Francisco and José—ran home, unaware that Marcial had been left behind in the Figueroa hotel. Earlier that evening, at dinner, they had announced that they were going out to see the movie. Marcial had asked to go along. His father had said "no," but he went all the same. Scared by the shooting and the commotion, and trying to get out into the square, Marcial took a wrong turn and ended up in the hotel kitchen. "But—what are you doing, güerito?" asked a woman named Mrs. Tolento.

> She took me up the stairs to the roof, and then they brought me and another group down a stairway to a neighboring house. We spent the night there. At sunrise,

[25] Marcial Maciel LC (10 March 1993)
[26] *ibid*

the Cristeros had gone to the mountains, so they [the soldiers] left town.[27]

While Marcial passed the night safe and sound, his mother was crying and praying. They told her that her son had likely been hit by bullets on the street, but she couldn't go out to look for him. It was a night full of anguish. How relieved she was the following morning when she saw Mrs. Tolento appear with a sheepish Marcial in tow! Several years later Mamá Maurita would take care of two women who had contracted leprosy: Mrs. Tolento and her sister. She cared for them until they passed away.

It is difficult to read Father Maciel's description of what he witnessed and lived as an 11- or 12-year-old without being moved. "You all know already how leprosy eats away at people," Father Maciel later said about his adolescent years when his mother, that "living Gospel," cared for Mrs. Tolento.

> It rots their flesh; their fingers fall off in pieces, pieces of hand and nose. You can see their teeth until they fall out too; the ears: that is how death picks away at them, stricken. They are a mass of pus. I was very struck by my mom's charity when she went to take care of her [Mrs. Tolento], washing her clothes, bringing her meals . . . . Each evening she would take a trusted maid and one of us along with her, and she'd leave us there in front of the house, so that the leprosy wouldn't spread to us. One night I let my curiosity get the better of me and went in to see what it was all about, but I could do no more than stick my nose around the door before I went running out . . . from that stench of leprosy.[28]

After the rowdy night in 1927 when the Cristero uprising reached Cotija, many residents left to join the Cristero fighters in the mountains.

Jesús Degollado Guízar, Mamá Maurita's brother, was initially the Cristero division general and chief of operations in

---

[27] Marcial Maciel LC (10 March 1993)
[28] *ibid*

Michoacán-West, Jalisco-South, Colima and the State of Na-yarit. When the Supreme Commander of the *Cristero* National Army—General Gorostieta—died, Jesús Degollado took his place. Another brother, Rafael, also fought in the war. Inter-viewed at the age of 98, he still got worked up when asked why the Cristeros fought:

> We fought . . . for human rights. To implant human rights, to respect human rights in Mexico. . . . We weren't allowed to hear Mass; we weren't allowed to get married in the Church. . . . If they found a priest saying Mass (let's say in my house in Sahuayo)—just imagine this, if you can—they'd seize him, arrest him, and shoot him. Or they'd banish him, they'd leave him half-dead, they'd cast him out. My house in Sahuayo was turned into the local Mayor's house. It was unbearable.[29]

In his own way, he explains it well: human rights were being violated in Mexico: one of these rights was the right to re-ligious freedom.

In 1854, liberal factions took power in Mexico with the tri-umph of the Ayutla Plan, and began promulgating increas-ingly anticlerical laws. In 1855 the Juárez Law suppressed ec-clesial jurisdiction in the civil and criminal spheres. The following year, 1856, the Lerdo Law led to the expropriation of Church property, and a 1833 decree, recognizing no religious vows, was re-proposed. The liberal Constitution of 1857 disre-garded the Catholic identity of Mexico, and Article 123 made worship and any external practice of religion subject to civil laws. The end of a three-year war between liberals and conser-vatives spelled the end of this "moderate" constitution, as the government of Benito Juárez began to decree radically anticler-ical measures through the Reform Laws (1859–1860). These laws expropriated all diocesan and religious priests' goods,

---

[29] Rafael Degollado (21 November 2001). Rafael, now 100, is still alive at the moment of publication.

suppressed religious orders and outlawed religious life, and recognized only civil marriages as valid. Cemeteries and works of charity were placed in the hands of the state, and the Church was prohibited from running its schools. The apostolic delegate was banished, and Mexico's representative to the Holy See was called home. Most bishops were expelled from the country.[30] With Article 123's power to interfere with public worship, the government declared a separation between church and state that meant, in effect, the state's total liberty to bar any religious activity. This one-sided and hostile separation was cast in iron when, on 25 November 1873, President Sebastian Lerdo de Tejada incorporated the Reform laws into the national constitution.

The 1900s began with the Mexican Revolution, a civil war that developed into a violent persecution of religion. The Villistas of Pancho Villa, the Zapatistas of Emiliano Zapata, and the Carrancistas of the radical Venustiano Carranza struggled against each other to gain control. Carranza came out triumphant. He persecuted the Catholic Church and promulgated the violently anti-religious Constitution of 1917: elementary education was to be religion-free, all public manifestations of the Faith were prohibited, and the practice of religion was henceforth permitted only in houses or places of worship monitored by civil authorities. Episcopal residences and seminaries were to be liquidated, and any real estate administered by the Church was to be expropriated. Article 130 declared that all priests were to be Mexican, that they did not have the right to vote nor did they have a right to associate for any political purpose, and that their studies had no civil value. Furthermore priests were prohibited from publicly criticizing the law. Diverse Mexican State legislatures appointed themselves to determine the maximum number of priests permitted, "according to the needs of the area."[31] It was, in other words, open persecution. The exiled Mexican bishops raised their voices

---

[30] In January 1861 alone, the Mexican government expelled 6 bishops from the country.
[31] cf. Mexican Constitution of 1917, Article 130

from their lands of exile, but their pleas—like the pleas of Popes Benedict XV and (later) Pius XI—fell on deaf ears.

The situation was exacerbated when Plutarco Elías Calles came to power on 1 December 1924. He shut down Catholic schools and churches, and had the archbishop of Mexico City put on trial (he was subsequently exonerated). Calles expelled foreign priests on 15 March 1926 and the Vatican's apostolic delegate to Mexico, Jorge José Caruana, two months later, on May 10. On 14 June 1926 he signed certain amendments to the Penal Code that were promulgated on July 2. They made worship-related infractions into crimes punishable by law. Priests had to "register" with the state if they wanted to exercise their ministry. The Mexican Catholics asked for a referendum to propose amendments to the Constitution, and presented Calles with two million signatures, but the president would not bend. After the bishops received a not overly explicit answer to their consultation with the Holy See, they called the faithful to offer "peaceful resistance," suspending all public worship.

In their Pastoral letter of 25 July 1926, the bishops announced to the Mexican faithful that from that day forward, finding themselves unable to comply with the government's dispositions, all public acts of worship requiring the presence of a priest would be suspended, effective 31 July 1926.

The people were not left without priests or without the sacraments: the Church had simply been forced underground. The faithful rallied around their bishops. Almost no time passed before the government responded by locking the churches. Many priests were tried and sentenced, and in one state of the Mexican Republic, the governor threatened to shoot anyone who brought a child to be baptized, attempted to get married within the Church, or simply listened to a sermon. The bishops insisted on the route of dialog, but the people finally lost patience and took up arms. These were the "Cristeros" (a name given to them by the Federal Army soldiers, who heard them die to the cry of "Long live Christ the King!": *Viva Cristo Rey!*). The first manifestations of the Cristero War emerged at the end of 1926, and by January 1927, urged on by the *National*

Religious Liberty Defense League, it had spread to a number of states. The conflict would continue until July 1929, and it would leave Mexico's soil stained with the blood of innumerable martyrs.

The State of Michoacán, with its profound Catholic roots, ended up deeply involved in the Cristero uprising.

Marcial clearly recalls having witnessed El Tacotal in the summer of 1927, a skirmish mentioned in General Jesús Degollado's memoirs.[32] He was in the garden when he heard the shouts and the gunfire not far off. Climbing up a tall ash tree, he could clearly observe Corona Hill, "the high hill with pine trees that you see from my house on Mina Street," and he tried to follow the progress of the clash between the Cristeros and the Callistas.[33]

It is likely that it was on this occasion, a few days before the actual confrontation, that he and his sister Olivia saw a battalion of more than 300 thirsty Mexican Army soldiers marching past in the heat. "We walked along beside them, offering them water."[34] They were federal troops sent to fight the Cristeros, but that was not the point. They were human and they were thirsty, and the Catholics of Cotija walked along with them, giving them something to drink.

"The battle took place a few days later, and we had 50 to 80 wounded men stretched out on the sidewalk of this block," recounts Father Maciel,

> There was one doctor to attend to them, and we—my brothers and I and other families—helped the doctor, following his instructions to assist those with gunshot wounds. There were some who were bleeding to death, so we'd tourniquet the arteries to stop the bleeding, and for others, we'd put some substances that the doctor gave us on their wounds. We'd help them all to pray and

---

[32] Jesús Degollado Guízar, *Memorias,* Mexico, ed. Jus, 1957, pp. 58–66
[33] cf. Marcial Maciel LC (24 September 2002)
[34] Marcial Maciel LC (9 October 1999)

ask God for pardon and—if it were his will—to cure them.[35]

Mamá Maurita had taught the children how to accompany those who were dying. They would still have much more to learn. Battles may not have been very common in Cotija— but executions were. There were many martyrs.

> There, in front of the parish church where the school is now (back then there was no school; it was a field), they'd keep the prisoners, the ones they had brought down into town, and they'd shoot them. They'd always shoot them between 2 and 3 in the afternoon. I remember one redhead in particular, and another man. . . . I have all the faces here before my mind's eye, and the firing squads, and all of them shouting, "Long live Christ the King!" and falling down, shot dead.[36]

Those killed would often be put on public display, hanging from the cedar trees in front of the parish.[37]

> When we went to the 6 a.m. morning Mass, there'd often be a man, or two or three, hanged from the trees in the town square. They were Cristeros who had been caught. They would hang them because they belonged to the side that was helping to fight to defend the Faith.[38]

The Maciel family fled Cotija for Jamay and Zamora, because the Cristero general Jesús Degollado was Mamá Maurita's brother, and this put the whole family in danger.

---

[35] Marcial Maciel LC (9 October 1999)
[36] Marcial Maciel LC (25 August 2001)
[37] *ibid*
[38] Marcial Maciel LC (10 March 1993)

The martyrdom of José Luis[39]

At the beginning of February 1928, Marcial was in his grandmother's house in Sahuayo[40] when he heard news in town that made his blood run cold: José Luis had been captured!

His name was José Sánchez del Río, but his friends called him José Luis. He was a 14-year-old who, despite the age difference, had been a good friend of Marcial's for several years. They played together, and José Luis would invite him to visit the Blessed Sacrament. Marcial was seven years his younger, and admired him. A year earlier, before turning 14, José Luis had proposed going off to the mountains with the Cristeros. Marcial went home to ask his parents for permission, and logically (he was six) had to bring back a negative answer to his friend: *I can't. My mom won't let me.*

José Luis's parents didn't authorize him to go either, but he wrote several letters to General Prudencio Mendoza, asking to be admitted into the Cristero's ranks. Because the boy was still so young, the general refused. José Luis insisted, saying that even if he were not strong enough to carry a rifle, he could at least help the soldiers take off their spurs, prepare their meals (he could fry beans and cook), and grease the weapons. After several months of persistent petitioning, the general assented, and put him under the orders of Cristero leader Luis Guízar Morfín. His mother was still against it. "Mom," said José Luis imploringly, "it has never been easier for us to win heaven than now."[41] He left for the mountains.

---

[39] Information mentioned in this section can be found in: Promoters of the Cause for Canonization, Informative Bulletin *"El mártir de Sahuayo,"* (Sahuayo, Michoacán, June 1997), Knights of Colombus, Council 4627, Sahuayo, Mexico (an account of José Luis' death prepared by the commission promoting his beatification) as well as: Lauro López Beltrán, *La persecución religiosa en México*, Tradición, Mexico, 1987, pp. 216–223; Marcial Maciel LC (10 March 1993); Antonio Rius Facius, *Méjico Cristero*, 2 volumes, Mexico, Asociación Pro-Cultura Occidental, 2002

[40] The Guízar-Valencia side of the family.

[41] Lauro López Beltrán, *La persecución religiosa . . .* , p. 219, Promoters of the Cause for Canonization, *"El mártir de . . . "*

There was a clash near Cotija seven months later. When government troops shot the horse Cristero leader Luis Guízar was riding, José Luis jumped off his own mount. "Here, take my horse. Save yourself, even if they kill me. I'm not essential here: you are."[42] Luis Guízar accepted, certain that they would spare José Luis's young life. The boy, rifle in hand, covered his retreat until he ran out of bullets. He was taken by the Federal Army. They locked him up in Cotija on 6 February 1928, and brought him to Sahuayo, his native town, the next day.

That was when the news spread: *They've captured José Luis! He's being kept in the church baptistery!* The local mayor, Rafael Picazo, had converted the parish church into barracks and horse stalls, and it would now also serve as a prison. On the night of February 7, José Luis killed the deputy's fighting cocks. Picazo, infuriated, came to see him on Wednesday morning, and José Luis told him: "God's house is a place for coming to pray, not for keeping animals."[43]

General Guerrero of the Federal Army asked 5,000 gold pesos in ransom for the boy. It was an exorbitant sum. Although several men from Cotija and Sahuayo (Francisco Maciel among them) tried to help José Luis's father Macario Sánchez round up this quantity of money, they were unable to get anywhere near the necessary amount. In exchange for his son, Sánchez offered everything he owned, house and furniture included, but Picazo was bereft of reason: "Money or no money, I'll order him to be killed right before his father's eyes!"[44]

"We all knew about it by then, and we were worried," says Father Maciel, who was just about to turn eight.

> All his friends, we got together to pray. You can imagine what kind of emotional state we were in. We were sad, and cried a lot, asking the Blessed Virgin for him not to

---

[42] Lauro López Beltrán, *La persecución religiosa . . .* , p. 219, Antonio Rius Facius, *Méjico Cristero . . .* , p. 312
[43] Lauro López Beltrán, *La persecución religiosa . . .* , p. 220
[44] cf. *ibid*, p. 221

be killed. At the same time, we asked that he'd not betray his Faith.[45]

From the street José Luis' strong voice could be heard singing inside the church: "To heaven, to heaven, to heaven I long to go . . . "[46]

Around 6 p.m. on Friday, 10 February 1928, José Luis was brought out from the church and taken to the *Refugio* hostelry, where a military operations center had been set up. José Luis seemed as content as could be: they were offering him the crown of martyrdom. He wanted nothing more; he was going to die for Christ. He asked for some paper and ink, and wrote to María Sánchez, one of his aunts:

> *Sahuayo.*
> *February 10, 1928.*
>
> *Dear Aunt,*
> *I have been sentenced to death. At 8:30 tonight the moment I have desired so much will arrive. Thank you for the favors that you and Magdalena did for me. I find myself unable to write my mum. Tell Magdalena that I've received permission to see her one last time and I think she won't refuse to come.[47] Give my regards to all, and— as always, and for the last time—receive the heart of your nephew who loves you a lot and longs to see you. May Christ live, may Christ reign, may Christ rule over all! Long live Christ the King! Long live Blessed Mary of Guadalupe!—José Sánchez del Río, who died to defend the Faith. Be sure to come. Farewell.[48]*

The federal soldiers removed José Luis' shoes, sliced the soles of his feet with a knife, and then beat him forward, shoeless and bleeding, forcing him to walk towards the cemetery. His friends and relatives accompanied him, and Marcial would never forget the heroic example his friend gave them in the last moments of his life:

---

[45] Marcial Maciel LC (10 March 1993)
[46] Promoters of the Cause for Canonization, *"El mártir de . . . "*
[47] This was so that she might bring him communion.
[48] Lauro López Beltrán, *La persecución religiosa . . . ,* pp. 221–222

They took him out of jail and led him along the street of the town with his hands tied behind his back, to shoot him. . . . At the corner of each block the mayor would stop them and say:

"We are going to kill you. We are going to shoot you, to torture you. Why don't you just shout 'Death to Christ the King'?"

"Long Live Christ the King!" was the answer. [49]

Once they reached the cemetery, the soldiers drove everyone out from the area where he would be killed. They had already dug a grave for the boy, and he stood next to it.

"Do you have a message for your father?" the chief of the guard said with a sneer in his voice.

"That we'll see each other in heaven," responded José Luis firmly. *"Long live Christ the King! Long live the Virgin of Guadalupe!"*[50]

Shots rang out. The coup de grâce brought José Sánchez' life to an end with his battle-cry still on his lips.

Father Maciel says that the slaughter of José Luis left a lasting impression on everyone, especially those who were only children at the time.

It has always been beautiful to remember; but there's always a touch of sadness to it. I'd say to our Lord: "Why did you choose him to be a martyr, and leave me behind?" I greatly envied this friend of mine, because he had succeeded in giving his life for Christ.[51]

By 1929, neither army had achieved victory. Despite superior numbers and military power, the soldiers of the federal government had not succeeded in quelling the activity of the Cristeros. They never would. The Cristeros, however, were limited by scarce resources, and had to face the difficulty of obtaining both arms and ammunition. The Catholic population

---

[49] Marcial Maciel LC (10 March 1993)
[50] Promoters of the Cause for Canonization, *"El mártir de . . . "*
[51] Marcial Maciel LC (10 March 1993)

continued to suffer violent wrongs and there was a ceaseless shedding of blood. That was when the United States of America began diplomatic negotiations through their ambassador in Mexico, Dwight Morrow. Ambassador Morrow proposed a peace agreement between the opposing parties, represented by President Emilio Portes Gil for the one side, and by the archbishop of Morelia and apostolic delegate Leopoldo Ruiz y Flores, and the bishop of Tabasco, Pascual Díaz Barreto, for the other. Archbishop Ruiz y Flores had sent a consultation to the Holy Father Pius XI, and the telegram response came dated 20 June 1929:

> 1. *Holy Father anxious for peaceful, lay solution.*
> 2. *Complete amnesty for bishops, priests and faithful.*
> 3. *Devolution of bishop's houses, parishes, and seminaries.*
> 4. *Unhindered relations between the Vatican and the Mexican Church. Only under these conditions can you sign, if you judge it appropriate before God."*[52]

On June 21 an agreement was reached (known in Mexico as the *arreglos*) and President Portes Gil declared amnesty. It fell to General Jesús Degollado Guízar through his representative Luis Beltrán to work out the deal to disband the Cristero army, and peace agreements between the Church and the Mexican government were completed during July 1929.[53] In August, General Degollado asked his Cristero troops to lay down their arms in a gesture of heroic obedience, and with tears in his eyes said:

> His Holiness the Pope, through the apostolic delegate— for reasons of which we are ignorant but which, as Catholics, we obey—has indicated that public worship resume, without the repealing of laws . . . As Christians, however, we can cling to an intense satisfaction, much

---

[52] José Gutiérrez Casillas, *Historia de la Iglesia en México*, Mexico, Porrúa, 1974, p. 413

[53] cf. Jesús Degollado Guízar, *Informe rendido al vicepresidente de la Liga Nacional Defensora de la Libertad Religiosa, licenciado Miguel Palomar y Vizcarra*, (21 November 1953). As quoted by Antonio Rius Facius, *Méjico cristero . . .* , pp. 390–391

richer for the soul: to fulfill our duty, and to offer the Church and Christ our most precious holocaust, that of seeing our ideals shattered before the world. But yes, by the Living God, we harbor the supernatural conviction, supported and nourished by our Faith, that in the end, Christ the King will reign in Mexico: not partially, but as absolute sovereign of all souls.[54]

The Mexican government had promised amnesty to the entire Cristero Army, but the reality was very different once weapons had been laid down. One by one, the Cristeros were assassinated by low-ranking federal authorities acting on government orders. General Jesús Degollado escaped with his life only by fleeing to the United States.[55]

Mamá Maurita—along with General Jesús Degollado, their brother Rafael and their other siblings—had learned from their mother[56] that real respect for the Catholic Church must translate into a sincere veneration for bishops and priests, Christ's representatives, and loyal, simple adherence to the Church's teaching. Going back a generation further, Prudencio Guízar and his wife Natividad Valencia had done their best to form a Christian family. Two of their sons (Mamá Maurita's uncles) were consecrated bishops: Blessed Rafael Guízar Valencia, bishop of Veracruz, and Bishop Antonio Guízar Valencia of Chihuahua. Through another son, Emiliano, they would become the grandparents of Luis Guízar Barragán, future bishop of Saltillo. Marcial Maciel was their great-grandson.

Life in Cotija was seen through the prism of faith. One day, after an informal conversation about the events of his childhood, Father Maciel remarked, "You'd breathe in the Church's

---

[54] Jesús Degollado Guízar, *Proclamation,* in Alfonso Alcalá Alvarado (coord.), *Historia general de la Iglesia en América Latina, V: México,* Mexico, Paulinas, 1984, p. 333

[55] General Jesús Degollado was later able to return to Mexico; he lived in Guadalajara until his death in August 1957. The classic Spanish book on the Cristero Wars is Jean Meyer's 3 volume *La Cristiada,* Mexico, Siglo XXI, 1973. See also: Jean Meyer, *La persecución religiosa en México,* in "Ecclesia," vol. 14, 2000; Antonio Rius Facius, *Méjico Cristero . . . ;* and Lauro López Beltrán, *La persecución religiosa . . . .*

[56] Mamá Maurita's mother was also named Maura.

teaching all day: regarding life, death, suffering, the value of faith, of giving their lives for Christ. Everything."[57]

Everyone has childhood memories, and certain episodes are recalled with particular fondness and introspection. The things that Father Marcial experienced in a strong Catholic family during a religious persecution helped forge his values, interests and attitudes into a life of service to Christ.

Why did the spark of Marcial's vocation flare up so quickly and keenly, and why has it been able to burn with such unchanging intensity? From among the many elements that came together to shape Marcial in his childhood and adolescence, it is possible to underline two. First: he saw the bright light of many men and women who died for their faith, especially the example of his friend José Luis. Second: he experienced the intense, ardent, warming fire of love that burned steadily in the center of their home—Mamá Maurita's constant, tactful charity and her limitless love for others. Two elements, one lesson: to love Christ to the point of death and, in the meantime, to spend it loving others with authentic Christian charity, as Christ would.

There was another lesson, as well. At home, in the cemetery, on the hill overlooking his town and during long, thoughtful teenage afternoons, Marcial had meditated upon the value of time and eternity. Time was short: he would have to use it well. His thoughts had become certainties, and these certainties led him to make a decision: he would spend his entire life loving and serving others; he would dedicate his life to Christ.

---

[57] Marcial Maciel LC (25 August 2001)

Marcial Maciel was born in Cotija de la Paz, Michoacán, México, on 10 March 1920.

Marcial Maciel was baptized in the parish of Cotija de la Paz on 18 March 1920. In less than a century (1860–1940) Cotija gave the Church six bishops and four founders, two of whom have already been beatified. The following are related to Father Maciel: bishops Rafael Guízar Valencia (beatified), Antonio Guízar Valencia, Francisco González Arias, Luis Guízar Barragán and José María González Valencia, as well as the Servant of God María de Jesús Guízar Barragán, founder of the Guadalupan Servants of Christ the Priest (Siervas Guadalupanas de Cristo sacerdote).

View of Cotija's town square in 1929, after the government pardoned the Cristeros who fought for religious liberty in Mexico during the Cristero War, to defend their Faith. Jesús Degollado Guízar, Father Maciel's uncle, was the last General-in-Chief of the National Army of the Cristeros.

Marcial Maciel's parents, Francisco Maciel Farías and Maura Degollado Guízar (Mamá Maurita) on the wedding day (Zamora, Michoacán, 23 November 1912), along with Mamá Maurita's parents, Santos Degollado Carranza and Maura Guízar Valencia (center) and her brothers and sisters.

Marcial Maciel heard the call to be a priest when he was 14.

Father Maciel's mother, Maura Degollado Guízar (1895–1977). Because of her Christian testimony as wife and mother, her loving dedication to the poor and her veneration for priests, the cause for her beatification has been introduced in Rome.

During his years as a seminarian, Marcial Maciel actively participated in the demonstrations that led to the opening of the churches
in the city of Orizaba, and later in the state of Veracruz. The
churches had been closed because of the government's policy of
religious persecution. This 1937 photograph is from Father
Mondragón's pictorial-historical photo album dealing with those
events in Orizaba. Young Marcial appears in the center.

From 2 September 1938 to 17
June 1940, Marcial Maciel
was a student at the inter-
diocesan seminary of Mon-
tezuma (New Mexico, USA).

III

Called to Found

The neighbors were not supposed to know that there was a clandestine seminary on 43 Aquiles Serdán Street in Atzca-potzalco, Mexico City.[1] If word reached the government, the Veracruz minor seminarians would be evicted, and the property confiscated. To keep their presence secret, therefore, the students rarely left the house, and they talked in whispers all day—even during recess. "When we played, it was in silence . . . so as not to attract attention. A very sorry way of living . . . ," remembers José Refugio Rodríguez Hernández, a fellow seminarian of Marcial's in the seminary of Veracruz.[2] It was hard for young teenagers to refrain from shouting and cheering as they played soccer and basketball, but, conscious of the danger, they succeeded in doing so.

Due to the seminary's considerable financial difficulties, the seminarians lived in poverty. The house was what it was, and no more: one room had been converted into their dining hall, and the boys' common living quarters was an improvised construction made of wooden planks ("a type of big box" is how Father Maciel now describes it[3]).

Despite the many things they lacked, the boys took the first steps of their vocation there with exuberance. At least that was Marcial's experience:

> Really, it would be extremely difficult for me to express all the happiness, all the joy with which I lived those

---

[1] More information on the Veracruz Seminary during the period 1936–37 can be found in Celestino Barradas, *Seminario, trayectoria . . .* , pp. 148–149.
[2] Father José Refugio Rodríguez (14 August 2003)
[3] Marcial Maciel LC (January 1992)

months, my first months in the seminary. The Lord
poured himself out into my soul and heart. . . . For me,
the days passed by like a dream: no sacrifice was too
costly, and there was no sacrifice I didn't seek out in
order to please God. I always tried to have an ear open
to the Holy Spirit, alert to perceive what he wanted from
me, and I always tried to buckle down to doing my duties as perfectly as possible, considering them as the
most genuine expression of God's holy will for me. So,
my days passed in silence, studying, working, playing,
praying. Recreation periods and holidays: what beautiful hours spent at Jesus' feet before the tabernacle! I'd
give my whole life to be able to relive one of those moments there with him.[4]

The Lord poured himself out into my soul and heart: this inner
experience of Christ's fidelity and love must have provided
ample compensation for a great many sufferings—because
young Marcial did not find seminary life easy.

Marcial was homesick for the first month or so. He would
sometimes cry at nights remembering Cotija, his family, his
mother . . . and his horse. He attempted to offer God his sadness, concluding that it was all worth it, "because to love God,
you have to do this—and much, much more."[5] This thought
would help him get to sleep.

Then there was the question of studies. Marcial had left his
hometown with a sixth-grade education. In Cotija de la Paz, he
had gone to the school of María Neri, an unmarried woman
who dedicated her whole life to giving catechism classes, per-
forming Christian works of mercy, and teaching the children.
The whole town loved her, and during times of persecution she
had been arrested on several occasions for refusing to stop offering religion classes. In Cotija there was no junior high school.
Young people who wanted to study had to go to cities like

---

[4] Marcial Maciel LC (January 1992)

[5] *ibid*

Zamora or Guadalajara, often as boarding school students in institutes run by religious congregations.

"I didn't know what a verb was, or a complement or a subject," explained Marcial. "I started to find out in January, 1936."[6]

With a great deal of effort, Marcial caught up on grammar and math in the seminary, and began studying Latin, which he found difficult. "I didn't have a good memory," he claims. Perhaps that was true when it came to memorizing verb charts, but much of what is written in these pages is taken from Father Maciel's personal recollections; and at 60, 70 or 80-odd years of age, he has proved capable of recalling names, dates and places; prices and menus; geographical and historical details, and even the weather conditions at the time. His Latin studies were a continuous effort to "keep at it, over and over and over," Father Maciel says, "but the Holy Spirit helped—because I came up with some formidably lucky answers!"[7]

Food in the seminary was poor, usually little more than black coffee in the morning, rice, beans and chickpeas. As a child, Marcial had come down with typhoid fever that had almost left him dead for lack of antibiotics. He had been confined to bed for 40 days with a high temperature, and it permanently affected his gastrointestinal system. In the seminary, the harshness of the menu caused him to develop a stomach ulcer. Many years later he would confess that he lived in "a tremendous state," and that he sometimes "couldn't sleep."[8]

They were not easy months, but despite it all, he was happy.

Vacations alongside Father Maldonado

Vacations rolled around quickly, just three months after his arrival. On the last day of March, his companions from Veracruz went home to spend the holidays with their families. Marcial and the rest of the seminarians from other parts of the

---

[6] Marcial Maciel LC (January 1992)
[7] *ibid*
[8] *ibid*

country who were unable to travel home could spend their vacation in different parishes of the diocese of Veracruz. The parish in Ixhuatlancillo, to the north of the city of Orizaba, fell to Marcial and another seminarian. It served several rural communities (called "congregations") under the care of Father Antonio Maldonado. The parish included many little towns where the native tongue was not Spanish, but Náhuatl, an Uto-Aztecan language.

From Father Maldonado—who was, according to Father Maciel, a very holy, very zealous priest, and an indefatigable missionary—Marcial learned what it meant to give one's life to save souls, even those in the remotest corners of the world. Father Maldonado visited all the hamlets right up to the foot of the extinct *el Pico de Orizaba* volcano (Orizaba Peak), taught the catechism, and prepared everyone he could to receive the sacraments. He would bring them the Eucharist, celebrate Mass, and care for the sick and dying. Giving yourself totally to others and giving yourself totally to Christ were two sides of the same coin.

The seminarians lived in Jesús María, the town that Father Maldonado used as his base.[9] In the morning the priest gave them Latin and Spanish classes, and in the afternoon they would do pastoral work in the surrounding communities. Outings with the priest turned into genuine missions. "I'd take them to the sierra on horseback, getting soaked and sleeping on bedrolls. I'd warn them," recounts Father Antonio, "'if you want to suffer: let's go! And they'd say: 'Yes, don't worry, that's what we came for, Father!'"[10] Esther, his sister, added: "He—Father Maciel—was very self-sacrificing. He'd give up his bed . . . sleep on the floor and send his blankets and pillow and everything to Victorita in Texmalaca."[11]

---

[9] *Jesús María* is now called *Mariano Escobedo*. Its name was changed in the times of the anticlerical governor Adalberto Tejeda.

[10] Javier García LC, *Interview with Father Antonio Maldonado and his sister Esther* (Salamanca, 25 August 1965)

[11] *ibid.* Victorita was a woman actively involved in her parish who assisted the poor and those most in need.

Besides Ixhuatlancillo, Marcial also accompanied Father Maldonado to congregations such as Santa Ana, Tusantla, Mamantla, La Perla, La Ciénega, and Chilapa. Nature is breathtaking at the base of Orizaba's majestic Peak: Madonna and calla lilies flower like tropical reefs along the roadside, and the branches of banana, mango and avocado trees—adorned with fresh orchids—bend under the sweet weight of their fruit. The tracks and trails wind by waterfalls and through craggy mountain passes, rising and falling with the rugged terrain, obliging wayfarers to travel on horseback, by donkey or on foot.

Getting from one place to another required long hours of travel—sometimes days—under a broiling sun. Upon arrival to a settlement consisting of perhaps 10 or 12 houses, they would sometimes find that all the country-folk were out working in the fields, with no one at home to greet them. They would wait, and then teach catechism or pray the rosary with the people, visit the sick and get them ready to receive the sacraments. Marcial appreciated the opportunity to do all this pastoral work, working all day and even part of the night.[12] His seminary vacations were physically taxing, but Marcial considered them a piece of heaven on earth.

As he lived with Father Maldonado in the "congregations," the sight of simple, humble, pure-hearted faces would remind the young seminarian of the *Los Tazumbos* workers and the poor people he loved so much in the Rinconada area outside of Cotija. As a boy, he used to explain the sacraments to his father's employees. Marcial's favorite task then had been to help prepare the children for their First Communion. Bishop Pío López, who was bishop of Tacámbaro at the time, would come to the Maciel's *Los Tazumbos* ranch each year for a large festival. The town would meet him half a mile out and greet him with banners and flowers and songs. Once in the hacienda, there would be Mass and the bishop would give first Holy Communion to the children who had been prepared.

---

[12] Marcial Maciel LC (January 1992)

There were Confirmations and marriages too. The town then celebrated by organizing a rodeo.

Just like the poor outside Cotija, the poor of these mountain communities around Jesús María were hungry to hear about God. Marcial had no problem adapting the Gospel message: he used songs, skits, pictures and props to get everyone involved. There are still people in Jesús María who remember having catechism classes with Marcial. "He was very enthusiastic and lively," says Clemente Hernández. "He had a great voice for proclaiming the word of God, and singing and all."[13] He also remembers a Holy Thursday in La Perla where "Father Maciel" had preached to them (they addressed him as "Father", even though he was still a 16-year old seminarian).

"He got everyone crying on that occasion," recalls Esther Maldonado, "because he would say: 'Look at the scene! Just look at the scene! If it doesn't move you to see the sight of the Blessed Virgin with her son, our Lord . . . if you don't weep, may the very stones shed tears!'"[14]

"I was very discouraged with the town," narrates Father Maldonado, "and I said, 'Look, the people here are low-spirited. They don't want to help fix the church. I don't know what to do with them.' So then he [Marcial] got the people enthused; he put on a raffle, and things were a bit better."[15] His chicken and goat raffles turned out to be memorable.

The church in Jesús María didn't have a statue of the Sacred Heart, and so, in order to raise the funds needed to purchase one, Marcial decided to raffle off a goat. The farm folk liked the idea—so much so that they gave the goat back to him after the first round so that he could raffle it off again. And again. Sometimes the lucky winner would accept the chicken or goat; others would return it so he could continue raising money. Marcial succeeded in collecting enough money to buy them a wooden statue of the Sacred Heart which had been carved in Barcelona.

---

[13] Clemente Hernández (1997)
[14] Javier García LC, *Interview with Father Antonio . . .* (25 August 1965)
[15] *ibid*

The system convinced Father Maldonado. "Those were the first raffles we put on," he said. "Later we caught on to the method, and put on more."[16]

The call, the mission

The summer ended and the new school year began. Although Marcial had arrived near term's end the year before, and had only had three months of classes, he advanced to second-year with his classmates (for Latin, too). He quickly adapted to the seminary schedule: studies, prayer, games, classes, and work.

Marcial put his whole heart into his formation (his adult life would confirm that half-measures weren't for him). If he decided something was worth doing, he did it wholeheartedly—and to the very end. When God's will was involved, he didn't even waste time to think twice. He simply took the step and dove in, head-first. Things have not changed: it is Father Maciel's characteristic style. First he exclaims "Of course!" and then he figures out how to go about it. He once mentioned that from the time he entered the seminary, he had promised the Holy Spirit two things: first, that he would always listen to him, and secondly, that he would never refuse him anything. Maybe God wanted to see if he could take him at his word, because it was not long before the Holy Spirit did speak to him, clearly.

God had something to ask of him.

Friday, 19 June 1936, was a big day in the seminary. It was the solemnity of the Sacred Heart. Marcial had helped out the day before, doing some chores and preparing the chapel for the feast day. On Friday, the seminarians had a special breakfast: two sweet rolls, bananas and hot chocolate rather than the humdrum coffee and re-fried beans. They had the usual time to clean their rooms and study, and time for recreation. Marcial took the opportunity to pay a visit to Jesus in the chapel. The

---

[16] Javier García LC (25 August 1965)

chapel was resplendent for the festivity, and he took it all in: the tabernacle, the candelabrum, a profusion of tuberoses and lilies . . .

There in the chapel, telling Christ how much he wanted to give himself to the mission of saving souls, he realized that Jesus was asking him to form a group of priests.

> They would dedicate themselves without measure, to-
> tally given to preaching and establishing God's King-
> dom. It seemed impossible to believe that in the world
> there were people who didn't know him, who were un-
> able to enjoy the beauty of his love, the sweetness of his
> love, the serenity and confidence his love inspires. And
> without comprehending, of course, everything I was
> committing myself to, I answered the Lord that I'd do
> whatever he wanted of me. My answer, then, was an un-
> conditional "yes." I myself didn't know what that "yes"
> would entail, but he—bit by bit—has been unveiling it.
> And he has continued to reveal what it entails my whole
> life long. It is a "yes" that crucified me forever; a "yes"
> that filled my young years with peace and joy—just as it
> does now, during these last years of my life. I don't
> know why I thought about forming this group of mis-
> sionary priests; I don't know why I accepted."[17]

It was a moment wrapped in mystery. Time and time again, Father Maciel has narrated—and been questioned about—this experience, in an effort to better explain and understand the how, why, and what-for behind his vocation.

Time has shown, however, that it was not just a stray idea, like those that occur while speculating about the future or doz-ing in the shade of an apple tree or daydreaming at school. It wasn't one of those regular adolescent-type things. It was what Father Maciel would later call a "motion" of the Holy Spirit: a clear, definite, out-and-out irruption of God's grace that simply disarmed any possible resistance, and definitively changed the

---

[17] Marcial Maciel LC (January 1992)

course of his existence. This new light struck Marcial's conscience so profoundly that, subsequently, he would never doubt what he had experienced.

Father Maciel explains that it is not as if he understood in detail that his vocation explicitly implied "founding a congregation." He is the first to admit that at that age he did not have the faintest idea of what a religious congregation was. "I was going to join the Carmelites," he said once, "like I would have gone to . . . I don't know . . . like I'd have gone to the army, if they ordained priests there."[18] What he did feel, with a power and clarity that precluded all doubts, was that God wanted him to form a group of priests who would dedicate their lives "wholeheartedly to preaching the Gospel—missionary priests who would live the Gospel thoroughly, love Christ with all their strength, be missionaries of that love, and preach Christ's new commandment of love among all people."[19]

For him, the question was simple: God loved him and he loved God, and God was asking this of him. That meant his response would be an unconditional *yes.* It was the same God for whom he had left behind all his loves in Cotija: his family, his friends among the poor, his horse. It was the same God to whom he wanted to give his whole life. He later said that he could not doubt that God truly wanted him to do this.[20]

When Marcial left the chapel, his heart and mind were quivering, and sentiments and ideas were buzzing through his head like bees in a hive. Recreation was over. He sat down at his desk. He would need some time and some silence to ponder over what had just happened.

Form a group of priests . . . he wondered what type of priest God wanted him to be. Should he write? Should he open a school or university? Should he dedicate himself to missionary work, or go and work among the poor? Working with the

[18] Marcial Maciel LC (January 1992)
[19] Jesús Colina, *Christ is My Life: Interview with the founder of the Legionaries of Christ and the Regnum Christi Movement,* Manchester (NH), Sophia Institute Press, 2003, p. 17
[20] *ibid*

poor was, he admitted, what he liked most.[21] His great desire was to live his priesthood just as Father Maldonado did, just like his uncle, Rafael Guízar: in some far-off village, full of souls waiting to be saved. A life full of missions, preaching and spending one's life for the people, tending to the poor and transmitting God's love to one and all.

Father Maciel admits that embracing God's plan for him was costly. Over the following days, he was assaulted by the fear of failing, of not being able to carry out a mission that he felt surpassed him. At prayer, Marcial even suggested to God the names of others who would be better founders than he: wiser men, older men, men of renown. In the end, however, he was hit by an idea that left him at ease:

> You sink. You sacrifice yourself. You fulfill God's will. Form others and send them into the world. They will preach to many hearts for you. They will start schools, universities, missions, and all the rest—so many things that you cannot do on your own.[22]

If he wanted to transmit God's love to many people, the best thing he could do was to form missionaries, authors, preachers and teachers: to form formers. This is what God was asking of him. It would be obedience and love for God—cost what it may—and not his personal qualities that God would have to bless and bring to fruition. It was obedience to the Father's will that had redeemed humanity; it was Christ's infinite love that moved him to accept the greatest sacrifice of all time, a sacrifice that only love could inspire and only love could bring to completion.

That very day, the feast of the Sacred Heart, Marcial told his spiritual director in the seminary about the call to found a group of priests. The priest encouraged him to press onward, telling him that—even though it was not yet possible to ascertain whether this was or wasn't an inspiration of God—it

---

[21] Marcial Maciel LC (13 September 1986)
[22] Marcial Maciel LC (Summer 1971)

would be advisable to buy a notebook and jot down in its pages everything that came to mind.

Marcial purchased three notebooks: one for him, and one each for two deans of the minor seminary. Both deans welcomed the project with enthusiasm and wanted to assist him with the foundation. As the days and weeks passed by, Marcial scribbled down all of the ideas that occurred to him: the congregation-to-be's organization, its essence, its mission.

The sad reality is that these three notebooks have all since disappeared. The two deans, theology students at the time, did not continue on to ordination, and they took their copies with them. Marcial's copy too, with the passing of time, has been lost to history.

IV

Church Bells Ring in Orizaba

Marcial's stomach ulcer had worsened so much during his second year of seminary studies that Bishop Rafael Guízar thought it best to send him for a month of rest to the city of Córdoba, Veracruz. Marcial stayed in a parish and lent a hand to the parish priest, Father Ignacio Lehonor Arroyo,[1] while he was there.

Back in Veracruz

Father Ignacio Lehonor celebrated an open-air Mass every day, hidden away in some ravine or cave because of the persecution.[2] At the end of Mass, he would entrust consecrated hosts to Marcial and some of the other young men helping out in the parish so that they could bring the Blessed Sacrament to the people he was unable to visit. To get an early start in the morning, Marcial would sometimes have to keep the Blessed Sacrament overnight. "I knelt down before going to bed, and then would go to sleep talking with Christ in the Blessed Sacrament, there at my side."[3]

The parish priest and the seminarians ran the risk of having soldiers discover that they were secretly carrying the Blessed Sacrament. They employed different strategies to keep

---

[1] Father Ignacio Lehonor Arroyo would later become the first bishop of Tuxpan.
[2] After the agreements between the Church and the Mexican government, which concluded the Cristero War in 1929, the Catholics of Mexico enjoyed greater freedom to worship in peace in the majority of the states of the Republic. Nevertheless, in the state of Veracruz, although there was no longer an armed uprising, the religious persecution continued. Consequently, priests had to exercise their ministry clandestinely.
[3] Marcial Maciel LC (Summer 1971)

them fooled, and usually went out at daybreak wearing street clothes.

"We would pass by the barracks of the federal troops and their outposts singing *Cuatro Milpas*,[4] jumping, skipping around and whistling, as we carried the Eucharist, passing from one house to another," Father Maciel remembers.

> We would give the Eucharist to sick people who were unable to take the host themselves. Others would take the host with their own hands. . . . I'd take note of those who wanted to go to confession, and the priest would pass by under the cover of night . . . [5]

No reply

Since the end of 1936, many parish priests and thousands of Catholics had flooded the state governor's office with telegrams and letters, asking the governor to comply with the law, end the persecution and give the faithful their churches back. No satisfactory reply was given. The state government sent the request to the federal capital, and the federal capital replied that it was an issue for the state. The Catholics should work out a solution with the governor of Veracruz himself. But this had already been tried.

The Veracruz town of Jesús María, for example, had written a letter with 1162 signatures to Mexico's President, General Lázaro Cárdenas, on 31 December 1936,[6] in which they stated that they had already filed several petitions with him and with the Governor of Veracruz.

> [We] reiterate our request for our churches to be re-opened and for its ministers to be allowed to exercise their ministry in accordance with the law. Among these petitions we can cite those of March 9 and April 4, di-

---

[4] *Cuatro Milpas:* the name means *Four Cornfields.*
[5] Marcial Maciel LC (Summer 1971)
[6] Other townships sent similar or identical letters.

rected to you, and those of March 10 and 30, directed to
the State Governor, all of this present year.[7]

A few lines later they showed great hope that the situation
would improve under the new state governor, Miguel Alemán,
who took office on 1 December 1936. They were hopeful, as "he
has already seen the spirit of order and submission that animates the Catholic citizens he governs."[8]

Leonor Sánchez shot dead

After a few weeks of rest with Father Ignacio in Córdoba,
Marcial's ulcer was a good deal better, and he returned to the
seminary. He was sent to Veracruz a short time later, probably
when school was dismissed for end of term towards the end of
January 1937. He was again assigned to Jesús María for vacations, and was pleased to think that he would see Father Antonio Maldonado and all of the people he had served a year
earlier. He was enthusiastic about going back, wanting to dedicate himself wholeheartedly to the mission: preaching, visiting the sick and riding the mountain paths on horseback to the
farthest congregation. The people welcomed him warmly
when he arrived, and he immediately resumed his pastoral
work at Father Maldonado's side.

A few days after his arrival news out of Orizaba spoke of
the tragic death of a Catholic girl at the hands of federal soldiers. People in Orizaba were organizing demonstrations to demand that the churched be reopened.[9] Graham Greene wrote

---

[7] —, *Letter to the president of the Republic from 1162 residents of Jesús María,* (Jesús
María, Veracruz, 31 December 1936)

[8] *ibid*

[9] The events that follow are narrated in many sources. Among them: Carlos
Aguilar Muñoz, *Un capítulo de la historia de Orizaba: Apertura de templos,* Mexico,
—, 1952; J. Mondragón A., *Album gráfico-histórico de los sucesos del 7 February 1937
en la ciudad de Orizaba,* Veracruz, J.P. Talavera, no date. The events were also covered in international newspapers such as the New York Times (9–14 February
1937), as quoted in John B. Williman, *La Iglesia y el Estado en Veracruz: 1840–1940,*
Mexico, SepSetentas, p. 171, and Orizaba's paper "Los Sucesos" (Orizaba, Veracruz, 12 and 24 February 1937).

about these dramatic historical events in his 1939 book *The Lawless Roads*: a girl shot by the police for going to Mass; an outburst of religious fervor in Veracruz; the people storm and bar the churches; the clanging church bells are given no rest . . . [10]

Father José María Flores, Orizaba's parish priest, was celebrating Mass in secret for about 30 people in someone's home on February 7 when the police burst in. Father Flores was taken into custody. Leonor Sánchez, the young daughter of a local laborer, had been at the Mass and fled as the police arrived. She was pursued and shot in the back. She died almost immediately.[11] News spread throughout Orizaba and the neighboring towns, and the following day, February 8, vast crowds attended the young martyr's funeral.[12] This mass gathering triggered a wave of peaceful demonstrations by Catholics and by the factory workers of nearby towns such as Río Blanco, Nogales, and Santa Rosa, demanding that church property be returned. The first such public protest took place on February 9 and the second was scheduled for February 11. People came into Orizaba from the nearby ranches and towns to take part in the demonstrations.

On the morning of February 11, Father Maldonado took Marcial along to accompany his parishioners to the demonstration. As they approached the city they joined up with the mass of country folk who had come down from the sierra. They soon realized that the army had blocked all the roads leading into the city. Marcial somehow found himself in the western guard-

---

[10] cf. Graham Greene, *The Lawless Roads,* Bodley Head, 1978.

[11] Leonor died in the *Ignacio de la Llave* Hospital at 10:15 a.m. from bullet wounds, cf. –, *Account of Leonor Sánchez López' Death,* in Orizaba's Civil Registry, *Deaths, Book 412,* 1937, vol. I, section 133, pp. 71–72.

[12] The informal use of the term martyr reflects the appraisal of her contemporaries. On February 8, Blessed Rafael Guízar, bishop of Veracruz, wrote to Father José María Flores, in jail for having celebrated what turned out to be Leonor Sánchez' last Mass, from Tacuba, Mexico City: "Far from exchanging words of condolence, I warmly congratulate you: the young martyr is already in heaven and you and the group of Catholics suffered in jail out of love for our Divine Redeemer." Rafael Guízar Valencia, *Letter to Father José María Flores* (8 February 1937)

house speaking with the leader of a group of soldiers, Captain Guerra, trying to persuade him to let them in. The hours passed. Eleven o'clock. Noon. The people kept coming.

"Look, Captain," Marcial said to Guerra, "Let us in: we haven't come here to disrupt the peace."[13]

The Captain continued to deny passage, and the people began to grow restless.

"Captain," Marcial insisted, "what do you prefer? To let us in, or to have a bloodbath here between your guards and these people? They won't understand. All they want to do is to go through. Your guards will open fire; but they're carrying machetes and will defend themselves. There will be a useless slaughter here, and there's no reason for it."

The captain finally gave the order to open the barricades. The multitude entered the city singing peacefully.

When Father Marcial related this incident to some Legionary seminarians, he explained that he really doesn't know why he always seemed to find himself in the middle of things.[14]

They went to the main church first. Then the crowd marched peacefully towards city hall, to chant and demand that the churches be returned. There were rallying cries and rousing speeches. Tempers started to rise. Miguel Alemán, the new governor, happened to be in Orizaba that day. He went out onto the balcony of city hall in an effort to calm the crowd. He assured them that they would get justice and invited them to observe the law. However, the crowd wasn't convinced and Alemán felt compelled to make a hasty exit. Hidden from the multitude, he withdrew to the Hotel Francia and then left Orizaba. Marcial, who was at the front of the crowd facing city hall, was led inside by the federal police. In the meanwhile, a young man called Carlos Villagómez and a railway worker named Salinas unsuccessfully tried to diffuse the tension from the balcony.

---

[13] Marcial Maciel LC (January 1992). All unreferenced dialogues of this chapter have been taken from this conference of Father Maciel.
[14] cf. Marcial Maciel LC (January 1992)

Rumors began to circulate among the people. "They've taken Father Marcial prisoner!" "Hey! They've carried off the güerito . . . " "Where's the seminarian?" He was only 17, but for a lot of people he was a point of reference. They had traveled the whole way with him, he used to teach them the catechism, he had visited their homes with Father Maldonado or on his behalf . . . The crowd started to shout, and tempers began to flare. "Let us see the güerito! Let us see him!"

Inside city hall, Colonel Baltasar Treviño led Marcial to the balcony.

"Speak to them, and tell them to keep their cool."

"But what kind of speech do you want me to make? What they want are the churches. Can I tell them that we can have the churches back?

"Look here: if you don't get them out of here, there are going to be a lot of dead people laying around. Get them away and then we'll talk. This is something that depends on the president of the Republic, it doesn't depend on me. Lead them away to pray in the streets."

"All the people were out in the streets protesting," recalled Mrs. Lupita Aguilar years later. She was an Orizaba resident who had taken part in the demonstrations. She said:

All the soldiers were ready, and we weren't retreating.
"Hit us, kill us, but we're not leaving."
"We'll fire," said the soldiers.
"Shoot, then—but we're not budging."
Father Mondragón was there, too, dressed in civies. You could recognize them [the priests] because I often dealt with them.[15]

By now tempers were well fired and the crowd was on the verge of breaking down the doors of city hall. Marcial came out onto the balcony and the crowd quieted down a little when they saw him. He tried to calm them by saying that he wasn't a prisoner; that the authorities seemed willing to give them

[15] Guadalupe Aguilar (c. 1970)

the churches; that he was speaking with them . . . but that the churches could not yet be turned over because that depended on the president of the Republic: they still did not have permission.

"Take note of how large masses of people behave," Father Marcial would later explain. "When they trust someone, just as when they don't . . . it's fearsome business. By that time they trusted me."[16]

Marcial asked the crowd to pass the word along to take six paces back, starting from the rear, and to move away from city hall. Time was needed for negotiations. Little by little the crowd drew back.[17]

From city hall the crowd headed for the jail to have some of the demonstrators set free. "I had said to Colonel Treviño," Father Maciel recalls:

> "Either you give us the prisoners or they kill me. Or I can listen to you, but then everyone will unite against you and city hall. Then try stopping this crowd!" So then they made annotations in the ledger and . . . handed over the prisoners. And with that, the demonstration broke up."[18]

The faithful in Orizaba opened the parish and several other church buildings on February 9 following the first rally, but the authorities had them closed on the night of February 10. After the governor appeared on February 11, several churches were occupied again at the end of the demonstration. Groups of men were organized, and they formed squads to guard the churches and prevent anyone from coming to close them. But the problem had by no means been resolved, as Carlos Aguilar Muñoz explains:

> The people, counseled by noted individuals, asked that the laws dealing with worship be repealed, that the churches be officially given back, and above all, that

---

[16] Marcial Maciel LC (January 1992)
[17] cf. Marcial Maciel LC (January 1992)
[18] Marcial Maciel LC (January 1992)

they be entrusted the church keys. They wanted to see
priests carrying out their duties in the churches.[19]

We want the keys!

Twelve days later, since the governor had still not responded
to their demands, another demonstration was convoked.

> The decision was taken to demand the church keys be
> handed over (the Federal Treasury was to give them to
> neighborhood committees[20]), as there was well-founded
> apprehension that they would be closed again each time
> the religion question was raised, and that the authorities
> would take no action.[21]

This time protesters from Fortín de las Flores and Córdoba
were added to the marchers from Orizaba, Río Blanco, Nogales
and Santa Rosa. "Since so many new people had come," says
Father Maciel, "half of the people in the demonstration didn't
know me. We got started, but things turned ugly, really ugly."[22]

They marched through the streets as before, but when
they came to the town square they found it sealed off by the
army. Things "turned ugly" indeed: Father Maciel still bears
the scar of a bayonet wound on his leg, inflicted by a soldier
who was trying to prevent them from moving forward. The
soldiers were edgy, but they had received orders not to fire.

Word was spread to disperse for the moment. Since the
governor's decision would be transmitted from the Federal
Treasury Office once it arrived, they decided to regroup there
at 6 p.m., renewing their demand that the keys be handed over.

In a letter that three Catholics sent to the Mexican president on 2 March 1937, there is a description of the happenings
of February 23:

---

[19] Carlos Aguilar Muñoz, *Un capítulo . . .*, pp. 26–27.
[20] This was the process that had been stipulated by the government. The
committees took responsibility for the church and were held accountable by the
government.
[21] Carlos Aguilar Muñoz, *Un capítulo . . .*, p. 27.
[22] *ibid*

> The undersecretary . . . said it was up to the governor to give him the orders . . . so that he, in turn, could inform the local offices. We spoke with the governor, and he said that the Catholics should go to the federal authorities. The people who kept on gathering outside the federal office were indignant. As there were armed troops monitoring the demonstration, the leading Catholics made superhuman efforts to maintain calm and order to avoid grave trouble.[23]

A Catholic women's group was able to enter the treasury and speak with Blas Camacho, the treasury official, in an attempt to work out a compromise. They received nothing but promises.

The tension grew as night came on, and the situation became worrisome. The army positioned itself in front of the treasury and around the building, brandishing bayonets to keep the people at bay. The crowd, numbering tens of thousands of demonstrators, unaware that bayonets had been drawn, pressed forward towards the door. Marcial was in the front row with Father Aburto and Father Lino. It didn't take long for them to realize the danger they were in. The crowd would continue to push forward. The first ones to die would be the priests. A massacre would ensue. Speaking with a megaphone from the roof of a truck, the priests and the leaders of Catholic Action took turns in an effort to restrain the strength of the crowd. They pleaded for calm, they sang songs, they launched cheers of Viva for Christ the King and for the Virgin of Guadalupe. The treasurer's promise, that the churches would not be closed again, "was transmitted to the marchers by Mrs. Carolina Ojeda de Islas, who used the very truck that contained the federal soldiers as her speaking platform."[24]

They had achieved little. Some of the demonstrators fired shots into the air—and the federal troops began to load their

---

[23] Virginia de Rebat, Lucía Fernandes Gertz, and a third unidentified signer, *Letter to the President of the Republic* (Mexico City, 2 March 1937)

[24] Carlos Aguilar Muñoz, *Un capítulo . . .* , p. 27.

weapons. Captain Guerra approached Marcial. "Now, güerito, you see what they're doing, the slaughter that they're going to provoke. Skip up there onto the truck and speak to these people."[25]

Marcial clambered up, and without too much thought took the megaphone and began to proclaim enthusiastically, "It's all set! We've got everything in our hands! Viva Christ the King! Viva the Virgin of Guadalupe!" The people took up his words. "Did you hear that? He says that everything's set, that it's all been taken care of . . . " And Marcial continued, "Now: to the churches!" This message, too, ran through the crowd. "It's all taken care of! We're going for the churches!"

Asked about these events in 1965, Father Antonio Maldonado said he remembered them well:

> Back then Father Maciel used to wear a straw hat, like the ones we had on the ranch. He got up to give a speech to the people, who were shouting, "We want the keys to the church, so that they'll be ours and so that they won't keep deceiving us!" And Father Maciel got up and said to them, "We already have the keys!"
>
> One of the federal employees got up to placate the people, because they were up in arms and had broken some windows. Nobody understood. Another one got up, but with the same result. And then Father Maciel gets up with his hat and says, "Yes, look! We really do have the keys!"
>
> "We can believe you" they shouted back, "because you're one of us!"[26]

The gathering were so convinced of what Marcial told them, that years later Guadalupe Aguilar would recall the episode saying that after chanting for the keys, they "went to the Treasury . . . there on Lerdo Street, and there they handed the keys over to us."[27]

---

[25] Marcial Maciel LC (January 1992)
[26] Javier García LC, *Interview with Father Antonio . . .* (25 August 1965)
[27] Guadalupe Aguilar (c. 1970)

Had they received what they wanted? In reality, they had not. They were requesting government authorization for public worship to resume in Catholic churches. As Catholics, they wanted to be able to make use of their churches. This had all been legally granted already by the federal government, and even though it had not been implemented in Veracruz, it was generally being applied in the rest of the states. Inasmuch as restoration of Church property was concerned, this demand has still not been met, not even with Mexico's new constitutional reform of 1992.[28]

Father Maciel said the idea of the keys just came to him: "I know where the keys are, and so I can just go and open the doors of the church and the people will think that the government has legally returned the churches to us."[29]

The massacre had to be avoided, and what the people wanted most was to be able to go to church in peace, to be able to have Mass, in short, to be able to practice their faith.

There he was, 17, someone who didn't even know how he had gotten himself involved in the whole thing. Thousands of demonstrators. Soldiers with bayonets. They had urged him up onto the truck, and the only thing that occurred to him while the people were singing and shouting was to tell them that everything had already been resolved, that everyone should please make for the parish. And that is what had happened.

The people began to draw back to head for the church. Surely the soldiers, too, breathed a sigh of relief, since they could let the people leave in peace. Many in the large crowd of

---

[28] The decree reforming the Mexican constitution on 27 January 1992, and the law of religious associations and public worship of July 14 of the same year (a regulatory law stipulating the practical application of the constitutional reform) were the legislative innovations which gave the Church in Mexico recognition as a juridical person. Property was not returned to the Church (existing churches are still state property) but it did recognize the Church's ownership of places of worship built in the future). The texts of these laws and their draft versions can be found in José Antonio González Fernández, José Francisco Ruiz Massieu and José Luis Soberanes Fernández, *Derecho eclesiástico mexicano*, Mexico, UNAM—Porrúa, 1992, p. 344.

[29] Marcial Maciel LC (January 1992)

demonstrators from outside Orizaba did not know who the "güerito" was, and there was no shortage of those who insulted him and called him traitor on the way to the parish church. "If you're trying to trick us," threatened one of the demonstrators, showing him an enormous knife, "this is for you."

When Marcial reached the church, he slipped into the sacristy, took the keys and opened the main door. Everyone went in singing and applauding, "Long Live Christ the King! Long Live the Virgin of Guadalupe!" The priests exposed the Blessed Sacrament, and after a while the people returned to their homes enthusiastic. In a 1997 interview, Clemente Hernández, a long-time resident of Jesús María, had no trouble remembering that day:

> I remember that one morning my mother told us, "They told me we have to go to Orizaba to participate in the demonstration to demand that they open the churches. I'm going, and don't worry about me. I'll return when I can." That's what my mother said to my brothers and me. Well, the whole day passed, and it was already getting dark when my mother arrived, extremely content because they had finally won. That is, they had given them the keys and had opened the churches. The people of the volcano mountain ridge, who lived up our way, were already coming back up, very happy that they had won. That's what I remember. I also heard them say that Father Marcial was one of those who had been most involved, that he went down to Orizaba on horseback, wearing his riding clothes and his big hat. He was the one who gave the boost to that demonstration, that goes without saying." [30]

To avoid provocation, the government would not close the churches again. That night, Orizaba's four other churches were opened in the same way, along with those of the nearby towns of Nogales, Río Blanco and Santa Rosa.

---

[30] Clemente Hernández (1997)

When, at last, Marcial arrived at the Aguilar's home to rest and have a cup of coffee early the next morning, the soles of his feet had become one big blister, bloodied and torn. His shoe-soles had worn out the day before, and events had been too hectic to bother replacing them. He hadn't even felt the pain—until that moment.

"There they were, working all night," Father Maldonado remembered. "And Father Maciel's shoes fell apart and his feet got blisters. That's when Lupita, the wife of Mr. Lino Aguilar, loaned him a pair of shoes." [31]

"Marcial was the one in the background who got things moving," said Mrs. Aguilar. "He convinced everyone. There's no doubt God was with him."[32]

Soledad Maldonado, one of Father Maldonado's sisters, offered her own interpretation of the young seminarian's involvement in the opening of Orizaba's churches:

> He would hold rallies in the public squares, like politicians today. The people of Orizaba would go to these meetings, but he also invited the people from the towns, despite the fact that . . . at that time it was a lot of work to go from Jesús María to Orizaba; it took two hours on horseback. He made a lot of sacrifices going and coming and organizing everything, and later intervening with the authorities. So that, after God, he's one of the ones who deserve most credit for public worship resuming in Orizaba.[33]

Christ pressed close

Marcial returned to Jesús María the following morning and again began the pastoral rounds with Father Maldonado. Days and weeks went by peacefully. He was happy to be doing missionary work, and when he contemplated the natural

---

[31] Javier García LC, *Interview with Father Antonio . . .* (25 August 1965)

[32] Guadalupe Aguilar (hacia 1970)

[33] Javier García LC, *Interview with Soledad Maldonado* (Salamanca, 2 August 1965)

beauty of his surroundings, it filled his mind with thoughts of God.

He did a lot of walking and riding, but one walk in particular remained forever engraved in his memory. It took place during that period, in February or March of 1937. He had gone to Chilapa with Father Maldonado. The way was long and winding, passing by waterfalls and along the edge of cliffs. The sun was setting when they arrived. The people were awaiting them. Before rosary and Eucharistic exposition in the church (dedicated to Saint Isidore), the priest heard confessions. It suddenly struck Father Maldonado that they had forgotten to bring the Blessed Sacrament along with them. In those days, Church law did not permit Mass to be celebrated at night so no hosts could be consecrated. The people had been expecting to have nocturnal Eucharistic adoration and Eucharistic benediction the next day, and he did not want to disappoint them. The only solution was to send the seminarian to fetch the Blessed Sacrament from the nearest village, La Ciénega.

The path to La Ciénega dropped through a steep, narrow mountain pass, and Marcial had to be careful not to fall off a precipice as he walked in the darkness. He reached La Ciénega an hour-and-a-half later. After some difficulties locating the chapel sacristan, he at last secured the Blessed Sacrament. Knowing that he would need to have his hands free to make his way back up to Chilapa, he placed the Eucharist in a small box, bound it tightly, and hung it from his neck.

It was raining and dark. The road was steep. Marcial walked with the Eucharist next to his heart. He went the whole way speaking with Jesus, holding him close and singing to him. He longed to love Jesus more and told him so, with simplicity, offering God the best of himself: that is his style of prayer.

> Lord, you loved me so much that you gave your life for me and stayed in the Eucharist to nourish me, accompany me, strengthen me. What can I do for you? Speak to me, Jesus; speak to my heart quietly. Let me hear you, Lord. What can I do to thank you for your gifts? How

much you love me! What else can I do, Lord, other than try to love you as you've loved me? [34]

Throughout his life, he has been in the habit of saying short, spontaneous prayers:

Jesus, I love you . . . What would you like from me?... Lord Jesus, help me, give me strength; I believe in you . . . Thank you for wanting to come with me tonight, to be so close to my heart . . . I am all yours; all yours. Ask me for anything, and it's yours . . .

What a difference between this peaceful moment of closeness with Jesus and the efforts and hazards among the crowds in Orizaba just a few weeks earlier! Marcial's life has been one of constant contrasts. He says that the turbulence of events has never robbed him of his deep-down peace of soul and friendship with God. He experienced God's immense love for him so strongly that his first, innermost impulse is to respond by completely giving himself and his love to God, no matter how small and limited these gifts might be. God, as it were, seduced him. Father Maciel frequently repeats that without his really knowing how, God's providence catapulted him into fulfilling his mission, conscious of simply being an instrument in God's hands.

It was an uphill trek to Chilapa, but for Marcial that night, the road just wasn't long enough.

Imprisoned

In early March, Marcial was present at the peaceful demonstrations to open the churches in Fortín de las Flores and Córdoba. Some time later, before the end of his vacation, he took part in a demonstration in Jalapa. Things didn't go so well there. Jalapa is the state capital, and for a long time the people had not had priests to give them spiritual attention. Moreover the in-

---

[34] Marcial Maciel LC, *Thanksgiving after communion* (29 June 1998) in Marcial Maciel, *Oraciones de corazón a Corazón,* Mexico, Contenidos de Formación Integral, 2001, p. 95

habitants, many of whom worked for the state government, were afraid to commit themselves. They did not respond like the people from the sierra. Only a few thousand demonstrators turned up in Jalapa, and they were easily dispersed. Marcial was sent to jail for rabble-rousing. He spent three days there.

The young governor Miguel Alemán would later become President of the Republic and a friend and benefactor of Father Maciel. Back then, so as not to leave Marcial in prison, the governor sent him to Tierra Blanca on the Tabasco state border, with the order not to return to the state of Veracruz. From there Macial traveled to Mexico City, and from the capital returned to Orizaba.

The date of the diocese of Veracruz annual pilgrimage to the Basilica of Our Lady of Guadalupe in Mexico City was approaching, and plans were being made to organize a demonstration there. The bishop of Veracruz, Rafael Guízar Valencia, Marcial's great-uncle, would celebrate Mass for them. A few days earlier, on March 6, seeing that the government's promises were empty, the bishop had sent a letter to President Lázaro Cárdenas in support of the recent demonstrations, asking him "to make use of his significant influence so that all the churches in the state of Veracruz would be opened, and later turned over to the resident committees, fulfilling the other requirements that the law prescribes."[35] The letter was co-signed by Bishop Nicolás Corona of Papantla, Bishop Jesús Villarreal y Fierro of Tehuantepec, and Francisco Miranda and José Pérez, representing the 72 Catholic commissions in the State of Veracruz.

Many people came to Mexico City from Veracruz for the rally. Motorized police were called in and the crowd was dispersed. Marcial was arrested again. He spent two days in jail, putting up with interrogations during the day and the bedbugs that prevented him from sleeping at night. On day three, it

[35] Rafael Guízar Valencia, Nicolás Corona, Jesús Villarreal y Fierro, Francisco Miranda and José Pérez. *Letter of the Bishops of Veracruz, Papantla y Tehuacán and the representatives of 72 Catholic commissions in the state of Veracruz to the President of the Republic, Gen. D. Lázaro Cárdenas*, (6 March 1937)

occurred to him to call his great-uncle Emiliano Guízar Valencia (Bishop Rafael's brother). He got through to Lula, Emiliano's daughter. She was worried when he told her his whereabouts, and soon a 20-peso bail had been paid for his release. He slept at Emiliano's house that night, and, since vacations were over, returned to the seminary the following day.

The seminary in Mixcoac

The Veracruz seminary had three campuses in Mexico City: one in Atzcapotzalco, another in Mixcoac, and a third in Tacuba. Marcial was transferred from Atzcapotzalco to Mixcoac, where some 200 seminarians lived. He spent another year studying there, still desiring to prepare himself to become a holy future priest, and still entertaining the idea of founding his group. "I had my head in the clouds a bit with this dream of foundation,"[36] he confesses, and adds that it was a joy for him to have the tabernacle always so close at hand.

His friends from the time remember him as a happy young seminarian who was generous with everyone, a young man with an intense prayer life and plenty of apostolic zeal. "The Lord has given you many gifts, and has multiplied your admirable work—founding the Legionaries of Christ—in full measure," Father Ignacio Villanueva wrote him in 1996: " . . . the fire and fervor of your youth, like when we prayed together in the memorable little chapel of Mixcoac and Atzcapotzalco, has now reached fulfillment."[37]

"Marcial was goodhearted indeed, and happy," recalls Father José Refugio Rodríguez, another seminary friend:

> Even then he gave a good example of charity to all. He was so fervent . . . for the feast day of the Sacred Heart, Father Maciel found a priest to preach us a novena: nine days to prepare for the feast.[38]

---

[36] Marcial Maciel LC (January 1992)
[37] Ignacio Villanueva, *Letter to Father Maciel* (3 January 1996)
[38] Father José Refugio Rodríguez (14 August 2003)

Father Rodríguez explained how Marcial, with the rector's permission, would promote the Marian Congregation[39] and the Apostolate of Prayer among them. "I'd like to speak with you . . . just for a moment. I won't take much of your recess." "All right," the seminarians would respond.

"It was quite something," concludes Father Rodríguez.[40]

Father Maciel remembers that from the age of 17 to 18, he chose the mystery of the Incarnation for the theme of his meditation each and every morning, except for Easter Sunday. *Et Verbum caro factum est*: "And the Word became flesh and dwelt among us" (*Jn* 1:14). Since then, Marcial has frequently allowed meditation on the mystery of the Incarnation and birth of the Son of God to engulf him. Christ came into the world because he loved God the Father, and because he loved every single human being: to redeem humanity by obeying the Father, even to the extent of dying on a cross. The young founder-to-be understood that if he and his future Legionaries wanted to bear fruit, they would have to make the simplicity and depth of Christ's mission their own. They would have to be united to Christ as branches to the vine, and work for the salvation of souls, moved by that same love for the Father and for all people. They would have to practice Christ's own charity, imitating the way Jesus obeyed the Father's will even to the cross, the path he chose to fulfill his redemptive mission. It is in the mysteries of the Incarnation and the Redemption that Father Maciel will always find the essence of Christ's message of love for humanity. This is the nucleus of the Gospel. It would also have to be the essence of his own founding charism.

In Mixcoac, a dozen or more of Marcial's companions became enthused with the idea of founding a new group, seminarians such as Jorge Abud, Alfonso Gutiérrez, Jorge Durán and Francisco Porras. The groundwork was going well for Marcial until, on 6 June 1938, his uncle Bishop Rafael Guízar died.[41] Father Pedro Castillo y Landa was named vicar of the

---

[39] A group that fostered devotion to the Blessed Virgin Mary.
[40] Father José Refugio Rodríguez (14 August 2003)
[41] Celestino Barradas, *Seminario, trayectoria . . .* , pp. 151–161

diocese on June 8, until a successor could be found. On 4 October 1939, Rome appointed Bishop Manuel Pío López of Tacámbaro, a friend of the Maciels, to the post.

While the bishop's post was still vacant, however, the seminary superiors became unhappy that Marcial had created a group within the seminary and was intent on founding a new congregation. They decided he would have to be expelled. They spoke with the diocesan vicar, and in the summer of 1938 they informed Marcial of their decision: he could no longer study in the Veracruz Seminary.

For an 18-year-old with so many aspirations, it was a hard blow. He knew he had done nothing wrong. Everything had always been done with his spiritual director's approval. With no real idea of what he ought to do, he set off for the home of Emiliano Guízar. His great-uncle suggested that he call his other brother, Bishop Antonio of Chihuahua, to tell him what had come to pass. Emiliano spoke to him first. The call turned out to be a good idea. "Don't worry," Bishop Antonio told Marcial. "Prepare your things, and I'll send you to Montezuma seminary from my diocese."[42]

Marcial moved to Chihuahua in August 1938. From there he was bound for the United States: he would be going to the inter-diocesan seminary of Montezuma in New Mexico.

---

[42] cf. Marcial Maciel LC (January 1992)

V

Montezuma Seminary
1938–1940

The Mexican bishops opened the new Montezuma Seminary, dedicated to Our Lady of Guadalupe, with the encouragement and economic support of the American bishops in 1937.[1] Years earlier, the Mexican episcopacy had resolved to open an inter-diocesan seminary in the USA, since violent government persecution and frequent raids made it nearly impossible for each diocese to maintain its own seminary in Mexico. To avoid the obvious difficulties of running a clandestine seminary, they decided to build it in the neighboring United States, in New Mexico. During its 35 years of existence from its inauguration in September 1937 until its move to Mexico in 1972, the seminary formed one-fifth of the clergy of the Mexican Republic. Alumni totaled 1707 priests and 16 bishops.[2]

Marcial arrived on 2 September 1938,[3] at the beginning of the seminary's second year of existence. He was tired after a train trip that had carried him across the Chihuahua desert to Ciudad Juarez (the border town across from El Paso, Texas) and from there through the New Mexican cities of Albu-

---

[1] It was known as the seminary of "Our Lady of the Americas" in English.

[2] There are several Spanish texts dealing with the Seminary of Montezuma: Luis Medina Ascencio, ed., *Montezuma Íntimo. Su escenario. Su gente. Su vida.*, Mexico, Ed. Jus, 1962, and, by the same author, *Historia del Seminario de Montezuma. Sus precedentes, fundación y consolidación. 1910–1953*, Mexico, Ed. Jus, 1962; José Macías SJ, *Montezuma en sus exalumnos 1937–1962. Bodas de plata.*, Mexico,—1962.

[3] José Macías, SJ, *Montezuma en sus exalumnos . . .* , p. 337. Whereas in the index of names Marcial is listed as studying for the dioceses of Chihuahua and Cuernavaca (p. 75), he is also mentioned as a student of the Cuernavaca diocese on page 337. The reason for this multiple-listing will become apparent in later chapters.

querque, Santa Fe, and Las Vegas,[4] the last stop before reaching Montezuma Seminary.

The seminary had an enrollment of 479 seminarians during the school year 1938–1939. With such a large number of students from all parts of the Mexican Republic, the seminary brought together many different degrees of cultural, human and religious formation. "I adjusted quickly," Father Maciel remembers. "I started to analyze everything around me. It was a very interesting mosaic of humanity—myself included."[5]

He made his first friend soon after arriving: Alfonso Sánchez Tinoco, the future bishop of Papantla. With Alfonso, Marcial attempted the foundation for the second time.

For young men studying to be priests, the years at seminary are years of prayer and study, a time to forge and strengthen their vocation and better understand their mission in the Church. They are years dedicated to studying Jesus Christ, seeking to know him deeply, to love him intensely and to let the Holy Spirit progressively shape their interior into the image of Christ. The future priest has to become "another Christ" for the world.

Seminarians nourish a pure, sincere, authentic love for Jesus through prayer spent in front of the Tabernacle. It is there that they increase their love for the priesthood, the Blessed Virgin Mary, the Church and the Pope. Since Jesus Christ is present in the Eucharist, it is there that they foster their desire to work for the salvation of souls.

Bishop Manuel Pérez-Gil y González, archbishop of Tlalnepantla,[6] then one of Marcial's companions in Montezuma, remembers seeing Marcial spend many hours in the chapel, wearing a white turtleneck sweater to keep warm as he enkindled his soul with love in prayer.[7] Father Francisco Porras, who

---

[4] Not to be confused with Las Vegas, Nevada.
[5] Marcial Maciel LC (January 1992)
[6] Manuel Pérez-Gil y González (1921–1996) was the bishop of Mexicali from 1966 to 1984. He was bishop of Tlalnepantla until it became an archdiocese in 1989, and he became its archbishop (17 June 1989). He died on 14 February 1996.
[7] cf. Manuel Pérez-Gil, *Testimony* (25 April 1990)

had been a fellow-seminarian of Marcial's in the Mixcoac seminary of Veracruz, was also in Montezuma. There is a certain degree of nostalgia in a letter he wrote to Father Maciel some forty years later:

> Together we made the effort to assimilate the humanistic studies taught by Father Araus, little Father Michael Lehonor and Father Manuelito, of the [Missionaries of the] Holy Spirit. Later we changed to Montezuma, and in so many of the recesses, I heard your invitation to visit the small chapel of the philosophy students for a few moments, to dialog with Christ, and so on. It's because of you that I began to leave behind a lot of other things to draw closer to the Tabernacle![8]

The New Mexico mountains are covered with snow for six months of the year, and winter was harsh in Montezuma Seminary. The chapel may have been cold, but it was nonetheless capable of setting young hearts ablaze.

Missionaries of the Sacred Heart

Membership slowly grew, and Marcial encouraged his companions to work for Christ's Kingdom, to flee mediocrity and to strive to fulfill their duty 24 hours a day. He urged them to set a good example and to spread devotion to the Sacred Heart in the seminary.

Father Gabriel Soto, a priest for the diocese of Zacatecas, Mexico, explains how Marcial began forming a group, the base of what would later become his congregation:

> He gathered a small group of us seminarians together and told us of his interest in founding a fellowship of priests who would expend their lives loving Christ and working so that Christ would reign in souls . . . I participated in the group. I liked the idea, although later on I realized that I did not have this charism, and I also had

---

[8] Francisco Porras, *Letter to Father Maciel* (30 January 1995)

a debt of gratitude to my bishop to return and work in my home diocese."[9]

In 1938, these seminarians went by the name of "Missionaries of the Sacred Heart." For them, as for the group that would eventually be renamed the Legionaries of Christ, the ideal of spending one's life even to the point of death while working for Christ and souls formed part of the charism. "It made for a beautiful environment," recalls Father Maciel.

> All of them with the same concern, with the same zeal for the salvation of souls and with the same promise to work until death—but to work well and to be exemplary priests who would waste no time, spending themselves completely in their pastoral work to save souls.[10]

From the moment Marcial felt the strong interior movement of the Holy Spirit to found a new group of priests, he understood intuitively that they should give themselves to Christ and to souls fully, "without holding anything back." He said they should work in such a way that their lives might be short, that work might consume them, but that they wouldn't be priests who were "just there to waste time or simply let life roll by."[11]

To preach until their voices failed. To work until they fell exhausted. Marcial had known parish priests like that since his boyhood at home in Cotija, especially during the period of religious persecution. He had seen this attitude of total self-giving out of love for souls in the life and death of his uncle Bishop Rafael Guízar, and in the examples of Father Antonio Maldonado in Jesús María and Father Ignacio Lehonor in Córdoba. They were priests who always had time to accompany Christ in prayer, and to attend to the needs of their people, at any time of day or night, even in the small hours of the morning. Often, they scarcely had had time to eat and sleep.

---

[9] Gabriel Soto, *Written testimony* (17 January 2004)
[10] Marcial Maciel LC (January 1992)
[11] *ibid*

That was our whole program: to do God's will, to save souls, but with 100% self-giving. Not wasting time. Not putting on a show. Even if it meant dying; even if a life that could have lasted 60 years ended up lasting only five or ten. It didn't matter, as long as it was consumed fulfilling the mission. Enough of spiritual lukewarmness! Enough of settling ourselves down comfortably into priestly life, just to drift along![12]

Since they would need to be strong to serve the Church, it was not a matter of despising one's health. Rather, it was a question of a spirit, an inner attitude, a mentality of giving without limits, without selfishness and without laziness or mediocrity. Their ideal was to die serving, to die from pure exhaustion, when the body could no longer take it because it was not possible to love God nor serve the Church more.

While still in the Mixcoac seminary in 1937, Marcial had written to his mother who was concerned about his ulcer: "Pray to God that I die from nothing other than the great love that I have for him."[13] Priests are called to be *alter Christus*, "another Christ," and their mission consists in offering their lives for the salvation of others. Marcial decided to love to the point of offering his live: for Christ, for humanity.

With the approval of the seminary superiors, the Missionaries of the Sacred Heart at Montezuma established times to meet, and in addition to what the seminary already offered them, they chose ways to grow and persevere in their spiritual life. They formed new teams each week. Each team proposed its own themes for the week's meditations and its own apostolic intentions for which to offer their prayers and sacrifices. Marcial wrote them a monthly bulletin to encourage a deeper understanding of their common spiritual goals. Every Friday the group held a meeting for what they called a "review of life," where they offered each other brotherly correction with

---

[12] Marcial Maciel LC (11 February 2002)
[13] Marcial Maciel LC, *Letter to Mamá Maurita* (8 November 1937)

straightforward, tactful simplicity. They encouraged one another, and out of love for Christ strove to fulfill their duties
meticulously: studying well even when they might not feel like
it, keeping silence according to the seminary norms, taking
part in sports when it was time for recreation, cleaning when it
was time for cleaning and praying when it was time to pray.
Above all, Marcial insisted that they live genuine charity,
which meant fostering a spirit of unity, never allowing themselves to make negative comments about others, and offering
help to everyone, especially the seminarians who were most in
need.

Although Marcial was younger than some of the others,[14]
he was recognized as founder and organizer of the group.

"I remember that his face reflected goodness, pure good-
heartedness," says Father Gabriel Soto.

> I always trusted him. He was a very humble man be-
> cause for me, he was a man who was always on the side
> of truth, and that is what distinguishes a humble man.
> He was also very friendly, not pompous, always ap-
> proachable and accessible. Well then, that was the Mar-
> cial I knew."[15]

The Missionaries of the Sacred Heart were committed to
helping their fellow seminarians better know and love Christ.
They encouraged them to honor Jesus by "enthroning the
image of his Sacred Heart" in their dorms. It was a common devotion of the time, and meant more than the mere gesture of
putting a picture up on the wall: what counted was the love
and enthusiasm it nurtured. To "enthrone the Sacred Heart"
meant making a firm resolution to fulfill one's duties as perfectly as possible out of love for God and souls. The image was
like a loved one's photograph, helping each seminarian to remember their friend and Lord, and to foster the desire to speak

---

[14] Several of the Missionaries were theology students, which means that they
had already studied classical humanities and philosophy, and would soon be
ordained.
[15] Gabriel Soto, *Written testimony* (14 January 2004)

with him and see him, the very reason they had entered the seminary in the first place. The initiative to spread devotion to the Sacred Heart was a success, and a considerable number of the seminarians got together with their roommates to see when they could enthrone the Sacred Heart in their rooms.

Two years later, Marcial would leave behind a united, well-organized group of 34 seminarians.

> From this group, which had already committed to found with me, came the bishop of Papantla [Alfonso Sánchez Tinoco] . . . , the bishop of Matamoros [Sabás Magaña García], the bishop of Toluca, who is still alive [Alfredo Torres Romero], the archbishop of Morelia [Estanislao Alcaraz y Figueroa], the bishop of Tlanepantla, Manuel Pérez Gil; Victorino Álvarez, the first bishop of Apatzingán and later the first bishop of Celaya; and then another who has since passed away, Fidel Cortés, *Fidelito* we called him, bishop of [Chilpancingo-] Chilapa.[16]

When Archbishop Luis María Martínez of Mexico City visited the seminary in September 1939, Marcial made the most of the opportunity, telling him about his project of founding a group of priests and asking his advice. The archbishop expressed interest and offered him guidance. Marcial continued to keep in touch with the archbishop by letter, and on December 29 of the same year, the young founder wrote him the following lines:

> All of us future Missionaries of the Sacred Heart of Jesus have put into practice the wise, fatherly, and holy advice that Your Excellency gave us when you passed through this beloved seminary.
>
> I personally spoke with the superiors, asking permission to work so that all the students at this school consecrate themselves in a special way to the Sacred Heart. From Father Rector down to the deans, they completely approved the project. And not only this, but even Father

---

[16] Marcial Maciel LC (January 1992)

Rector took a large number of the holy cards of the Sacred Heart and has given away many to the young men.

Moreover, God's grace has been so effective in the soul of each of the students that the result of their personal consecration has been the ardent desire to enthrone the Sacred Heart in their dorms. The superiors said they were totally free to do so, and to date it has been enthroned in more than 10 rooms.

After the last enthronement, made earlier today, we raffled off books about devotion to the Sacred Heart of Jesus. Before the raffle, we read a work which I have included with this letter, so that Your Excellency will realize . . . what kind of ideas circulate among our companions about this.[17]

The first year and a half at Montezuma went by peacefully and fervently. Marcial lived the typical life of a student, and formed friendships that would last a lifetime. There were small triumphs and failures, he made the effort to forge his character or to learn to pray, and there were times of loneliness when letters from home caused homesickness or worries. Both moments of happiness and moments of sadness, he found, could bring spiritual joy and interior peace when lived at Jesus' side. These were the threads that formed the tapestry of Marcial's weeks and months in the seminary.

Changing bishops again

At the end of October 1939 the superiors recommended that Marcial travel to Mexico to have a doctor examine the delicate state of his ulcer. While he was there, he was to ask some of Montezuma seminary's contacts for scholarships to support the seminarians with no financial resources. Marcial set out for Mexico, and along the way stopped by Chihuahua to say hello to his uncle, Bishop Antonio Guízar. The bishop had heard

---

[17] Marcial Maciel LC, *Letter to Archbishop of Mexico Luis María Martínez* (29 December 1939)

from the superiors at the seminary that Marcial was founding a congregation with some of the young men at Montezuma, and he told Marcial to think it over seriously. If he persisted with his plans, Bishop Guízar said, he would no longer be able to sponsor him as a seminarian of the Chihuahua Diocese.

"Let me check with my spiritual director," Marcial said. "I don't feel that I can make a decision about something so important on my own. At least for me, it's something very important."

"Fine, but let me know what you decide."

Marcial continued his journey to Mexico City, reflecting on what had happened and speaking to the Holy Spirit about it. He couldn't play games with what he clearly saw to be God's will for his life; the group was not something that had simply occurred to him. God was the one who had asked him to be a founder and who had placed in his hands a mission whose fruit was destined not for him personally, but for the Church. If it was something God wanted, Marcial felt he could not treat it lightly.

On November 28, Marcial received a letter from Bishop Antonio Guízar informing him that he would no longer be able to attend Montezuma as a student for his diocese.

Marcial did not know what to do. He asked the advice of Father Luis Vega SJ, who worked at Holy Family Parish in Mexico City, and was told, "Well, if you want to, you can return to Montezuma sponsored by another bishop."

Here was a ray of light. There was no shortage of bishops in his family. The name of Bishop Francisco González Arias[18] of Cuernavaca came to mind.

The bishop of Cuernavaca was known to be a man of God with a principled conscience—prudent, upright and attentive to God's will—and several Mexican bishops were in the habit of asking him for advice. Marcial went to see him, entrusting himself to the Holy Spirit. He introduced himself as the son of Francisco Maciel and Maura Degollado Guízar.

---

[18] A brief biographical sketch of Bishop Francisco González Arias can be found in: Lauro López Beltrán, *Diócesis y Obispos de Cuernavaca, 1875–1978,* Mexico, Jus, 1978, pp. 171–204.

"Ah, Maurita's son!" the bishop exclaimed cheerfully. "That makes me your uncle."[19] Marcial explained everything that had happened, including the latest letter from Chihuahua, and he asked his uncle to send him back to Montezuma as a seminarian for the diocese of Cuernavaca. Bishop González Arias heard him out and agreed to the idea.

Full of hope and extremely relieved—not only was his ulcer a good deal better, but he had also found a way of returning to Montezuma—Marcial prepared his bags. On 12 December 1939, he arrived as a seminarian for the Cuernavaca diocese, looking forward to the years that lay before him in New Mexico.

God, however, had other plans. Only a few months remained for Marcial in Montezuma.

---

[19] cf. Marcial Maciel LC (January 1992). As the reader will already have noticed, in Mexico terms like "uncle" and "cousin" have a much wider meaning than in English. Bishop Francisco González Arias was, in fact, a second-cousin of Marcial's grandmother.

The congregation of the Legionaries of Christ came into existence with 13 seminarians and a 20-year-old founder on 3 January 1941, in the borrowed basement of this house at 39 Turín Street in Mexico City.

In May 1941, the members of the new congregation moved to a property at 21 Victoria Street in the Tlalpan neighborhood of Mexico City. They set up their dining room outside, with a table and benches made of planks, and an awning of sheets for a roof.

In the apostolic school of 21 Victoria Street, Marcial and the seminarians built themselves additional rooms, since the house was not large enough for all of them.

On 2 July 1945, Bishop Francisco González Arias of Cuernavaca and Archbishop Fernando Ruiz Solórzano of Yucatán visited the apostolic school of the "Missionaries of the Sacred Heart" (the future Legionaries of Christ) located at 12 Madero Street.

Bishop Francisco González Arias of Cuernavaca encouraged the foundation of the "Missionaries of the Sacred Heart" from day one, and with fatherly concern he supported Father Maciel with unconditional help, advice, and protection.

Marcial Maciel was ordained a priest on 26 November 1944 in the original Basilica of Our Lady of Guadalupe (Mexico) by His Excellency Francisco González Arias, bishop of Cuernavaca. In prayer that day, Marcial offered his whole life to Christ through Mary.

2 September 1946. Father Marcial Maciel brought a group of 32 future Legionaries to Spain to study at the Pontifical University of Comillas (Comillas, Santander). They flew from Mexico City to Cuba, and from Havana they crossed the Atlantic by steamship.

Legionary students talk with one of their professors in front of the main entrance of the Pontifical University of Comillas. The years spent in Comillas (1946–1950) marked a fruitful period of maturation, formation, and growth for the young congregation.

VI

The Founding
1940–1941

Seminary life in Montezuma progressed smoothly for Marcial during the first few months of 1940. Although the superiors had now become somewhat hesitant regarding the meetings of the Missionaries of the Sacred Heart, they nevertheless encouraged the individual members to continue working to elevate the spiritual and disciplinary level of the seminary, and showed support for the young founder.

Gabriel Soto, a fellow seminarian of Marcial's while in Montezuma, spoke about what Marcial did and promoted while in the seminary:

> We would frequently go to the chapel for adoration of the Blessed Sacrament. That was the number one thing. I don't remember how long we would stay in adoration, but we did spend many hours in prayer. We also offered up many sacrifices—each one freely decided what he thought best on his own . . . [1]

He was a friend who stood by Marcial through thick and thin as seminary life went on, and he agreed with Marcial's assessment that a priest's life should be solidly built upon the bedrock of prayer: that was the top priority. Like the other members of the group, Gabriel made small, simple, voluntary sacrifices throughout the day—restraint at meals, self-control at play, dedication and constancy in study. He explains that this spirit had a positive influence upon the other seminarians:

---

[1] Gabriel Soto, *Written Testimony* (17 January 2004)

[All these things] had a notable impact on the seminary. He, along with the seminarians who followed him, prompted an environment of fervor, intense Eucharistic life, charity, and good, positive conversations; they did so always respecting the activities that were part of the normal seminary schedule.[2]

Being a close friend to Marcial, Gabriel also saw how much he suffered at Montezuma for his ideas and ideals:

Marcial sought to serve others, never himself, with his life. Nevertheless, he suffered a lot in the seminary: he suffered perhaps more than he himself remembers, because he has that striking gift of forgetting all those things and concealing the evil he received . . . When someone throws himself into these "humanly speaking" crazy ideas, he always becomes the target of criticism. His companions caused him suffering, but the superiors did, too. I think he underwent it all for the assertiveness and commitment with which he sought to set up his congregation. Everything spoke to him of this one idea. In a special way I believe it was prayer that gave him such impressive strength of soul.[3]

Expelled

In June 1940 the rector, Father Agustín Waldner, spoke with Marcial to inform him that after summer vacation there was a possibility that he would not be allowed back to Montezuma. The rector explained his concern that some of the Mexican bishops would be annoyed if they found out that a congregation was being formed in the very heart of an inter-diocesan seminary. The final decision had not yet been made, and the rector promised to let Marcial know once he had given it some more thought.

---

[2] Gabriel Soto (17 January 2004)
[3] *ibid*

"I don't think it was so much the superiors who were against it," clarifies Father Gabriel Soto, sixty-four years later:

> I understand, rather, that it was a certain bishop; but I don't recall which one [it was who] categorically opposed Marcial's ideas . . . That was the reason Marcial left Montezuma in 1940: due to the seminary superiors' opposition to the new congregation he was forming. That was why they told him he could no longer continue there. I think it is understandable that the superiors didn't find it appropriate to have a group or institute being formed within the seminary. That is why I say that he had to carry his mission forward despite so many problems . . . "[4]

Marcial understood what the rector had said—but not completely.

The superiors had voiced their concern, but nothing concrete had been decided upon. The fact is that Marcial had already been toying with the idea of founding a separate house for his Missionaries somewhere in Mexico (probably in Michoacán's capital, Morelia, if the archbishop approved) so as not to complicate the normal running of Montezuma Seminary. The formation team in the seminary had expressed support for this idea, but for the young founder it was still just one possibility among many. He never doubted that, if his project were to fail, he would be able return to Montezuma to continue with his studies without difficulty.

When Marcial left for his summer vacation on 17 June 1940, he was happy, enthusiastic—and unaware that, in Montezuma's official logbook, he was now registered as *Marcial Maciel: ex-student.*[5]

Several days later, in Mexico City, Marcial met the archbishop of Morelia, Leopoldo Ruiz y Flores, who listened to the seminarian and invited him to accompany him back to his dio-

---

[4] Gabriel Soto (17 January 2004)
[5] Father José Macías SJ, *Montezuma en sus exalumnos . . .* , p. 337.

cese the next day, so that they could talk at greater ease during the trip.

When they arrived in Morelia, the archbishop asked his secretary Monsignor Fernando Ruiz Solórzano to analyze the young seminarian's situation. Monsignor Fernando prudently cautioned against trying to set up a separate house since Marcial was only a seminarian, and still so young. Marcial accepted God's will, but the secretary must have noticed a touch of sadness cross his face. "Don't let it discourage you," he said, "God often asks for this type of sacrifice when an important enterprise is at hand. If I'm still alive when you're ordained, you can be sure that I'll be able to be of greater help."[6] Monsignor Fernando Ruiz Solórzano would later become the much loved and revered bishop of Yucatán in southeast Mexico, and Father Maciel did enjoy his steadfast help and esteem after ordination. He offered the founder support in difficult moments, opened up doors to him in Rome by writing letters of recommendation, and ensured that he rested in moments of particular physical debility. He wrote to defend him against the calumnies that people were beginning to spread in an effort to destroy the new congregation and tarnish the founder's reputation. Bishop Fernando died with a wide-spread reputation of holiness.

For young Marcial, the secretary's words of assurance were heartening. As for the idea of founding a new house in Morelia, he gave it no more thought: if God did not want it to happen, well then, that was that.

After four weeks of vacation, he left for Cuernavaca to say hello to Bishop González Arias. When he arrived, he was surprised to find no one at home but the secretary. His "uncle" had been having heart problems, and his doctor had recommended he go to the coastal city of Veracruz to rest and recuperate.

"Did you know that the rector of Montezuma sent word saying you'd left the seminary for good?" inquired the secretary. "What did you do?"

"Well really I . . . ," stammered Marcial. "Are you sure?"

---

[6] cf. Marcial Maciel LC, *Annotations regarding the years 1939–1940*

"Well, I just don't know if you can return or not. The best thing would be to go to Veracruz to speak with the bishop. He'll tell you what you can do."[7]

As on similar occasions of hardship, Marcial turned to Jesus Christ in the Eucharist for comfort and strength, repeating short prayers over and over again: *Jesus, I believe in you, Jesus, I trust you* . . . . Kneeling in front of the tabernacle, he left his worries in God's hands and made a resolution. He was willing to defer any idea of founding until after he was ordained, if they would only allow him back into the seminary to finish his studies.

Marcial decided that he would track down his uncle. Five days later he boarded a bus bound for Veracruz. To his dismay, Marcial noticed that he had climbed on the wrong bus. Instead of the one that stopped only in the major cities of Puebla, Orizaba and Fortín de las Flores (cities he knew well), he had gotten on the one that stopped in many of the smaller towns on the way to Jalapa, the state capital. "Oh well," he thought to himself, "it's all the same. The important thing is to get to Veracruz." At lunch time, the driver announced that the bus would make a one-hour stop at San Salvador el Seco.[8]

Marcial figured that if it looked halfway decent, he would get a few tacos at the eatery by the bus stop. He went to investigate, and saw Bishop González Arias seated at a table with his sister Plácida and a priest named Father Antonio Rábago, having lunch.

"Marcial! What are you doing here?"

"Well, I was looking for you, believe it or not—I have a few things I wanted to speak to you about."

"Sure, I'd be happy to talk."

"Can you accept me in Cuernavaca as—?"

"Hold on! Look, here's what we'll do. I always take a walk after lunch: you can tell me what's on your mind then, all right?"

---

[7] cf. Marcial Maciel LC, *Annotations* . . . .
[8] "Holy Savior, the Dry"

"Look," said the bishop as they walked the little town after lunch, "forget about the bus going to Veracruz, and take the one headed for Mexico. There's no way I'm going to stand in the way of an enterprise that—as far as I can see—is inspired by God. So I give you total liberty to work and study wherever is best. You'll remain under my guardianship. But write to the rector anyway, to see if he'll let you go back to Montezuma."[9]

Letters went back and forth. The bishop wrote. Marcial wrote. Father Waldner, the rector in Montezuma, sent answers to both, saying that he couldn't take the young seminarian back. At the end of August, however, the bishop told Marcial to return to Montezuma to speak with the rector personally and ask to be admitted.

Questions and emotions jostled within Marcial's heart. To appear before the rector again would be a bitter pill to swallow, but—if the bishop asked it of him, that was what God wanted, and God loves obedience. On the one hand, all of his Missionaries were there in Montezuma, and for now they were his surest hope. How would he proceed with founding, if he weren't allowed to stay? On the other hand, if he promised not to speak about any foundation until he was ordained a priest— he had already contemplated this as a possible solution—he would most likely be able to continue his studies. It was hard to understand what God wanted. While he waited for his visa to the States, he asked some contemplative nuns to pray for his intentions and offered his anxieties to Jesus Christ. He could trust in God; he loved God. This gave him hope, and brought him some consolation. After all, God knew what he was doing, and this whole project was God's idea, not his.

Marcial left for Montezuma in early September 1940 alongside three other young men the bishop of Cuernavaca was sending to the seminary. They traveled by taxi, having agreed to split the fare four ways. Marcial was calm, certain that everything would work out. God had not let him down so

---

[9] cf. Marcial Maciel LC, *Annotations . . .* , and *idem* (January 1992)

far. He had practically convinced himself that his petition to be readmitted would be granted.

Everything would work out: but according to God's plans, not his.

At about three o'clock in the morning in the middle of the desert between El Paso, Texas, and Las Vegas, New Mexico, they stopped to take a short rest and have a bite to eat. Marcial remembers it all: a road-side eatery, the notes of *South of the Border* hanging in the night air (a song that would always remind him of this fleeting moment of rest in the midst of life's hustle and bustle), a full moon, and a silent, star-filled sky. His mother, Mamá Maurita, had taught him to contemplate God and enjoy his company through the beauty of nature, and he can still remember the thoughts that went through his head that night:

> Beautiful nights like those really preach to us about God, about his immensity and beauty. They offer us an extraordinary way to understand and contemplate his omnipotence, his beauty, his wisdom, his love—they can evoke so many things."[10]

As it turned out, Marcial would not have many tranquil moments like this one over the next few years. Perhaps he remembers it so intensely precisely because it was followed by such profound misfortune.

Once at Montezuma he was assigned a room, and ordinary seminary life started up again. Marcial was studying in his room after lunch three or four days after their arrival when someone knocked at his door. It was Brother Molina.

"Father Waldner says that we have to leave for Albuquerque right away, because you have to return to Mexico."

"Oh, right—, right . . . but— Brother, for what reason?"

"Look, I don't know. Pack your suitcase and come on. I'll wait for you here."

"Right—but I want to speak with the rector; or with one of the priests . . . "

---

[10] Marcial Maciel LC (January 1992)

"No. No, there's no time. The rector told me to tell you that there was no time for that. So let's go. Get your things together. We're leaving."[11]

The lay brother had the car waiting. Marcial could only drop into the chapel to make one last quick visit to Jesus Christ, and murmur a quick farewell to a few of the Missionaries he happened to pass by in the hallway.

Expelled again. First from the Veracruz seminary, now from Montezuma.

The car wound its way down the road, and Marcial saw the beautiful seminary building disappear around a corner. He wept in silence.

> It is very difficult to express the sentiments that overwhelmed my heart and the thoughts that flashed through my mind. Really, I don't know how a human being can resist so much agony at certain moments of life without dying. I remember that in the car I could practically only pray and cry, not knowing the reason or the purpose of it all. I must have felt an immense desolation, as if the whole world was collapsing under me."[12]

He took the train to Juarez City. Monsignor Pelayo, the parish priest, kindly offered him lodging and paid for his ticket to Chihuahua the next day. From there he continued on to Mexico. He spent the long hours of the trip trying to understand what had just come to pass, and wondering what he would do next.

Studying for the priesthood

Marcial looked up his spiritual director, Father Álvarez SJ, and told him what had happened. The priest encouraged him, telling him to keep at it without getting discouraged, since it was God who wanted the foundation.

---

[11] Marcial Maciel LC (January 1992)
[12] cf. *ibid*

If God wanted it, that was how it would be. Bishop Francisco González Arias confirmed this conclusion, telling Marcial:

> You aren't going to go back home. I am going to support you, and I am going to help you to bring about what God has inspired you to do, because it seems to me to be something that comes from God. Today I commended you at Mass. I fervently asked the Holy Spirit and the Blessed Virgin Mary to illuminate me. I received light and strength, and what is more, I felt it necessary to take you in, support you and help you in whatever way I can, in anything that is needed for you to carry out God's work.[13]

The bishop of Cuernavaca planned to send him to one of the other Mexican seminaries. However, after several different seminaries refused to accept him, the bishop settled on another solution. He would provide theology professors to tutor Marcial one-on-one, and the new foundation could begin once he was ordained.

Marcial began his theology studies. They would continue until ordination four years later. He received private classes, studying the treatises one by one and presenting his exams orally in Cuernavaca before a four-man tribunal. It was a demanding set of examiners: first, Bishop Francisco González Arias himself; second, Monsignor Gregorio Araiza, who had studied philosophy in Rome's Angelicum University of St. Thomas Aquinas and theology at the Gregorian, chief apostolic notary and juridical advisor to the Mexican Episcopate;[14] third, his professor Monsignor José García Ortiz, later named general vicar of the diocese, who had also studied at the Gregorian University in Rome (doctorate and gold medal in philosophy,

---

[13] Marcial Maciel LC (January 1992)

[14] Besides being a canon lawyer well-respected by the Mexican bishops, Monsignor Araiza was also a Latin scholar. On 6 June 1951 he was named a canon of the metropolitan cathedral after the death of Monsignor Jesús Mier y Terán. He continued to exercise a variety of special tasks for the Church in Mexico until his death on 25 May 1966.

doctorate and gold medal in theology, doctorate in Canon Law);[15] and fourth, his professor Doctor Manuel G. Rojas, an experienced theologian. They didn't hand Marcial his philosophy and theology credits on a silver platter. The bishop was aware that he was preparing a priest who had been called to found a religious congregation.

Father Maciel's intellectual formation was undoubtedly up to the mission God gave him. On numerous occasions throughout his priestly life, he would manifest a precise knowledge of the Catholic Faith that he received from his four theology professors. His preparation would enable him to orient his Legionaries in their academic formation, choose the best schools for them, and help them to keep the Deposit of the Faith (*depositum fidei*) intact in the midst of widespread doctrinal confusion. Father Maciel has often said that "faith is worth more than life itself." His wisdom does not come from books alone, but also from the light of faith, fully accepted and embraced.

Marcial had just settled down to his studies when, at the beginning of October 1940, he received a letter from his family telling him that his brother Alfonso was gravely ill with typhoid fever and that they doubted he would survive. Bishop González Arias gave him permission to go to Cotija to be with his brother and family.

Alfonso, closest to Marcial in age, was 22 at the time. Their father had put him in charge of *Los Tazumbos*, his largest ranch, and Alfonso—equipped with pistol and riding on horseback—administered it ably. He was pure Mexican, and "Cotijan" to the bone: headstrong, happy and noble. Father Maciel recalls that once, as a seminarian, he had been conversing with his brother when some men within earshot began to use coarse language. Alfonso was so upset that he jumped to his feet and confronted them, indignantly demanding that they keep quiet. "Don't you realize that my brother is here, and he's going to be a priest?"

Penicillin was not yet available. Alfonso's strong constitution did its best to resist the typhoid fever, and he had actually

---

[15] Father José García Ortiz obtained his doctorate in philosophy on 11 December 1915, in theology on 5 November 1919, and in Canon Law on 6 November 1924.

seemed to be slowly improving. At one point, however, a shot caused an infection that his debilitated body could not counter.

"I'm going to ask God to cure you quickly," Marcial reassured him.

"No; I'm ready to die. I've already suffered a lot. I want to go to be with God."

"Well, but it's better that God's will be done, isn't it?"

"Yes—but why don't you ask God to take me to be with him instead . . . ?"[16]

Alfonso died on 4 November 1940.

After Alfonso's death, Marcial stayed with his family, spending two or three more weeks in Cotija and the surrounding region. During that time, he and his brother José assisted at the deathbed of not less than 10 people who died of gunshot wounds or pneumonia.

Marcial had been in Cotija all October with his brother, and he had found time to gather together a group of eight adolescents who said they wanted to be priests. Without really planning it, his third attempt to found a congregation suddenly blossomed into what he named the "Immaculate Conception Apostolic School." Several women prepared the boys' meals and looked after the house his father had lent him in Cotija. Anita and Sarita Ochoa and Guadalupe Oseguera, teachers in the town, offered to tutor the boys and prepare them for the seminary. For five pesos a month, Marcial rented another house that served as their classroom, where the eight boys spent their day. He succeeded in convincing Father Jesús de la Parra, a retired priest who served as chaplain in St. Joseph's parish, to be the new school's rector, since he would have to return to Cuernavaca to continue his studies at the bishop's house.

Sunrise on the horizon

By November 25, Marcial had gone back to continue his schooling, and he had a chance to speak with the bishop of Cuernavaca. He told him about his new project, the apostolic

---

[16] cf. Marcial Maciel LC (January 1992)

school in Cotija, and said that he had been thinking about following up on it during his vacation periods. Bishop González Arias interrupted him. "Look," he said, "we'll do the following. You keep on studying, and I'll find you a house. I give you permission to set up the apostolic school here in Cuernavaca, so that you don't have to be going back and forth to Cotija: it's too far."[17]

The bishop offered him a church and an old Franciscan convent with gardens just outside Cuernavaca where he could live with his Missionaries. Marcial was still pondering the offer and praying about it days later: the idea had not totally convinced him. Where could he find qualified teachers for the boys in Cuernavaca, and enough people to support them? Would he be able to find young men who wanted to be priests? On these points it would be more advantageous for him to found in Mexico City.

Bishop González Arias had reservations about that proposal. Was a 20-year old seminarian going to set up a school all by himself in Mexico City? Who would help him? Nevertheless, the bishop did not write off the possibility, and asked the Holy Spirit for light. A few days later, the bishop accepted his nephew's idea, having reached the conclusion that it was God's will. He personally visited Archbishop Luis María Martínez of Mexico City, asking permission to open an extension of Cuernavaca's minor seminary in his diocese, which could later become the apostolic school of the Missionaries of the Sacred Heart—the future Legionaries of Christ.

It was God who wanted the foundation, but it was Marcial who had to put his hand to the plow. He had already made three attempts: one in the Mexican capital (at the seminary of Veracruz in Atzcapotzalco and in Mixcoac), one in the United States (Montezuma), and another one in Cotija. "I didn't exactly have well-defined plans," he says.

> Really, it wasn't I who did it. I was only the tool of God's providence, and day after day I tried to carry out his will for my life and the project of the foundation. I didn't

---

[17] cf. Marcial Maciel LC (January 1992)

exactly have well-defined plans—actually, quite the opposite. My idea was to do my best not to get in the way
of God's grace, and to offer myself as an instrument for
him to do with me as he saw fit.[18]

God led him from one place to another, offering no expla-
nations. Marcial's efforts had often ended in grievous disappointments.

There was a reason behind the jostling that he had experienced. He had been brought back to the capital because God
must have wanted the Legion of Christ to be founded in Mexico City, under the tutelage of the bishop of Cuernavaca, with
a group of adolescents and a founder who was still studying
theology. He must have wanted the founder to be a 20-year-old
who had learned to follow God's lead, even despite trials and
adversity.

This was the fourth attempt, and it would be the definitive
one. Marcial moved to Mexico to prepare the groundwork for
the founding. Friends of the Guízars, the Retes family, had a
house on Turín Street, number 39, and they agreed to lend Marcial the rooms of the basement in order to begin the apostolic
school, until he could find somewhere else to house his Missionaries. Starting in December 1940, Marcial studied in Mexico from Monday to Thursday, and dedicated his weekends to
look for vocations in the capital and other cities of Michoacán,
Jalisco and Querétaro. The bishop of Cuernavaca gave him a
recommendation letter requesting that bishops open their
doors to him, and in this way he could get in touch with parish
priests and local families. He walked miles, visiting schools
and parishes, and succeeded in finding about 30 adolescents
who were interested. At the same time, he knocked on doors in
the more affluent zones of Mexico City asking for donations
whenever he had a gap in his study schedule. But after several
exhausting days and weeks, he had collected no more than 100
pesos. "And that," commented Father Maciel, took "into con-
sideration that to save money, I always took along a roll with

---

[18] Jesús Colina, *Christ is My Life . . .* , p. 28

beans and a small, 3¢ can of *Sidral Mundet* pop[19] . . . because if I didn't, I'd end up spending more on food than what I collected all day."[20]

Miss Conchita Cañedo, a friend of the Retes family, donated 500 pesos. Marcial's first thought was to buy what was truly essential: not beds, chairs, tables or plates, but an altar, a chalice and other items needed to celebrate Mass. Once these had been purchased, he bought the cheapest 15 desks and chairs he could find. And that was all: the money couldn't be stretched any further.

On December 8, the feast of the Immaculate Conception, the Retes family offered him a substantial loan with which to found the congregation. "But what happens if I can't pay it back afterwards?" Marcial asked.[21] If he couldn't pay, they'd pardon the debt; if he could, and they needed it, they'd accept the money back; if they didn't need it, they'd let him keep it.

Everything was finally in place. The only thing left to do was to go and inform Bishop González Arias, and ask his permission to begin.

Here and throughout the history of the congregation, Father Maciel discovered that when God has plans, he usually likes to bring them about through Mary, his Mother. It was on December 8, a Marian feast day, that he received the news of the Retes' loan. Four days later, on December 12, the feast of Our Lady of Guadalupe, Marcial was in Cuernavaca telling the bishop about the opportunity to carry out the foundation.

"Let's go pray in the chapel," his uncle replied, "to ask God to enlighten us and help us see if this is what he wants."[22]

They entered the chapel together, and the minutes ticked by: half an hour, an hour, two hours. Marcial was asking Jesus Christ to illumine the bishop; the bishop was doing the same. Finally Bishop González Arias stood up and left the chapel, with Marcial at his heels. "Look, Marcial, I believe God wants

---

[19] An apple-flavored soft-drink produced in Mexico.
[20] cf. Marcial Maciel LC (January 1992)
[21] *ibid*
[22] *ibid*

us to begin, and since we have that financial backing, we also have a good human starting point."[23] He told Marcial to propose an appropriate day for the foundation.

Foundation Day

Marcial opted for January 1. After Christmas, he went to visit the boys and families who had said they would take part in the foundation. Some of the boys had changed their minds, and others were not allowed to go. In the end, Marcial succeeded in bringing together 13 future apostolics. However, Father Daniel Santana, the Salesian priest assigned by the bishop as future rector and chaplain of the apostolic school fell ill, and could not be there on January 1. Marcial took the 13 boys to the Basilica of Guadalupe, and entrusted the foundation to her motherly protection. Father Santana arrived at 39 Turín Street on January 2, and on 3 January 1941, a First Friday, he celebrated the inaugural Mass of the "Sacred Heart Apostolic School."[24]

Marcial realized that it had also been a First Friday January 3 that he had left his family five years ago as a 15-year-old and slept under the cold stars at the Tingüindín train station. He was grateful to Jesus for the coincidence: two January 3's, two First Fridays, two days dedicated to the Sacred Heart. He took it as a clear sign of God's blessing.

Many things had happened since leaving Cotija, and that was how God wanted it. Marcial's only desire then had been to spend his life for Christ as a priest, and his plans had been to join the Carmelites in Puebla. He had loved God and had been faithful, and now he was surrounded by 13 boys in the borrowed basement of a house in Mexico City, founding a congregation at 20 years of age. Even he would admit that the situation God had placed him in seemed unbelievable.

---

[23] Jesús Colina, *Christ is My Life . . .* , p. 29

[24] —, *Diary of the Missionary Apostolic School of the Sacred Heart of Jesus* (Mexico City, 3 January 1941). It was called a "missionary apostolic school" (*apostólica misional*) because its aim was that of forming missionary apostles. It was the common name for minor seminaries in Mexico at the time.

On the day of foundation, Marcial felt overwhelmed by the responsibility placed upon his shoulders. Father Santana had just celebrated Mass on 39 Turín Street: the apostolic school was born. The boys were studying. Marcial suddenly felt a terrible sense of desolation inside, as if he were submerged in some type of deep darkness. Much later, he would tell the Legionaries of Christ in Salamanca, Spain, about the sentiments he had experienced.

> The only thing I could do was go to the tabernacle and say to the Lord: "Don't you see that this just can't be? It's too much for me."
>
> I felt that I didn't know what I should do—but I had his company; I had him. I had someone to talk to, someone to speak with. . . .
>
> Time and time again I went to pray in the chapel, always saying the same thing. . . . It occurred to me to open the Gospel, the missal . . . and I read this phrase: "Commit your way to the Lord, trust in him, and he will act" (Psalm 37:5). So I said, "If this is your answer: here I am. I am your instrument: act through me! I will do everything I can, but you are going to be the one who carries the baton." That brought me tranquility.[25]

---

[25] Marcial Maciel LC (1981).

VII

The Early Years
1941–1946

During their first months at 39 Turín Street in 1941, the Missionaries of the Sacred Heart and their founder slept on the floor until they had enough money to buy beds. Winter was cold. They covered the floor with newspapers to keep out the dampness, spread their sheets over the papers, and slept wrapped in their blankets or *zarapes*.[1] It was hard to fall asleep.

From January until May, Miss Natalia Retes Quezada[2] (usually addressed as *Talita* by those who knew her) prepared meals for the boys. She served things like beans or rice soup, with an inexpensive fruit sauce made of blended sapodilla plum[3] mixed with sugar and orange juice for desert. The apostolic boys loved it. Despite her protestations, Marcial paid her 25 centavos per boy per day to help cover the expenses.

From the first day of the apostolic school, Marcial drew up schedules with designated times for prayer, classes, recreation and study. He was able to hire a number of teachers. Manuel González Rojas taught Latin, and others teachers taught Greek, Spanish, History, Math and Geography. Father Santana, the rector, celebrated Mass, heard confessions and sometimes gave classes and talks on the spiritual life. The Salesian priest knew how to relate with young people, and Marcial continually thanked God for the providential, tranquil way that all the

---

[1] A zarape is a Mexican garment similar to the ponchos worn in Chile, a heavy cloak draped over the body, front and back.

[2] Natalia Retes was a spinster in her fifties. She helped the Missionaries of the Sacred Heart until her death in December 1948. The Legionaries of Christ gratefully remember her as the congregation's first benefactor.

small difficulties common to all beginnings were gradually taken care of—including their material needs.

Holy Week in Veracruz

When Holy Week 1941 arrived, Marcial decided to take the apostolics to the town of Jesús María in Veracruz for two weeks of vacation. He was having difficulty finding money for the boys' upkeep, and guessed that between Father Maldonado and his parishioners he would be able to find food and lodgings. He was right. Father Antonio Maldonado and his sister Esther were overjoyed to receive the seminarian and his spiritual sons. It had been three years since he had last visited them.

Years later, Father Maldonado and his sister Esther would narrate the boys' visit to their town. Father Maldonado recounts:

> That Holy Week, there was only one palm branch left over [from Palm Sunday Mass], and there were no other palms in town, so I gave it to Father Maciel, who gave a palm leaf to each one of the boys. He always took care of them, as if they were his own sons. He was careful to ensure that they were always together; they all needed to arrive punctually to lunch, breakfast, afternoon snack and prayers . . . all together, so that they wouldn't get scattered. They were always very orderly, going from one activity to the next just like in school.[4]

"And I would tell him," added Esther, "'Oh, Father—let them be! They're outdoors!' But he [Marcial] would say, 'No, Esther, you don't understand. I'm responsible for all of them.'"[5]

When they returned to Mexico City, Marcial learned that he would need to look for another home for the apostolic school. Someone had denounced the seminary to the govern-

---

[3] The sapodilla plum (*zapote*) is a savory tropical fruit.
[4] Javier García LC, *Interview with Father Antonio* . . . (25 August 1965)
[5] *ibid*

ment, and the Retes family was in danger of having the house confiscated. The Retes family donated him another house in far-off Mazatlán. He sold it, and with the money from its sale and a 4,000-peso loan from Bishop Gonzalez Arias, he was able to buy a house at 21 Victoria Street, in the town of Tlalpan on the southern outskirts of Mexico City. Although the house was small, it had ample lawn and garden space. The move itself was easy, and did not cost them anything. The founder and the 13 boys only needed a small truck loaded with 15 desks, 15 chairs, the altar, the few household goods that belonged to them, and some pots Talita lent them for cooking.

They would live at 21 Victoria Street for almost three years, until 1944, when the Archdiocese of Mexico asked to buy the property for its own seminary. They then moved a short distance to 12 Madero Street. This house was large and well-suited to accommodate a continually growing apostolic school for several years.

Beginnings are never easy. To begin a work of God in poverty implies immense faith and trust in providence. It also implies hard work and a great deal of wear and tear. Despite it all, the early years were a time of high hopes and happiness for both the founder and the apostolics, full of enthusiastic self-giving for love of God. They were so happy that they scarcely realized they were poor.

Marcial dedicated himself to his three top priorities: forming his Missionaries, looking for whatever they needed to survive, and studying.

They had a grove of fruit trees at 21 Victoria Street, as well as a coop for chickens and turkeys, and two milk cows. The first cow Mariposa ("Butterfly") was a gift from Mr. Alfredo Porras, and a few months later a certain Mr. Eustaquio donated Presumida ("Show-off"). Marcial would get up before sunrise to milk the cows, and then go out to sell the milk and buy breakfast for the apostolic boys from what he earned. When he got home, he would wake the boys, direct a meditation for them in the chapel, and prepare breakfast after going to Mass with them.

The apostolics had time to clean their rooms and do some household chores before going to class, though most of the housework fell to Marcial. He was in charge of cooking, cleaning, and washing the boys' clothes each day (by hand, of course): muddied and stained shirts, socks, pants . . . Once classes started, Marcial spent the morning selling flowers or fruit from the garden and begging for alms door-to-door, so as to collect enough money to buy lunch, which usually consisted of beans, bread, and rice. It was a hand-to-mouth life.

Only on one occasion did Marcial fall short of money to buy bread for the apostolics. They got by on lemon tea that day until nearly 8 p.m., when Marcial, seeing the expression on their faces by that time, went out and asked a store to give him a tin of sardines and 15 rolls on credit. With this and another cup of lemon tea, the boys were able to go to bed with something in their stomachs. Father Maciel explained later:

> Thank God, with the exception of that day we always had what we needed, though certainly it was all very poor. But everyone was happy because we knew we were starting something important for the Church, and in doing so we were pleasing God.[6]

On occasion Marcial would beg for donations in the afternoon, but normally he made sure to stay at home to form the apostolics. He had to teach them how to pray, how to shine their shoes and even how to brush their teeth. He organized their sports, and encouraged them by taking part. Whenever the opportunity arose—in homilies, informal talks or one-on-one conversations—he would pay special attention to helping them form their consciences. He encouraged them to be sincere, honest and open with their superiors, and motivated them to act according to higher motives like love for Christ or for their future priestly mission rather than for the desire to be seen or appreciated, or for any other lesser reward. Most of all, he made sure that their young hearts nurtured a personal, con-

---

[6] Jesús Colina, *Christ is My Life . . .* , p. 32–33

crete, ardent love for Jesus and for souls, and thus a high regard for their vocation and for the Church's mission.

He encouraged them to prepare themselves conscientiously, and talked to them about the schools and universities they would establish to help the Church and to teach all men and women about Christ and his love. The boys, who just days earlier had survived on nothing but bread and sardines, firmly believed that they would build those schools and universities, and redoubled their efforts to improve their handwriting and spelling, since they knew that they needed to achieve a level of preparation that would measure up to the standards of the times.

In the midst of his comings and goings, Marcial set aside long moments to pray the breviary in the chapel and to talk with Jesus, his Friend and Teacher. For Marcial, Christ was a living fountain of love, a source of strength and his model of self-giving.

When the boys finished studying around 9:30 p.m., Marcial was just beginning his own studies as a seminarian. Manuel González Rojas, the apostolics' Latin teacher, agreed to come at night to tutor him, and thanks to his availability, generosity, and teaching skills, Marcial managed to do his philosophy and theology studies at a quick pace, bringing him ever closer to ordination. After two or three hours of class or study, an exhausted Marcial would at last fall into bed around midnight to sleep for a few hours. But sleep was brief. He was up again before cockcrow to milk the cows and start his daily routine all over again. For two years he lived in these conditions. "God always strengthened me and held me up,"[7] Father Maciel explains.

New rectors

Because of a painful illness that provoked intense headaches, Father Daniel Santana asked to be relieved of his duties

---

[7] Jesús Colina, *Christ is My Life . . .* , p. 32

as rector. Bishop González Arias had to look within his own diocese and inquire in neighboring ones to find someone to replace him. A succession of priests followed Father Santana in governing the apostolic school. One in particular, Father Antonio García Esparza, a late vocation to the priesthood, occasioned many dilemmas for Marcial. He was rector from 1943 until early 1944, and had a different concept of how a minor seminary should be run. Even in the presence of the apostolic boys he would oppose the decisions Marcial took as founder and which the bishop of Cuernavaca had already approved.

Marcial waited for an opportunity to speak with the bishop, explaining what was happening and the harm it was causing the boys' formation as they prepared for priesthood and religious life. That was his chief concern. Bishop González Arias gave Marcial an option: he could stay at 21 Victoria Street and bear with the situation as best he could, or else move to the seminary in Cuernavaca, leaving the apostolics at 21 Victoria Street until the bishop figured out what could be done for them.

Marcial spent a sorrowful night on the living room sofa of Emiliano Guízar, his great-uncle, contemplating a picture of the Sacred Heart, praying and asking for enlightenment.

The following morning the bishop of Cuernavaca asked him to stop by, and told him that he had rethought his decision from the day before. The bishop had been unable to sleep, thinking that he had made a mistake. He told Marcial to return to 21 Victoria Street, promising to remove the rector from his duties and look for another. That was the end of Marcial's problems.

Ordained a Priest

Marcial finished his theology studies at long last. He went on a week-long spiritual retreat to prepare himself for ordination, and was ordained a priest on 26 November 1944. The particulars are few and simple: the ceremony took place in the Basilica of Our Lady of Guadalupe in Mexico City,[8] and Bishop

---

[8] The old basilica, later closed to the public on account of structural problems.

González Arias presided. Along with all of the apostolics, several family members, benefactors and friends took part.

Returning home from the basilica, Marcial and the apostolics went straight to the kitchen to prepare some sandwiches, because in the midst of all the emotions and preparation, they had forgotten that they would still need to eat on ordination day. They spent the day in great simplicity.

Beyond the external events of November 26, it is possible to discover what Father Maciel's spiritual experience was like on the most longed-for moment of his life:

> I had to suffer enormous tribulations even to take the step to priesthood, interior tribulations, because I never believed myself worthy of receiving the sublime gift of the priesthood. Besides, I could never accept before God that I—as poor, pitiable and incapable as I was, in short, all that infinite personal smallness—was the one who would have to carry forward the founding of the Legionaries of Christ. But God had things planned otherwise.[9]

Marcial had spent practically the whole night in prayer before the Blessed Sacrament to ready himself to receive the sacrament of priesthood. On the morning of the 26th he had left for the Basilica of Guadalupe, placing himself before God.

> I went up to the altar like a grain of wheat that longs to come to the mill to become flour, to be made a host with him who is the Host, with him who is flour, [a grain of wheat] that has been through the mill and suffered all the griefs and martyrdoms that a human being can suffer in this world, just as he suffered.
>
> Once again I placed my life in God's hands through the Blessed Virgin Mary. There on Tepeyac,[10] beneath her sweet immaculate gaze, I left everything in her hands,

---

[9] Marcial Maciel LC (1980s)
[10] Tepeyac is the hill where Our Lady of Guadalupe appeared to St. Juan Diego. The Basilica of Our Lady of Guadalupe was later built on this site.

under her protection, and I went up the steps of the altar to fulfill God's will.[11]

Marcial went to Cotija de la Paz as a newly ordained priest to celebrate his *cantamisa* ("First Mass") on 6 January 1945. Archbishop José María González Valencia of Durango was the main celebrant. He greatly esteemed Marcial and would support him throughout his life.

Difficult Moments

In the first months of 1945, Marcial finished the first draft of the constitutions of the Legionaries of Christ, still known at the time as the Missionaries of the Sacred Heart. He would need to present the constitutions to the Holy See to be examined and approved by the Congregation for Religious.

Towards the end of May, the Latin scholar who had been translating the constitutions from Spanish to Latin decided to "charge for his services," holding the constitutions ransom for a sum that Marcial could not afford. Marcial offered him a car, the second-hand model that a benefactor had given him for his birthday. The offer was unsatisfactory. Several days later, the scholar left with the originals in both Spanish and Latin. Marcial, asking the Holy Spirit to illuminate him, had to sit down in front of a blank sheet of paper and start rewriting the constitutions from scratch.

Talita Retes came by the school to deliver the apostolics' clean clothing a week later, at the beginning of June, and she saw in Marcial's face that he was not well. He had been feeling ill for days, trying simply to ignore the pain and continue working.

"Something's wrong," she said.

"Never mind; it's nothing."[12]

Talita insisted. She obliged him to go to the *Italian Hospital* for a check-up, and it was just in time. He nearly died from a case of appendicitis with complications resulting in peritonitis,

---

[11] Marcial Maciel LC (1980s)

[12] cf. Marcial Maciel LC (January 1992)

leaving him in critical condition. They operated and were able to save his life.[13]

Marcial had harbored high hopes of celebrating the mass of the Feast of the Sacred Heart that Friday—his first time as a priest—but he would have to accompany the Sacred Heart from his hospital bed instead.

---

[13] It was one of the first times penicillin was used in Mexico

VIII

God in a Hurry
1946

Looking after the Missionaries became considerably simpler for Marcial after being ordained a priest, since he could now celebrate Mass for them and be named officially as their rector. It was also easier for families to entrust their sons to a priest than to a seminarian.

Novitiate

The apostolic school was growing steadily, and so were the boys. It was time to set up a novitiate. Marcial was able to buy a house for the new community right next-door to the apostolic school, at 10 Madero Street. Since two houses meant two rectors, the archbishop of Morelia permitted a priest from his diocese, Father Luis Ferreira (a fellow-seminarian of Marcial's in Montezuma), to temporarily assist the founder as rector of the apostolic school.

The novitiate was founded on 25 March 1946, and Father Maciel took charge of the 13 older boys who had been preparing for a year to become novices.[1] Since opening a novitiate constituted a decisive step towards the congregation's definitive approval, he had been spending long hours in prayer asking Jesus what the essence of their spirituality ought to be, and what concrete path they should follow. He received an answer that morning, and it was simple: their entire spirituality should be Christ-centered; their path, to follow the footsteps of Christ.

---

[1] Young men preparing to enter novitiate are commonly called "postulants" or "candidates." The novitiate is a one- to two-year period that lets young men learn about religious life.

> I had a clear idea, of course, regarding our founding and our aims, but what wasn't so clear was the idea of how to define the Legion of Christ's spirituality. That day (first as I was praying, and later during the Eucharistic Celebration) God gave me a very special light. I think that this was the starting point for our Christ-centered spirit, our compact spirit as Legionaries of Christ: "Follow in Christ's footsteps"; no complications.[2]

It was Christ who had come to earth to redeem humanity. He had been obedient unto death, "death on a cross", and spared no sacrifice in carrying out his mission. As a proof of love, Christ had lain down his very life, Marcial reflected, and if he remained with his followers in the Eucharist and the Gospel, it was so that they would come to know him, and learn to imitate him.

> There was no other way, no safer way, to fulfill our vocation as Legionaries of Christ and priests of Christ (that is: without euphemisms, without wrenching it out of shape, without being hypocritical) than by imitating him, letting our feet fall precisely within his footprints. For me, it was that day, 25 March 1946, that sparked off the unity, the certainty, the depth, and the harmony of what every Legionary of Christ's and Regnum Christi[3] Movement member's spirituality is, and always will be.[4]

This was the light he received the day the novitiate began. It was a question of knowing, loving, and imitating Christ, and as a direct consequence, of loving all men and women just as Christ did: even to the point of laying down one's life for them.

Over the front door of every Legionary novitiate throughout the world, the following three words are inscribed: *Christus Vita Vestra* (Christ Your Life). For Legionaries and Regnum Christi members, Christ is the Way, the Truth, and the Life. Jesus

---

[2] Marcial Maciel LC (1980s)
[3] Regnum Christi ("Christ's Kingdom") is the name of the Movement of apostolate that Father Maciel would found several years later.
[4] Marcial Maciel LC (1980s)

Christ, the Son of God who became man out of love, and who gave himself up to save all men and women, is the center of their lives. Their ideal is to give themselves totally to Christ and to others, out of love, thus taking part in the work of the Church, where Christ continues his saving mission in the world.

A providential encounter

A few weeks later, Marcial went to seek spiritual guidance from Archbishop Luis María Martínez, the Primate of Mexico, something that he had been doing rather regularly since first meeting him as a seminarian in Montezuma. As he waited to see the archbishop, he began to speak with a Spanish priest who was also waiting his turn, Father Francisco Javier Baeza, the rector of the Pontifical University of Comillas, Spain. He was traveling through Latin America to promote a scholarship program for his university sponsored by the Spanish government. "I'd be very interested in that," exclaimed Marcial. He wasted no time explaining the founding of his congregation to Father Baeza, and how he wanted the Missionaries to receive their formation at the very best universities. They got along immediately. Marcial invited him to Madero Street, and a few days later, the rector of Comillas visited the apostolic school to see an academic presentation that the boys had prepared.

"I don't have to tell you, Father Maciel," said Father Baeza, "that if you go to Spain, come and see me. I'll speak with the government and help you get the scholarships you need."[5] Father Marcial agreed to visit him in Spain within a few weeks. He planned to do so en route to Rome, where he would present the congregation's constitutions to the Holy See along with the request for the *nihil obstat*, to pave the way for the congregation's official approval.[6] In his naivety, the young founder believed he could ask for and receive an appointment with the Holy Father just as easily as he did when he wanted to see

---

[5] cf. Marcial Maciel LC (January 1992)

[6] *Nihil obstat*: the name of document issued by the Holy See's Sacred Congregation for Religious that states that there is "nothing to prohibit" the canonical establishment of a new religious congregation on a diocesan level.

Archbishop Luis María Martínez. He imagined that he would simply explain his foundation plans to Pius XII and then ask for his blessing, and that would be that.

There is a popular Mexican phrase that runs to the tune of: "Slow down, Jack: I'm in a hurry."[7] They would need to find another refrain for Marcial, perhaps something like: "Brace yourself! God's in a hurry!" Marcial was 26 and God was driving him along. He had left Cotija some ten years earlier at the age of 15, thinking that he would soon be in Puebla with the Carmelites. God had other plans for him. Marcial had been expelled from seminary three times. He had been in jail. The constitutions he wrote had been held for ransom; he had to write them twice. He had seen his first groups unravel three times. He spent the last two years living on an average of two to three hours of sleep, and had had peritonitis. He had purchased three houses and finished his Juniorate,[8] philosophy and theology studies. He was now a priest, at the head of a group of more than 40 boys, all sustained on donations. And this was just the beginning. "Really, my whole life has been a type of whirlwind," confessed Father Maciel a year after the congregation's 50th Anniversary:

> It is as if I had stepped out for a pleasant walk in the countryside on a mild day, and without knowing why or whence, something came along, something like the wind. It caught me up, and without letting me think much, without giving me time to reflect and take all the measures of time-frames and prudence . . . I began to act—or to "let it act" through me . . . [9]

After speaking with the archbishop of Mexico, Marcial began his preparations to visit Spain and Rome, a necessary

---

[7] The actual saying is: *"Vísteme despacio, Juan, que tengo prisa."*
[8] The Juniorate was a stage of priestly formation that preceded philosophical and theological studies, dedicated to the study of classical literature, language, and culture. In Spanish-speaking countries it was sometimes referred to as the *Latinado*, and its students were nicknamed *Latinos* ("Latinists").
[9] Marcial Maciel LC (January 1992)

step if the congregation was to be officially brought into canonical existence and recognized by the Church. He needed to give a copy of the constitutions to the Sacred Congregation for Religious, and present the formal petition of his bishop—Bishop González Arias of Cuernavaca—to the Holy See (this request would be accompanied by the recommendation letters of 23 different bishops and archbishops from across Mexico).

Father Oñate's Report

Marcial asked Archbishop Luis María Altamirano y Bulnes of Morelia to lend him the services of Father Alfonso Sánchez Tinoco, another classmate from Montezuma, to take care of the novices during his trip to Europe. Father Luis Ferreira would be in charge of the apostolics.

Several months earlier, Bishop Francisco González Arias had assigned a priest to visit the Legionary of Christ's house and write a report on the nascent institute. He had entrusted the task to Father Ángel Oñate of the Missionaries of the Holy Spirit (M Sp S).[10] He interviewed the teachers, the superiors, and each of the 32 boys. After a period of careful observation, he prepared his report.

> From the conversations I have held with their superiors and teachers, I was able to verify that all have the capacity for a refined spiritual formation and that, in fact, the young men's spirits are cultivated with great care in the seminary. . . . In general, the students are very fervent. They ardently love "their Missionary vocation", possess an edifying devotion to the Sacred Heart of Jesus and the Blessed Virgin Mary, are obedient, docile, joyful, very respectful and deferential towards their teachers, and attentive; and there reigns among them great unity and fraternal charity.[11]

---

[10] Father Ángel Oñate would later become the second Superior General of the Missionaries of the Holy Spirit (M Sp S).
[11] Ángel M. Oñate, M Sp S, *Report to his Excellency Francisco González Arias, Bishop of Cuernavaca* (Mexico City, 8 October 1945)

The report covered the various spheres of their formation: spiritual, physical, intellectual, and so on. Regarding their studies, Father Oñate noted that, "To a greater or lesser degree, they all have the capacity for a good intellectual formation, and there are some who stand out for their intelligence and have a gift for studying. . . . Their marks are generally good."[12]

It is surprising to note that, four years after founding, and with a 25-year-old founder to guide them, the group of 32 adolescents and young men already reflected all the attributes of integral formation (spiritual, intellectual, human, apostolic) that characterize the Legion's and Regnum Christi's particular style of teaching and formation. They are the same traits that are currently to be found in their formation houses, apostolic schools, novitiates and Centers for Higher Studies.

Father Oñate offered an extensive description of his impressions of the founder. Among other things, he wrote:

> He is a man of profound, deeply rooted piety and sound virtues that have been proved true by many years of hard trials and setbacks borne with exemplary patience and authentic Christian charity. He is young (25 years old), but his experience and maturity exceed his age. The sound judgment and prudence he has shown, knowing how to bring the Work to its current state, are noteworthy. . . .[13]

He concluded his report to the bishop of Cuernavaca with the following recommendation:

> In all sincerity, I believe that a great enterprise is being prepared there for the glory of God and the good of the Church, something that will be glorious for Mexico, at times so greatly discredited. [I believe] that the work is already mature enough for you to request the necessary approval from the Holy See, and to officially establish

---

[12] Ángel M. Oñate (8 October 1945)
[13] *ibid*

the religious congregation of the Missionaries of the Sacred Heart of Jesus.[14]

First trip to Europe

On May 15, Bishop González Arias signed the document asking the Holy See to grant the *nihil obstat*. Ten days later, on May 25, Marcial departed for Europe on a trip that would imply seven exhausting days of take-offs and landings. The first plane took him through Brownsville, Houston, Temple, New Orleans, Atlanta, Washington and New York. From there he caught another plane to cross the Atlantic. Before landing in Madrid, it made stopovers in Gander (Canada), Shannon (Ireland) and Lisbon (Portugal).

In Madrid, Marcial stayed with the Paulist Fathers on García de Paredes Street. When he went to see Father Baeza the next day, he was received warmly, but the rector had some bad news for him.

"My! I didn't expect to see you so soon!" exclaimed the rector.

"Well, there you go, Father; here I am!"

"Look, Father . . . I'm terribly sorry to tell you this, but I have already talked with the university advisory board, and the priests feel that I shouldn't present your petition since we are asking for scholarships from the Ministry for External Affairs ourselves . . . "

"Well, Father, then I'll go on to Rome. But—if I obtain scholarships, would you have anything against letting us study in Comillas?"

"Of course not! On the contrary, we'd be delighted. It would be an honor to have more Latin American students here with us."[15]

Marcial headed back towards García de Paredes after the interview. As he walked through the streets of Madrid, it sud-

---

[14] Ángel M. Oñate (8 October 1945)
[15] cf. Marcial Maciel LC (January 1992)

denly struck him how alone he felt in a strange land—even though Spain and Mexico spoke the same language. He went to the Paulist chapel to talk with Christ and to discuss the situation with him. Without scholarships, the idea of coming to Comillas collapsed. He tried to understand what it all meant, asking God if he wanted them there or not. If so, he, Marcial, would do everything he could to make it happen.

> I prayed and came to the conclusion that I ought not to cease looking for some way to obtain scholarships there in Madrid. So, with all the obstinacy of someone who believes he's received a mission from God—great or small, it doesn't matter—I set out to walk the streets of Madrid, knocking on one door after another.[16]

He would walk up to the front door, speak with the doorman, ask to see the head of the house, and introduce himself. "I'm a priest from Mexico. I've come to Spain in order to . . . " (and here he would explain his plans). He then continued: "so, since Spain is such a Catholic country and is so fond of Mexico, I wanted to see if a few people could help me obtain these scholarships so that my Missionaries can come to study at the Pontifical University in Comillas . . . "[17]

Even though some may have refused to receive him, many Madrileño families came to his aid. Some promised him 25 pesetas a month, others 50 or 100. One man promised him a monthly 300 pesetas for his Missionaries, and such was the gratitude of Father Maciel that he still has not forgotten the man's name: Mr. Baltasar Márquez.

Marcial was troubled that he was not in Mexico guiding the apostolics and novices. He wrote them extensively in his free moments. It cheered him up, and gave him a chance not only to encourage them, but also to reflect upon and spell out his own deepest convictions. On 4 June 1946, he wrote:

---

[16] Marcial Maciel LC (January 1992)
[17] cf. *ibid*

Day after day I think of you, alone in your struggles, and the thought that Jesus is looking after you lifts my spirits.

We are not alone. . . . there are many others on the battlefield like us. We should push on fearlessly in faith, and hope. . . . If we could only exercise our faith! If you have faith, you will hope, and if you hope you will be master of yourself. So, in the hour of struggle, accept it . . . silence . . . peace . . . God's hour will come. Never fear the blows of God: they are blows of love. Forward! Always forward! . . .

Today I've been sick, I've been sad, I've been alone, I have wept. And then, suddenly, I'm struck by the thought of the most magnificent reality we live as Christians. I have God in my very heart . . . everything is solved! Goodbye loneliness, goodbye sadness, goodbye tears! I have everything! He is with me, he comforts me, he will heal me . . .

Seek God always. Never depend on the consolation and esteem of others: the day you do will be your ruin. God alone, God alone . . . God heals the deepest wounds, he brings joy to the saddest moments of life . . . God is worthy of being loved with all our heart. He is friend, father and brother. God is always there . . . God is faithful . . . .[18]

Another providential encounter

One day, looking for a certain house in Madrid, Marcial stopped to ask for directions. The man responded with an accent that was familiar. "Excuse me," Father Maciel exclaimed, "you're Mexican, aren't you?" He was. It was Jorge Ignacio Rubio Mañé, a historian from the Yucatan state of Mexico, who was finishing up some research in Madrid, in the *Archivo de Indias*. Marcial told him about his activities and his difficulties, and the historian responded, "I'm going to have dinner with the Minister for External Affairs this very evening!

---

[18] Marcial Maciel, *Letter to novices* (Madrid, 4 June 1946)

I'll tell him about your predicament, and see if I can't manage to get you an appointment. I'll call you tomorrow morning."[19]

All afternoon and until midnight that evening, Marcial spent long periods of prayer before the Blessed Sacrament in the perpetual-adoration church run by the Handmaidens of the Sacred Heart of Jesus, at 10 General Martínez Campos Avenue. The next day, at 10 a.m. sharp, the phone rang. "Mr. Alberto Martín Artajo, the Minister, was very interested in your plans, and he'll be waiting for you this evening between 7 and 9 p.m., at the Ministry for External Affairs in Santa Cruz Square."

Father Maciel spent an enjoyable 40 minutes speaking with the Minister, Martin Artajo, who told him that part of the Hispanic Culture Department's budget was earmarked for Latin America, and that they could help him out. To do so, however—since the Church had not yet officially approved the young congregation—he would need to get a recommendation from someone in Rome. "I'm a good friend of Cardinal Giuseppe Pizzardo,"[20] said the Minister by way of suggestion. Once again Marcial prayed until the small hours of the morning, this time to give thanks to God for all his help.

The Rome of 1946

Marcial left Madrid for Italy in June, 1946. Rome had still not succeeded in getting itself into order after the war: it was a city in disarray. Foreigners were mistrusted. It was not uncommon for them to dress as clergy to avoid attracting attention, and robberies abounded in hunger's vast domain. It was to this Rome that the young Mexican priest arrived. He was 26. He did not speak the language. He knew no one, but he had a dream that drove him onward: to speak to the Pope about his project of founding a new religious congregation. Alone in a strange city, Marcial was not sure where to go.

---

[19] cf. Marcial Maciel LC (January 1992)
[20] cf. Marcial Maciel LC (11 January 2004). Cardinal Pizzardo was then the Prefect of the Sacred Congregation for Seminaries and Institutes of Study (now: the "Congregation for Catholic Education").

The Allied Troops had not yet withdrawn, so there was not much room in hotels or boardinghouses; besides, he did not have much money. He knocked on the door of the Missionaries of the Holy Spirit, and then tried his luck at a few other promising addresses, but no one was able to take him in. He finally decided to sleep under a bridge. As he made his way down toward the Tiber, however, he met a young Belgian who suggested that he might try the Pío Latinoamericano, the college for Latin American priests and seminarians studying in Rome. Marcial was grateful for the advice, and had already set off when suddenly he heard a voice calling his name: *"Marcial!"* It was Father Maina, who had been his spiritual director for a time in the seminary of Montezuma. The priest was happy to welcome him in, sharing with Marcial his supper of a little mozzarella cheese and chicory coffee.[21]

A providential turn of affairs brought him into contact with some members of the Roman Curia. Before leaving Mexico, the chief apostolic notary Monsignor Gregorio Araiza[22] had entrusted to Marcial an envelope containing a confidential document and a sum of money destined for the Holy See: Marcial was instructed to bring it to Rome and give it to Cardinal Nicola Canali in person. The cardinal got along with Father Maciel immediately, and trusted him—also due, no doubt, to the fact that the Church in Mexico had commended such a delicate task to him. From then on, Canali would support and defend the Mexican founder, opening doors to him within the Roman Curia, and introducing him to his friends among the College of Cardinals.

First audience with the Pope

Marcial was still uncertain, however, about how to secure a private audience with the Holy Father. No matter whom he

---

[21] cf. Marcial Maciel LC (January 1992)
[22] As was mentioned in Chapter 6, Monsignor Araiza had been on the tribunal for Marcial's theology exams. He knew him well, and held the young priest in high regard.

asked, the answer was always the same: "Oh . . . —no, that's *very* difficult."

It was very difficult, and it is not hard to understand why. Pope Pius XII had been working non-stop since the end of the war. Even though the Nazi threat had been removed, Italy, like the rest of Europe, was trying to get onto its feet. The Pope was aware that changes were in the air and that neither Italy nor Europe could turn back the clock; he longed to see the birth of a new Christian civilization, one where the rapid cultural, social, scientific and technological advances could be set upon the solid foundation of unchanging Gospel values. He rose at 5 a.m. and went to bed an hour after midnight. The Pope had first-rate helpers—men such as the Cardinals Pizzardo, Tedeschini, Canali and Lavitrano—but they were few.

Marcial received some help from Carlos Quintero Arce, a friend he had met at the Pío Latinoamericano College where he was staying. Now an archbishop, Quintero Arce still remembers the circumstance well.

> It was the month of June, 1946, when I found out that a Mexican priest had arrived to the college. The day after he arrived, I went up to him very naturally to ask who he was, and if he was going to be studying with us. He responded saying that he was Father Marcial Maciel, that he had come to Rome because the bishop of Cuernavaca had given him some business to deal with at the Sacred Congregation for Religious, and that he wanted to have a meeting with the Holy Father. He immediately asked me if I could help him.
>
> We struck up a good friendship from the start. I realized he was a very smart, fervent priest. After passing the first few days in Rome with him, I also perceived that he possessed a powerful personal charisma and a prodigious memory for remembering all the people he ever met. I am convinced that God gave him these qualities thinking of the mission he'd put in his hands as founder of a new congregation. At the time, it consisted of perhaps a hundred members and they called them-

selves the Missionaries of the Sacred Heart. In fact, Father Marcial showed me a large photograph of the members of the congregation.

It was truly admirable to see that group of seminarians, who already had the bearing that is proper to the Legionaries of Christ—the present name of the congregation. What especially impressed me was the fact that Father Marcial was still such a young priest, but already had a large group of seminarians and a magnificent formation center in Tlalpan, in Mexico's capital.

When Father Maciel asked me how I could help him arrange a meeting with the Holy Father, I let him see that it wasn't easy since there was a strict protocol. I told him, nevertheless, that when we wanted to get near the Pope to greet him, the Pío Latinoamericano seminarians usually asked some cardinal friend to allow them to accompany him to some ceremony, like secretaries. That was how I proposed to Father Maciel that we do the same, so that he could get close to the Holy Father.[23]

Carlos Quintero took him to one of the Pope's Masses in St. Peter's Basilica. Many cardinals were present, and when the procession was formed to begin the ceremony, he suggested that Marcial stand close by one of the cardinals. Father Maciel does not remember which cardinal he accompanied,[24] but he does recall that he put on his surplice and had carried the cardinal's short red cape over his arm, as if he were one of his secretaries.

Father Maciel stayed with him during the whole Mass. At the end, the procession came back to its starting point

---

[23] Carlos Quintero Arce, Emeritus archbishop of Hermosillo, *Letter to Father Evaristo Sada LC* (Hermosillo, Mexico, 27 November 2003). He was the first bishop of Ciudad Valles, and after a period as coadjutor bishop, became the archbishop of Hermosillo, Mexico.

[24] Father Maciel has mentioned the name of Cardinal Giuseppe Pizzardo on occasion (cf. Jesús Colina, *Christ is My Life* . . . p. 40), but explains that he has no clear recollection of whom he accompanied.

next to the Pietà, by the elevator the Holy Father used to reach his chambers.[25]

At the end of the celebration, and before taking the elevator to his rooms, the Holy Father greeted each one of the cardinals, arranged in a semicircle on both sides of the elevator.

> According to custom, every cardinal came forward to the Pope for the formal greeting, accompanied by his secretary. It was in that moment that Father Maciel took advantage of the chance to introduce himself to the Holy Father and ask for an audience, so that he could present his foundation project to him. The Holy Father granted him the audience immediately.[26]

Father Maciel explains that after kissing the Pope's ring, he said: "Holy Father, I am a Mexican priest and I'd like to speak with you, but I have no one to recommend me." Pius XII turned to Monsignor Federico Callori di Vignale,[27] who was accompanying him, and said: "Tomorrow, at 12."[28]

Quintero helped Marcial clinch the appointment at the Papal Household, and accompanied him to the *Portone di Bronzo* the next day. Once in the Vatican, Marcial "went on alone to the hall where he had the audience with the Pope. It took place on Wednesday, 12 June 1946."[29]

The Pope was not miserly with the time he dedicated to Father Maciel. He listened to him, encouraged him to go ahead with his plans, and explained to him that the bishop of Cuernavaca's petition regarding the *nihil obstat* should be given to the Sacred Congregation for Religious, since they would be able to set the approval process in motion. Marcial described

---

[25] Carlos Quintero Arce, *Letter to Father Evaristo Sada . . .* (27 November 2003)
[26] *ibid*
[27] Monsignor Federico Callori di Vignale formed part of the Pontifical Court (now: Pontifical Household). He was one of a group of ecclesiastics who served the Pope directly in his personal concerns. In 1946 he held the title of *Copero.*
[28] cf. Jesús Colina, *Christ is My Life...*, p. 40, Marcial Maciel (January 1992)
[29] Carlos Quintero Arce, *Letter to Father Evaristo Sada . . .* (27 November 2003)

their charism and spirituality, the formation he wanted his Missionaries to receive, and the apostolates that they would carry out.

> During the interview, when I touched on our apostolic charism, the Pope insisted that we emphasize the thorough formation of Catholic leaders, especially for South America. I took this to prayer and tried to understand better, in God's presence, what he was asking of us through the mouth of his Vicar on earth.[30]

In obedience to this explicit recommendation of the Holy Father, forming Catholic leaders and encouraging them to launch apostolic endeavors is one of the priorities of the Legion of Christ and Regnum Christi, and one of the specific ways by which they seek to make Christ's Kingdom effectively reach all people and every society.[31] Father Maciel does not understand "leader" in elitist or class-related terms, or as someone who holds authoritative power over others, but rather as any and every person who is able to exercise a positive influence on others. In an interview with Jesús Colina he explains:

> To practice true charity and ardent, generous love for Christ and the Church he founded, you have to give yourself generously to all, without barriers. Therefore, the Legion of Christ and the Regnum Christi Movement strive to undertake those endeavors that in their depth and breadth will be most effective in establishing Christ's Kingdom among all people and in society, while maintaining utmost fidelity to the Church's Magisterium and full communion with the Successor of Peter, the Pope and all the Church's shepherds who are in communion with him. Regnum Christi is conscious that our action will be effective if we achieve the Chris-

---

[30] Jesús Colina, *Christ is My Life . . .* , p. 40

[31] This "Kingdom" would be best interpreted as the "Christian civilization love" that Pope Paul VI and Pope John Paul II have so frequently spoken of. Saint Augustine used similar terms when, at the beginning of his *The City of God,* he explained that "Two loves created two cities . . . ".

tian formation and apostolic deployment of those men and women who exercise the greatest leadership in the religious, cultural, intellectual, social, economic, human and artistic spheres.[32]

A few pages later, he adds:

It should be said that we seek the integral good of the human person, every person, be they rich or poor, wise or ignorant, regardless of race, language, nationality or talent. This is the example that Christ left us in the Gospel. Like him we approach people to bring them Christ's grace and redemption. We do not approach them for unworthy motives, economic gain, prestige or any other reason. We want to reach everyone, and for that very reason, just as Christ chose a group of apostles to take his Gospel to the whole world, we, too, begin by forming and training a given few, due to human limitations, so that their work will reach as many individuals as possible.[33]

Pope Pius XII suggested that Father Maciel ask the sub-secretary of State, Monsignor Giovanni Battista Montini (future Pope Paul VI) to help him revise the congregation's constitutions. This turned out to be the beginning of a personal friendship between Monsignor Montini and Father Maciel that would continue until the future Pontiff's death.

After speaking with the Pope, there was little else for Marcial to do in Rome. He dropped off Bishop González Arias' letter and the constitutions at the Sacred Congregation for Religious. Cardinal Nicola Canali helped him arrange an appointment with Cardinal Giuseppe Pizzardo, who kindly gave him the note of recommendation that the Spanish Minister for External Affairs needed to grant Father Maciel his scholarships.

Marcial also took advantage of free moments to visit the famous sites of Christian Rome, especially its many churches, the Major Basilicas and the Colosseum. Years later, he would write:

> I visited the Colosseum. It looked as if nothing had changed except for a great cross planted at the entrance. I saw the place for the gladiators and the dens of the beasts. The prayer that I tried to utter aloud froze in my throat. . . . These walls, witnesses to such faith and such hope, spoke to me of God's supreme presence. Here, I thought, thousands of my brothers and sisters consciously entrusted their souls to the love of the eternal God; and from their lips there arose perhaps, like a cry, one of the verses of blessing chanted by the young men in the furnace. And in the very depths of their horror the Father told them, "Today you will be with me in paradise" (Lk 23:43).[34]

Father Maciel marveled at the faith, hope and love of the martyrs: "I left there on fire to offer something similar to my brothers, in the total surrender and immolation of my life."[35]

His pilgrimage aroused his fervor and left him disillusioned at the same time. In the beauty of the edifices and the wasted walls of the Colosseum he saw etched the dazzling faith of martyrs and of yesteryear's Christians. But he also saw that Jesus was now being left to live in grey shadows, alone, seldom visited in the majority of the churches' tabernacles . . .

> It took many days to understand that times and society were undergoing rapid evolution, and that while we needed houses of worship where people could gather and give praise to the Lord, it was much, much more necessary and urgent to teach men that we are "living temples of the Holy Spirit" (2 Cor 6:16). Teach them faith, hope and love so that each of them would make

---

[34] Marcial Maciel LC, *Letter* . . . (Chicago, 20 December 1982—Rome, 29 May 1988)
[35] *ibid*

his heart and soul into a temple consecrated to the Holy Spirit.

My fears, anguish and anxiety subsided inasmuch as I grew more and more certain that the Holy Spirit gives life to his Church and makes it holy throughout the world, in the midst of the ebb and flow of human happenings.

As I contemplated this reality, light swelled up in me as to the essence of my Christian state and its destiny. It was necessary, imperative and urgent not to lose sight of it for a single instant of my fleeting journey on this earth. Awareness, then, that by baptism I am a son of God, a member of Christ's Mystical Body. With an inescapable commitment: to preach God's Kingdom and apply myself without any antics to the work of spreading his message to as many people as possible and giving them the joy of sharing in him the way I have.

This is my mission; for this and this alone will I have to give account to my Creator at the end of my earthly existence. . . . I want to end my existence with the peace of knowing for sure that all those assigned to me when I was created received the message of God's love and existence.[36]

Marcial understood God's mission for him and his Missionaries: to help all people experience the God of love like an inner fire. Only then would they be consumed by love, and transformed into flaming torches capable of bringing light and warmth everywhere they would go.

Some problems solved

Father Maciel was eager to tell Father Baeza about everything that had happened since their last meeting. He left Rome for Genoa on 15 June, where he boarded a boat to Barcelona. Once on Spanish soil, he caught a train and spent the night of

---

[36] Marcial Maciel LC, *Letter . . .* (Chicago, 20 December 1982—Rome, 29 May 1988)

19 June in Bilbao. He took a train to Santander the next day, and another train from Santander to Torrelavega. At Torrelavega he climbed aboard the dilapidated bus that served Comillas (which the apostolics would nick-name the *Antidiluviana*[37]).

As the old vehicle rumbled and rattled along the narrow road, Marcial gazed out of the window, appraising the houses and properties that whizzed past. "Nice—but pretty far . . . That one would suit us nicely . . . Too small . . . No, that one's too big . . . "

When he finally arrived at the university, Father Baeza was happy to hear the Mexican founder's good news. Marcial dined and slept in Comillas that night, and accepted the invitation to celebrate Mass for the seminarians at the Pontifical University the next day, 21 June. He left for Madrid immediately afterwards to arrange an appointment with the Minister for External Affairs.

Martin Artajo was pleased to receive news from Cardinal Pizzardo. Marcial asked for 32 scholarships, and the Minister granted them all.

As they were speaking, it dawned on Marcial that there was an entire ocean between his boys and the university. "Sir? I just realized that I don't have any way of bringing the boys from Mexico to Comillas."

Mr. Artajo dialed a number on his phone. "Hello, Juan Claudio, how's it going? Listen, I have a young Mexican priest here who's founding a congregation. We've given him 32 scholarships so he can bring his boys to Comillas, but he doesn't have any way of getting them to Spain. Can your company help them out?"[38]

Juan Claudio Güell y Churruca—Count of Ruiseñada and eldest son of the third Marquis of Comillas—invited Father Maciel to come see him. He was the owner of a Spanish shipping company, *Compañía Española de Navegación*, which transported goods between Spain and Cuba. The company had

---

[37] That is, "antediluvian": old enough to have come off Noah's ark.
[38] Marcial Maciel LC (January 1992)

been founded by the first Marquis of Comillas, his great-grand-father Antonio López y López. Saying a prayer asking the Holy Spirit to enlighten the count's response, Marcial presented himself at Juan Claudio's Castellana offices. When the owner of the shipping company offered to bring his Missionaries by steamer from Cuba to Bilbao for free, another idea flashed through Marcial's mind.

"Count, sir? Did you know that I still don't have a place for my boys to stay?"

"Why's that? Aren't they going to live in the seminary?"

"Well, no. They aren't going to be boarding students. Since they're Religious, I want to rent a house in Comillas, but I haven't really looked for one yet."

"Well," mused the count, "in Comillas we have the Sobrellano palace. It was my grandfather's.[39] We only use it for a month or two during the summer. I believe my grandfather would be very pleased knowing that you—coming from Mexico to be priests—would be able to stay there."[40]

Marcial's prayer that evening was bursting with gratitude for God's largesse. Everything had worked out in Spain—scholarships, lodgings, transportation—while in Rome they would already be examining the constitutions and considering his bishop's petition for the approval of the congregation. What remained to be done? Marcial decided that he could return to Mexico as soon as possible, to begin preparing for the expedition to Europe.

Father Evaristo Sada LC, the Legion of Christ's current general secretary (2004), once asked Father Maciel what plans he had made in order to take the first concrete steps towards the Legion's founding. He relays the founder's answer:

---

[39] His grandfather was Claudio López Bru, the second Marquis of Comillas. Work on the Sobrellano Palace (designed by the Catalonian architect Joan Martorell) had actually begun in 1881, at the initiative of his great-grandfather, but it was Claudio López Bru who first inhabited the palace, in 1888.

[40] Marcial Maciel LC (January 1992)

Nuestro Padre[41] told me: "Well, note that I didn't have a program. God was leading me, the Holy Spirit was leading me, and I didn't really have any idea of what I was getting into. A problem would present itself, and I'd resolve it, and then another, and another, and . . . really, God led me exactly as he wished."

After a pause, Father Maciel turned to him and said: "You know, Father, it's easier to do it than to explain it."[42]

To found the congregation, Marcial had not spent much time deliberating. He had had no pre-established plans, and he certainly hadn't foreseen the problems that would arise. God said "Walk!", and he had started walking; God marked the pace, and Marcial's only concern was to continue forward faithfully, step by step. He tried to do what God asked, following the Holy Spirit's advice. "God was illuminating me at every moment,"[43] he says.

At times, he might have imagined himself navigating through fog; but he knew that, for God at least, everything was crystal clear.

---

[41] The Legionaries of Christ and Regnum Christi members refer to Father Maciel as *Nuestro Padre*. In Spanish-speaking countries, this was how most religious institutes and congregations traditionally referred to their founders. As it would literally be rendered "our father", it is rarely translated into other languages.

[42] Evaristo Sada LC (19 January 1997)

[43] Marcial Maciel LC (January 1992)

July 1947. Some of the first Legionaries fixing up a cowshed they rented in Comillas for a dormitory. They lodged there until, in March 1948, they moved to the "Quiroz Institute" next to the Trappist monastery Via Coeli *in Cóbreces, a town a few miles away from Comillas.*

Bishop Alfonso Espino y Silva of Cuernavaca (seated, at right) and Archbishop Luis María Martínez of Mexico City (seated, at left) visit the apostolics at the Pacelli Estate during the first semester of 1950. Bishop Alfonso Espino y Silva succeeded Bishop Francisco González Arias as Bishop of Cuernavaca

The Legionaries inaugurated their first center in Rome in October of 1950, when Father Maciel was 30 years old. This photo shows the building, located on Via Aurelia, shortly after construction. Today, the building serves as the general headquarters of the Legion of Christ and the Regnum Christi Movement.

On 28 December 1950, Pope Pius XII received in audience a group of more than 50 Legionaries of Christ, who came to express their affection and filial support. Six days later the Legion of Christ would celebrate its 10th anniversary. By then, it already had two seminaries, one in Mexico and the other in Spain, and had just opened its first center in Rome, with room for 90 Legionaries

This photograph, taken in the early 1950s, shows Monsignor Giovanni Battista Montini with Mrs. Flora Barragán de Garza and her children Flora and Roberto, along with Father Marcial Maciel LC and Father Jorge Ruiz of the diocese of Querétaro (Mexico). Father Maciel first met Monsignor Montini in 1946, when the future Pontiff was the Holy See's sub-secretary of State. During the 1950s, Montini helped give impetus to the founding of the Cumbres Institute.

The first apostolic project of the Legionaries of Christ, the Cumbres Institute of Mexico City, opened its doors in February 1954. Archbishop Luis María Martínez of Mexico City presided at the official inauguration that April. In the photograph, from left to right: Roberto Garza (1), Mrs. Flora Barragán (3), Mrs. Edmé Barragán de Galas (4), Archbishop Luis María Martínez (6), Father Faustino Pardo (7), Father Marcial Maciel (8), Guillermo Barroso (9), Luis Barroso (10), Santiago Galas (11), architect Mr. Villagrán (12), architect Mr. Palazuelos (17).

On behalf of Pope Pius XII, Cardinal Clemente Micara asked Father Maciel to build a church in Rome dedicated to Our Lady of Guadalupe. In the photo, Cardinal Micara places the cornerstone (11 April 1955); Cardinals Pizzardo, Tedeschini, Piazza y Canali were also present at the ceremony. The stone, brought from Tepeyac hill in Mexico where Our Lady appeared to Saint Juan Diego, had been blessed by Pope Pius XII on 3 April 1955.

Pope John XXIII visits the church of Our Lady of Guadalupe in Rome on 20 November 1962.

IX

A Latin American Breeze in Comillas
1946–1947

Marcial had six weeks to prepare the trans-Atlantic voyage from Mexico to Spain for 32 of his boys. Their parents, in the presence of the notary public, signed forms authorizing them to leave the country—although some needed reassurance. This they received from Bishop González Arias, the bishop of Cuernavaca, who (despite being gravely ill) gave the founder his total backing. He was not able to see them off when they left, and would die on 20 August 1946, after having promised his nephew to continue blessing and protecting "this enterprise that God wants and loves so much" from heaven.[1]

Marcial worked hard to provide the Foreign Affairs Department in Mexico with all the necessary documents. He got the boys' passports in order, bought suitcases, purchased clothes, and collected the money they would need for the flight from Mexico to Cuba and to cover their initial expenses in Spain.[2] And he had to ensure that the apostolic school in Mexico had everything it would need to continue functioning. The days passed quickly, and the departure date drew near.

---

[1] cf. Marcial Maciel LC (January 1992). On 10 May 1984, Father Maciel LC addressed a letter to the Legionaries: "Bishop González Arias, bishop of Cuernavaca, was the person whom God used in his providence to protect the Legion's birth. A man of profound faith and understanding of the Church, we owe him our gratitude and respect, and a special place in our history. Although I am sure that we all remember him and acknowledge all that he did for us, I want the whole Legion to celebrate his birth into eternal life, August 20, as a feast day, as a sign of our warm appreciation and in memorial of his important, fatherly protection of the Legion."

[2] They had to take the boat from a neighboring country since there were no official relations between Mexico and Spain at the time.

Crossing the Atlantic

While the younger apostolics, feeling a little sad for the first few days, remained in Mexico with Father Luis Ferreira, the older apostolic boys, the novices and the founder flew to Cuba with *Mexicana* Airlines on September 2.[3] It would be three days before the Trans-Atlantic Company's steamer would weigh anchor in Havana on 5 September 1946.

The founder paid careful attention to every detail of the trip and to each of the boys. He felt the weight of responsibility on his shoulders. For their part, the boys were happy and confident, without a care in the world. It was enough to know that they were accompanied by their founder. They had a great time.

Marcial and some other Legionaries fondly remember certain stories from that trip, since it was an adventure for all of them. Marcial explains that Cardinal Arteaga y Betancourt arranged for them to stay in a Jesuit school called Belén in Havana, where they were welcomed with great kindness. It was there that they stayed until embarking for Spain. Father Carlos Mora LC, known for his mischievousness as an apostolic, remembers one episode quite vividly: the huge plateful of steaming mashed potatoes he had to finish off one day in the suffocating Cuban summer heat. He had served himself rather too generously—somehow mistaking mashed potatoes for vanilla ice cream.

Due to a dock-workers strike that kept the steamer in New York's harbor, the group was able to enjoy a couple of days in the city. Cardinal Francis Joseph Spellman received them, and they were thrilled to be able to buy trinkets and a few Coca-Colas with the American dollars he gave them.

Once the *Marqués de Comillas* was out at sea, the novices and apostolics returned to their regular schedule, with times for prayer, lessons, talks, study, recreation, Mass and Eucharistic benediction.

---

[3] Javier Bucio, a seminarian from the diocese of Mexico, also traveled by plane with them from Mexico to Cuba. This is why in the photo (reproduced in this book) 33 seminarians are visible. Bucio is the one in tie.

Samuel Lemus, a seminarian for the diocese of Morelia, Mexico, accompanied them from Havana to Comillas, where he was being sent to receive his schooling. In the summer of 1946, Archbishop Luis María Altamirano y Bulnes sent Samuel to meet Father Maciel so that they could travel to Comillas together, telling him, "Place yourself at his disposition. Help him in every way you can. But . . . there is only one thing: don't go off and stay with him, because I need you here."[4] Father Lemus admits, however, that in a certain sense he did "stay" with the founder.

> My heart stayed in his life and I have always prayed for him with all my heart, because his example, simplicity, humility, sincerity and friendship have meant a great deal to my priestly life. He has a deep sense of friendship: friendship with God that translates into a crystal-clear, luminous friendship with everyone he has dealt with throughout his life.[5]

Father Lemus retains agreeable memories of the voyage too:

> I remember that evening was falling in Havana. As we sailed away in the boat the *Marqués de Comillas* with the mountains and bay fading away behind us, Father Maciel was sitting there in the stern, looking off into eternity, like a modern-day prophet. I will never forget this image. He created a marvelous atmosphere for those 32 boys in the boat. He celebrated Mass. They made many friends, and sang popular Mexican tunes . . . They created a marvelous, happy, family atmosphere. Father

---

[4] It is possible that Archbishop Luis María had heard of Father Maciel through his good friend and fellow bishop, Rafael Guízar of Veracruz.

[5] Samuel Lemus (14 October 2003). As was mentioned earlier, Samuel Lemus was not the only diocesan seminarian to accompany the Legionaries on their first trip to Spain. Whereas Javier Bucio accompanied them on the plane, Samuel Lemus met them in Havana. Father Samuel Lemus has worked forming priests and in the media. He is the author of several books, and currently writes a weekly column in *El Universal*, a Mexican daily newspaper.

Maciel also spoke with the people on board who had problems. He began to do a lot of apostolate on the boat. He always acts naturally and simply, and soon everyone knew who he was, and knew he was there . . .

He paid attention to taking care of the boys, because when we passed by Newfoundland a bad storm hit us. The boat rocked and tossed, rose and plummeted; he dedicated himself to those who were most seasick (I was among them). He was always attentive to the needs of others. That reality stuck with me my whole life long, and it shaped my mind and my priestly activity: to help and serve everyone, with love . . .

I remember Father Maciel had a little mouth organ with him in the steamer. He would play it in the evenings, at dusk: it was beautiful. All of this provided a clean-spirited atmosphere of simplicity, warmth and generosity. Father Maciel has always been a clean, simple man, childlike and humble. That is why our Lord God has blessed him so super-abundantly."[6]

The other passengers may have given them sidelong glances for the first few days, but before long they had won everyone's good will. Here were Mexican boys who sang on deck during their recreation periods, and who organized such lively games and competitions that soon passengers were eager to gather around, watch and cheer.

On 27 September 1946 the steamer spent a few hours in Corunna, Spain, before finally docking in the Santurce Harbor of Bilbao. Marcial gathered together their packages and suitcases, and then he and the boys climbed aboard a train bound for the city center. All the money set aside for the trip had already been spent, and they survived their first few days in Spain thanks to a check that one of the apostolics had received from a generous fellow passenger.

They first found something to satisfy their hunger, and then looked for a place to stay, renting a few bed-and-breakfast

---

[6] Father Samuel Lemus (14 October 2003)

rooms where they could leave their things. They divided into two groups: half went off to sleep, while the other half toured the city for a while. Marcial's group ended up taking shelter from the rain that night under the public bandstand in the center of Arenal Square. Once the rain eased up they tried to get some sleep on the park benches. When the sun rose, the first group left the lodgings, and Marcial's group, who had spent the whole night outdoors, finally managed to get some sleep.

Several hours later and more rested, Marcial returned to the docks to pick up the second-hand bus that they had brought from New York. It had been donated by a Mexican benefactor, and was necessary to transport the 32 boys from one part of Spain to another (the boys baptized the green and white Chevrolet bus the "Wawa"[7]). They left Bilbao after lunch with Father Maciel at the wheel, and reached the town of Comillas just before midnight. Mugs of chicory and a little simple fare awaited them in the philosophy students' dining room at the university. A small group of seminarians, lanterns in hand, soon came to help them find their way down to the Marquis of Comillas' palace.

Father Jorge Cortés LC recalls their first night in Comillas:

> Once we arrived, Nuestro Padre settled us in. When you hear *Palace of the Marquis,* it might conjure up images of stately chambers, but there was nothing of that for us. It was the attic of the Marquis' palace, and there were no beds, no mattresses, nothing at all. There was a wooden floor.
>
> So we began the operation of unpacking. We opened our suitcases and took out the blankets and bedspreads we'd brought from Mexico (Nuestro Padre had bought them for us) and sorted out how we'd spend the night. There were no pillows.[8]

---

[7] In Spanish: *guagua.* Both in Cuba and the Canary Islands, buses were informally referred to with this term.
[8] Jorge Cortés LC (31 December 1997)

Welcome to Comillas

Even after 50 years, Father Gregorio López LC, a Spanish Legionary who was a Comillas student at the time, still remembers the impression that the Mexican Missionaries made upon the seminarians:

> It was October . . . and we were in Mass. Suddenly we heard noises behind us. Back then, we seminarians weren't curious—we just, well, took a look out of the corner of our eye to see what was going on! All of a sudden, toward the end of communion, we saw that there was a group of adolescents dressed in burgundy sweaters, white shirts and blue pants coming up behind the last theologian for communion. Very fervent. Then some seminarians: later we found out that these were novices. There were 12 or 14, I think, in cassocks with a white sash. They received communion. They went back to their places. . . .
>
> Sure enough: as soon as Mass was over, there we were: "Who are they?" "What was it all about?"
>
> "They're some young Mexicans who've come to study Latin."
>
> "Hmph," I said, "they're just kids."
>
> We were already philosophy students; they were in the minor seminary ...
>
> "And the ones in cassock?"
>
> "They're novices from a new congregation . . . ."[9]

The apostolics began their classes in the university at the beginning of October. Three weeks after their arrival, Marcial was obliged to travel to Rome, having received news from Mexico that Rome's Sacred Congregation for Religious thought the new congregation should be entrusted to an older superior, since Marcial seemed too young and inexperienced.[10] Their

---

[9] Gregorio López LC (January 2003)

[10] cf. Luca Hermenegildo Pasetto, Secretary of the Sacred Congregation for Religious, *Letter to the Bishop of Cuernavaca, Francisco González Arias* (Vatican, 2 September 1946). The bishop of Cuernavaca had just died on 20 August 1946.

concern was not groundless: he was young, and he didn't have experience. Nevertheless, God had placed this mission in his hands.

The Episcopal See of Cuernavaca was now vacant. Bishop González Arias, who had died on 20 August 1946, was no longer there to speak on behalf of the Missionaries.

Marcial did not succeed in resolving the problem during his trip to Rome, and the Vicar of Cuernavaca, Monsignor García, decided to study the situation from Mexico and propose a new superior. In the meantime, not wanting to leave his seminarians alone for too long, Marcial felt obliged to return to Comillas at the beginning of November. He was deeply concerned.

In January 1947, Marcial was in Rome once again. The Sacred Congregation for Religious proposed a compromise: instead of imposing a new superior, Father Lucio Rodrigo, a priest in Comillas, would be appointed as advisor to the congregation.

The attic of the Sobrellano Palace turned out to be a less than ideal place for 32 boys to live. The Missionaries moved out of the palace's attic towards the middle of November, relocating to two rented houses in the town of Comillas. The apostolics occupied the Sacred Heart house, so named because of the statue that graced its façade. Marcial and the novices moved into Santa Lucía (also known as "La Carranceda"), where they all had meals. Father Maciel celebrated Mass for them each morning in a hermitage half-way between the two houses, and after Mass he would take the apostolics to the university by bus. When it wasn't raining, or when he was unable to drive them, they went on foot, taking a steep shortcut they nicknamed the *despeñaperros*.[11]

While the apostolics were in class, Marcial went to pick up the daily rations of food from the cook in the university. He then returned to Santa Lucía to teach the novices, write letters

---

[11] Meaning roughly "Like dogs-over-a-cliff".

and prepare their meal before going back to pick up the apostolics. After lunch, the "Wawa" would make another trip up to the university.

Father Gregorio continues this account:

> Nuestro Padre and those apostolics began to attract our attention: the way they were, the way they acted, their formation, their manners. As we got to see him more close-up, Nuestro Padre was, for us, the discovery of a different style of priest. . . .
>
> The second World War had ended, but we were still coming out of the war. The truth is that Spain was really poor. And suddenly we see that a young priest had arrived with a bunch of kids, driving a bus. For us, that was really something: a priest driving a bus! We'd never have believed it. So much so that we'd all go down to see how Nuestro Padre managed to come through the front gate of the university with it. I don't think they built the university's entranceway with modern times in mind. Even though the bus was from the '40s, the kind they used for third-class travelers, for us it was, well, a bus!
>
> It fit. Just. A hair's breadth on each side, otherwise you'd pull the whole gate down. It was a real adventure. We'd go down to see him pull in. And when he squeaked through, there'd be lots of cheering because he hadn't scraped the sides. Then there was the first curve. It was a tight U-shaped curve, and no one used to take it, not even with little cars. They could never make it on the first try, and always had to do some maneuvering. This priest took the curve the first time around, without any maneuvers: another round of applause. It was impressive. Here was something modern, and novel and impressive.
>
> We admired the life the boys led. We hardly saw them, except when they walked across the campus or played soccer with the smaller seminarians, since they came down to play on our field. We were struck by the

fact that the bell would ring to go back to classes, and a couple of minutes later those boys were already there: hair combed and shoes shined. And extremely polite: "Good morning", "No, please, you first", "Excuse me, may I . . . ?"

And there we'd be, saying:

"Well, what planet did these guys come from? What's this all about?"[12]

Marcial usually brought the apostolics an afternoon snack (bread and figs or quince jelly). They would spend a few light-hearted minutes together, seated on the lawn by the university gate. Despite being so brief, the boys enjoyed these moments together with their founder, since they had such a tight schedule. With classes and study, they would be worn out when they came home in the evenings, and could do little more than have supper and pray before going off to bed.

In Santa Lucía, the novices followed the serene rhythm of the novitiate: prayer, study, silence, formation talks (given by Father Maciel), recreation and times of adoration in the presence of the Blessed Sacrament.

Father Javier Tena LC especially remembers the "Eucharistic atmosphere" that reigned in the house:

Nuestro Padre instilled in us a tremendous love for the Eucharist. He focused on this aspect: a sort of delicacy in our relationship with Christ. In the morning, for example, we'd wash and dress quickly in order to have more time there in Jesus' presence, alone, before morning prayers would start. We'd multiply our short visits to the Eucharist throughout the day—before going to play, or at the end of recreation periods. We'd all go to the chapel to be there, speaking with Jesus Christ in the Eucharist. I clearly recall that Nuestro Padre really inculcated this, at least during my time in the apostolic

---

[12] Gregorio López LC (January 2003)

school. I think that it is a habit that has lasted all through our formation and priestly life."[13]

Not only soccer

Marcial taught the novices and apostolics how to pray. He would frequently accompany them in their morning meditation, speaking to Jesus Christ out loud, contemplating and reflecting with them upon the mysteries of Christ's Incarnation, life, death and resurrection. This is how he had prayed during his own seminary years, and this is how Mamá Maurita had guided her children in fifteen minutes of prayer each day, in front of the picture of the Sacred Heart that she had in her room. It was a school of spontaneous prayer. The boys' hearts swelled as they acquired a personal, uncomplicated, one-on-one relationship with Jesus. In this relationship they stoked and forged their friendship with him, fostering a child's love for their Father and the love that redeemed creatures ought to feel towards their Redeemer.

On 6 November 1999, Father Maciel prayed aloud with a new generation of apostolics in Center Harbor, New Hampshire. In the moments for prayer after communion, he said:

> Christ is here, in my heart. What an extraordinary grace it is, to sacramentally have him present in my bosom, to be able to speak with him heart-to-heart. Close your eyes, enter within your heart and speak with Jesus. Learn from him all the lessons you need to learn. Listen to his words. Follow his advice, follow his example . . . Jesus is in your heart. Embrace him, speak with him, tell him that you love him more than anything else. Thank him for wanting to remain with us in the Eucharist, to come down into your heart. How much you love me, Jesus! You became man, you died on a cross, and you are in the Eucharist: to remain with me, to nourish my soul.

---

[13] Javier Tena LC (29 December 1997)

How much you love me! And I: what can I do for you? What do you want from me, Jesus?[14]

From the day he founded the Legion, Marcial dedicated the best of his time, attention and effort to the human and spiritual formation of his religious, a formation that encompasses not only general ideas but also the smallest particulars. In his 1992 book *The Integral Formation of Catholic Priests,* Father Maciel begins the chapter on human formation with the following observations:

> "Chosen from among men." The new and better wine of grace, with its gifts, commitments and demands, needs new wineskins to receive it fittingly, preserve it faithfully, and allow it to develop its sanctifying dynamism effectively. Supernatural grace does not suppress nature but elevates it (St. Thomas Aquinas, *Summa Theologiae,* I 1 8 c). *Spiritual formation presupposes and relies on the human formation* of the future priest. . . .
>
> Human formation does not only benefit the candidate but also profoundly influences his future ministry. His maturity, his psychological balance, and the strength of his will will greatly impinge, for good or evil, on the fruitfulness of his apostolate. A priest's human and social make-up (his way of thinking and acting, his personal presentation and manners, his way of expressing himself, etc.) opens or closes the door to dialogue, trust, and friendship. . . . Formation programs, activities in the seminary, and, above all, formators and candidates themselves have to confront this basic aspect of a priest's integral formation. The main goal of human formation for the seminarian is *full human maturity.*[15]

---

[14] Marcial Maciel LC, *Reflections after communion* (Immaculate Conception Apostolic School, New Hampshire, 6 November 1999) in *Oraciones de corazón . . . ,* pp. 183–184

[15] Marcial Maciel LC, *Integral Formation of Catholic Priests,* Circle Press, Hamden, Conn., 1998, pp. 103–4

On diverse occasions the Holy Father has recognized Father Maciel's work and experience forming priests. Pope John Paul II invited the Legion of Christ's founder to participate in the October 1991 Synod of Bishops on the formation of priests held in Rome. On 7 April 1992 he was asked by the Pope to take part in the press conference which presented the apostolic exhortation *Pastores Dabo Vobis* ("I Will Give You Shepherds").[16] Two years later, on 20 February 1994, the Holy Father appointed him an advisor to the Vatican Congregation for the Clergy.

When it comes to sculpting the image of Christ in future priests and religious, Father Maciel insists that no detail is unimportant. Even a game of soccer can be used well and transformed into an excellent means of formation.

Rumors about an "international game" between the apostolics and an all-star team from the seminary had been drifting through the university corridors for several weeks. The game took place on the university's main field during Christmas vacation. It was bone-chilling cold. The superiors of the seminary were present, and between theologians, philosophers, and juniors a crowd of 400 seminarians had gathered. Some were there to cheer on the home team, and others rooted for the missionaries from Mexico. As was customary at the time, the team of Comillas seminarians took to the field wearing their cassocks, over which they had donned the traditional white *guardapolvo* (an outer garment resembling a lab-coat, aimed at protecting their cassock from dust and mud). A spontaneous roar arose from the bleachers when the apostolics appeared— they were wearing shorts, a sports jersey, and soccer cleats.[17]

"Now that's courageous!"

"But it's freezing out here!"

"What's the spiritual director going to say when he sees them playing in shorts?" asked one of the seminarians.

---

[16] promulgated on 25 March 1992
[17] cf. Gregorio López LC (31 December 1997)

"Be quiet—that's how we *all* should play . . . "[18]

"That was the first time we had seen anything like it in the seminary,"[19] recalls Father Gustavo Izquierdo LC, who was a Comillas seminarian at the time.

But those were different times in Spain. The Missionaries of the Sacred Heart were "too progressive", "too liberal," some thought. "Modernistic seminarians" they were: playing soccer in shorts, going to the ocean in bathing suits . . . These things are considered normal now (Legionaries have always tended to be characterized by their normality and spontaneity), but in post-war Spain, all of these things were viewed as a tremendous novelty.

Surprise intensified as the game went on. Not only were the apostolics winning: they played with charity . . . and no swearing! As Father Gregorio López explained, it was surprise bordering on awe and incredulity:

> They played well, and if they fouled someone, they stopped the ball and gave it to the referee, apologizing to the other players. And we said: No. No, no, no, no. This can't be for real. As for us, if we could trip someone up and put in the ball with our hands, we'd put it in. How was it possible . . . ? No, no, no, no, no, no. What's all this? They were people who had come from another planet, no question about it.[20]

In fact, at one point the referees didn't realize that a missionary had called a foul on himself. The apostolic stopped, raised his hand, and said: "Handball!" The public was not used to this type of behavior, but for the Legionaries, it was—and continues to be—the most normal thing in the world. When Father Maciel talks about that incident, he explains it in this way:

---

[18] Gustavo Izquierdo LC, *Written testimony* (undated)
[19] *ibid*
[20] Gregorio López LC (January 2003)

It is a whole "way" of teaching. However, take note of its source: from the love of Christ and for the love of Christ. Conviction. Sincerity. Sacrifice. These are elementary things.[21]

I used to speak to them about Christ, about uprightness, about honor. I'd speak to them about sincerity; I'd speak to them about fulfilling their duty, about being honest in life. That's why there'd be: "Hands! It was a handball" or "I did such-and-such." I got rid of referees so that they'd be their own referees. If anyone tried to cheat, he knew it, but he also knew that he shouldn't be cheating. It was a mix of pedagogical elements that were intertwined throughout every moment of our life.[22]

Another teaching tool that Marcial used was the apostolic school's five-and-dime store. The boys were allowed to come and buy whatever they wanted, with no one to attend to them. They came, helped themselves, and deposited the coins in a moneybox placed amid the trinkets.

There were the exams as well: unsupervised. The exam was distributed to the class. There was no need for a teacher to stride the aisles, no need for him to be present: their consciences were enough. No one copied, and no one gave answers away.

The apostolics won the international game that December day in Comillas. They enthusiastically shouted a rhymed *hooray* for the seminary. "It wasn't usual here to shout encouragement to the opposing or losing team," explains Father Gustavo. After the game, the apostolics headed off to visit Jesus Christ in the chapel, to offer their triumph to him.[23]

For a long time, the game was commented upon in the hallways—the game, but not just the game.

---

[21] Marcial Maciel LC (23 September 2001)
[22] Marcial Maciel LC (29 December 1997)
[23] Marcial Maciel LC (23 September 2001)

Cofounders

Marcial's responsibilities as superior obliged him to be absent for weeks on end, and sometimes for months. He was gone for 20 days in January 1947, and traveled to Rome and Mexico from March to June to resolve ecclesiastical issues, look for new candidates for the apostolic school at 12 Madero Street, and beg donations to support them all. He was also looking for a new house for the apostolics in Mexico, since they needed a bigger place to fit all the boys. Many youngsters wanted to join and no more could be packed into the houses on numbers 10 and 12 Madero Street. Marcial sold those two properties, and before 1947 was over, with the help of some friends and benefactors, he bought what had been the estate of a certain Morones, famously anticlerical. Marcial changed the name of the apostolic school's new property to the "Pacelli Estate," in honor of Pius XII.[24]

When Marcial was away, the apostolics and novices followed their ordinary schedule, and one of the boys, appointed by Father Maciel before he left, took charge of the group. Their joyfulness, far from diminishing, continued to bubble over. There was no spiritual easing-off, and the house did not fall into disarray. At the seminary, these facts were spoken of with admiration: *Have you seen them, how they live . . . ?*

Father Gregorio López LC says that what most caught their attention was that the apostolics and novices didn't have a superior:

> Because Nuestro Padre wasn't there. Nuestro Padre had to travel to Mexico, and he left them there. He designated one of them to be the superior and so they, well, they obeyed. And we'd be saying: "How about that! If they'd leave us on our own, a fine ruckus we'd create!"[25]

---

[24] There are currently two schools on the property: the CEYCA for boys, run by the Legionaries, and the Godwin for girls, run by consecrated women of the Regnum Christi.

[25] Gregorio López LC (January 2003)

Father Maciel always asserts that he was not alone in
founding the Legion of Christ and Regnum Christi. He never
considered himself indispensable. In 1945, when he had nearly
died from peritonitis, he called Brother Alfredo Torres, a candi-
date who would soon join the novitiate, to his hospital bedside,
entrusting the congregation to him. "If I die, take my cassock
and go on to Rome."[26]

Many Legionary priests who were apostolics or novices
back then have grown up, fought, and persevered alongside
Father Maciel. They shared the young founder's ideal of loving
Jesus and giving up their lives for him by serving the Church
and bringing the Gospel's message to the world. If Marcial was
the founder, they knew they were cofounders. Together they
founded the Legion. They were there because they wanted to
be there; because they had freely decided to follow God's call.
For them, following the norms and obeying a superior (be he
young or old) was nothing more than a coherent, simple way
to follow Jesus Christ and accept God's will, made known to
them through human instruments.

It caused admiration in Comillas: boys who obeyed, and
who were obviously happy. Something similar happens when
people see the Legionaries of Christ today.

What moved them? Three concepts: *Freedom, Personal conviction,* and *Love of God.* They lived in an ambience of trust and
openness. They were free to make their own decisions and act
accordingly, striving to be faithful to their consciences and
faithful to Christ.

Recently a Legionary asked 81-year-old Father Maciel
how he had been able to travel so calmly, certain that the boys
would behave in his absence. He replied:

> The certainty was in the principles that all of you ac-
> cepted, the personal convictions that you had created in
> your lives: habits of living, of discipline, of prayer, of
> study. I'd be gone for a month or two, even up to three
> months. I left them on their own, with one of them in

[26] cf. Alfredo Torres LC (15 November 1989)

charge. I returned, and everything was the same as before.[27]

According to those who knew them at the time, they were bright, uncomplicated, spontaneous adolescents; they were mature and convinced regarding why and for whom they acted. They had not left their families in Mexico for a man called Marcial, and it wasn't for his sake that they were content to endure poverty and cold in Spain. It was for Christ.

From palace to stable

Marcial returned to Spain from Mexico towards the beginning of July 1947, and was greeted with the news that the Sacred Heart house would no longer be up for rent. They would have to move. Providentially, there was a cow stable behind Santa Lucía that the owner was willing to rent out as a dormitory for the apostolics. Marcial organized its "remodeling," and was the first to roll up his sleeves. It wasn't the Ritz. They scraped the floor, removed what seemed like decades-worth of spider webs and flies from the walls and rafters, and thoroughly cleaned every corner. The boys brought sand up from the beach, and Marcial mixed the cement to fix the holes in the walls. They purchased straw to use for bedding, and spread their blankets on top. To encourage the apostolics to accept their new lodgings in good spirit, Marcial placed a figure of Baby Jesus lying in a manger at the center of the room. As soon as an apostolic named Hector Manuel saw it, he jumped up and exclaimed with an air at the same time solemn and enthusiastic, "Brothers, Jesus left his palace in heaven, and was born in a stable out of love for us. Out of love for Christ, we left the palace of the Marquis, and we'll be sleeping in a cowshed!"[28] They all laughed, and agreed. The fire of the founder was already burning bright within these young men.

The new lodgings were "well ventilated" and even had some "running water": at night a steady draft whistled through

---

[27] Marcial Maciel LC (25 September 2001)
[28] cf. Marcial Maciel LC (January 1992)

the small pane-less windows, and on rainy days a trickle of water ran across the stable's floor. On nights with a strong northwesterly wind, when the lighthouses lit their lanterns and the bells of Santa Lucía rang to warn ships of their proximity to the shore, it is not hard to imagine that an apostolic or two would think about his own town, his home or his mother. However, another thought would give him courage, wrapped up in his blanket and nestled in the straw. *It's all worth it, for love of Jesus Christ . . .*

"It rained for up to three months at a time. There was no plaster, there was no paint, and the dampness and cold penetrated to the bone," remembers Father Maciel.

> Of course, they set an excellent example. Whatever sacrifice was asked of them, they absolutely never complained—not even once, not even one of them, the younger ones nor the older ones—about the life they lived, the food, their clothing, the things that were available to relax with or to live on. Everything was for Christ, always. They did everything for him and for the salvation of souls, and so that Christ would reign. That is why they lived it all with joy, and accepted it all with lots of enthusiasm.[29]

The times were difficult, since food was scarce in Spain and it was food stamps for everyone. Marcial's was a large "family," and their rations of rye bread and whatever little else they received weren't enough for the young (and growing) boys. They suffered most at the beginning, but as time went on Father Maciel worked things out with a few benefactors in Mexico and the Count of Ruiseñada, Juan Claudio Güell y Churruca. Thanks to their generosity, they were allowed to import sacks of sugar, coffee and other foodstuffs. Coffee was extremely expensive in Spain, and a merchant in Santander, Señor Martin, willingly exchanged bread, meat or fish for the coffee they offered him. The boys were fed. Nothing fancy,

---

[29] Marcial Maciel LC (1980s)

most of the time: chickpeas, beans, lentils, and oats (they had to pick out the weevils)—but they were fed.

There were no showers in the stable, and so when it didn't rain they had three choices for washing in the morning: the sea, the well in the garden, or water from the hose. In all three cases, the water was cold, and almost freezing in winter. They would douse themselves with a bucket of water, lather up, rinse themselves off with another bucketful, and: ready! For Father Maciel, that meant 32 bucketfuls times two, and his arms and back were often sore. They all welcomed the opportunities to go to the sea instead. During a recent visit to Comillas, Father Marcial stated:

> How odd the priests and seminarians thought it, because in the winter, each morning at sunrise, I'd go down to the beach with all the boys and novices and we'd wash there. We bathed: in, out, and off we went![30]

The boys would actually bathe twice a day. Although it was considered unusual at the time, Father Maciel insisted that the apostolics also wash a second time, after sports.[31]

Many years later, in the company of those same men, now Legionary priests, Father Marcial explained: "The thing is that, among us, we had a great spirit, and great dreams—didn't we?" He looks back with admiration:

> You had already determined your ideal. You were already set on actively surrendering yourself to Christ and being like him to the greatest degree possible. So all of these things helped us on another level. Humanly speaking, you can't explain it, can you? Humanly speaking, you can't explain it.[32]

They never complained or whined, and they didn't fall ill, either. They also studied very well, prayed with great fervor, and lived happily: always happy, and play-

---

[30] Marcial Maciel LC (22 September 2001)
[31] *ibid*
[32] *ibid*

ing. Father Rodrigo would come here to see them put on plays and other things . . . .[33]

On the days when they had no classes, the apostolics were constantly singing, acting, arranging pantomimes and dramatic recitations, and inventing new activities to do together. The novices, older and more mature, were enthusiastic too.

"It was a pleasant atmosphere," concluded Marcial, "An atmosphere of poverty bordering on misery, but one of boundless joy and total dedication. You look back on these years with delight, because you see God's hand at work.[34]

The murmur of admiration and surprise continued to drift through the university's corridors: about a Mexican founder and his Missionaries; about their life-style, their charity, their simplicity; about their sincere, fresh love for Christ and souls; about their mettle and their contagious happiness, despite the unenviable conditions in which they lived. Perhaps it was not surprising, therefore, that some seminarians ended up wanting to join them.

---

[33] Marcial Maciel LC (1 January 1998)
[34] *ibid*

X

Born into the Church
1948

Seeking Church Approval

The Comillas seminarians Marcial accepted into the Congregation between 1947 and 1948 could be counted on one's fingers.[1]

Considering the university had more than 300 students in the minor seminary and approximately 400 philosophy and theology students, this amount was relatively small. But the attitude toward the Missionaries of the Sacred Heart was generally favorable, and not a few seminarians went to Father Maciel for spiritual direction or confession. Young men frequently displayed an interest in joining. Since many Spanish seminarians felt drawn to missionary life in Latin America, and the Spanish bishops and the University of Comillas promoted and nurtured this missionary zeal, a few priests at the university, especially board members, began to fear that the phenomenon would spread. Initial signs of hesitancy were followed by reservations and then criticism. The same thing had happened in the seminary of Veracruz and at Montezuma: some people were beginning to see this growing congregation as a problem. Marcial was soon informed that until the congregation received official approval, no university seminarian was authorized to join the Missionaries of the Sacred Heart.

These circumstances, instead of hampering the congregation's canonical establishment, actually had the inadvertent effect of hastening it.

---

[1] They numbered less than ten, and included the Legionary priests Gustavo and Guillermo Izquierdo, Rafael Arumí Blancafort, and Antonio Lagoa (†).

Marcial had always wanted to receive the Church's approval as soon as possible. He thought—somewhat naively, he admits—that it was simply a question of presenting the constitutions and his bishop's letter of support to obtain instant canonical recognition. Given the circumstances, Marcial intensified his prayers and redoubled his efforts to get Rome's *nihil obstat* without further delay.

On 2 February 1948, both Father Francisco Baeza and Professor Lucio Rodrigo, the congregation's advisor, wrote favorable letters to the secretary of the Sacred Congregation for Religious, Monsignor Luca Hermenegildo Pasetto OFM Cap, and to Father Servo Goyeneche CMF, another member of the same Vatican body. The letters expressed their support for the idea of establishing the new institute canonically, and they were not sparing in their praise of the founder and his congregation. Father Baeza wrote:

> After a year-and-a-half of almost daily experience, I have been able to reassure myself . . . of the promise that this priest and his work hold for the greater glory of God and the good of many souls in Latin America. Father Maciel truly has a spirit that outstrips his age: his piety, zeal, and priestly efficacy are anything but commonplace. As he is a man with great tenacity and no less magnanimity, I don't think it is rash to assert that he will have a providential role in the urgent apostolic undertaking called for by Latin America. Judging by what we see daily, his young charges are examples of excellent novices and fervent religious.[2]

In one of his reports to Monsignor Pasetto, Father Rodrigo wrote:

> The religious life of the members of the institute emulates in a splendid way the life of a true religious house of perfect observance. It must be said that piety, modesty, fraternal charity and the exercise of self-denial,

---

[2] Francisco J. Baeza, *Letter to Father Goyeneche* (2 February 1948)

humility and obedience all flourish marvelously: they can rightly serve as an edifying example even to religious advanced in perfection. The same must be said for the apostolic boys. Their behavior is so unfeigned and well-rooted that even in Father Maciel's prolonged absences of days or weeks (from time to time, diverse matters of the institute demand his attention) they conserve the same fervent and constant tenor of life. I sincerely believe that this phenomenon must be attributed to some special assistance of the Holy Spirit, who thus manifests his pleasure in the institute, and how much glory it is destined to give to God and the Church.[3]

Monsignor Giuseppe di Meglio, an advisor to the nunciature in Madrid, wrote a letter to Cardinal Luigi Lavitrano, the Prefect of the Congregation for Religious in Rome.[4] He recommended the Missionaries of the Sacred Heart and highlighted their need for canonical recognition if they were to accept the young men who wanted to be admitted. He also explained and pondered the timeliness of the apostolate they proposed to develop, especially in Mexico.

Marcial was encouraged by this show of support.

Since he was still a stranger to his new bishop in Cuernavaca, Alfonso Espino y Silva, he left for Mexico on 10 February 1948 to introduce himself and place himself at the bishop's disposal.[5] He asked the bishop for his help and backing.

On 27 February 1948, Bishop Espino y Silva wrote to the Congregation for Religious in response to the letter from 1946,[6] and repeated his predecessor's request for the *nihil obstat*.[7] He asked the Congregation for Religious to disregard the objection

---

[3] Lucio Rodrigo, *Report to Monsignor Hermenegildo Pasetto* (2 February 1948)

[4] cf. Giuseppe Di Meglio, *Letter to Cardinal Luigi Lavitrano* (8 February 1948)

[5] Lauro López Beltrán writes about Alfonso Espina y Silva in *Diócesis y Obispos . . .* , pp. 205–245.

[6] cf. Luca Hermenegildo Pasetto, *Letter to the Bishop . . .* (Vatican, 2 September 1946)

[7] Alfonso Espino y Silva, *Letter to the Sacred Congregation for Religious* (27 February 1948)

over the founder's age in view of the excellent reports that he had received both from the rector of the university and from Father Maciel's assessor in Comillas.

As a result of the criticisms in Comillas, the Missionaries had to leave Santa Lucia and its cowshed. When Marcial returned from Mexico in March, he organized the move to Cóbreces, a town about three miles from Comillas. The Cistercian monks there agreed to rent him the Quiroz Institute adjacent to their monastery. To avoid so many trips back and forth in the Wawa, Marcial later rented a small house in Comillas, Villa Margarita, where the boys could go to eat and study during the day.

Rome, 1948

Marcial traveled to Rome in May, hoping to have his congregation approved. He had planned on going several weeks earlier, but the apostolic nuncio to Spain, Bishop Gaetano Cicognani, recommended that he wait until after the Italian elections. There was a reason for this.

The elections, the first between the Italian Communist Party and the new Christian Democratic Party, caused considerable social unrest in Italy at the time. The nightmare of Nazism had passed, and Communism had become the Church's most dangerous external enemy. In Croatia, the communists had condemned Archbishop Aloysius Stepinac to sixteen years of forced labor. Ukrainian Metropolitan Archbishop Josyf Slipiy was deported to a Siberian gulag. Soon afterwards, in December 1948, the cardinal primate of Hungary, József Mindszenty, was also arrested: a month later he was condemned to life imprisonment and all of his goods were confiscated. News continued to reach Rome from the Underground Church. On Easter Sunday 1948, just before the Italian elections, Pope Pius XII addressed a powerful, straightforward message to the many Catholics gathered in St. Peter's Square: "There is no room in our conscience for faint-heartedness, for comfort, for the indecisiveness of many who, in this crucial hour, believe they can serve two masters."[8] The elections of 18 April 1948 went in favor of the Christian Democrats.

In Cóbreces, Marcial and his young men had kept vigil in Eucharistic adoration from April 17–18, praying for the election outcome along with the Pope and the Church in Italy. Marcial left for Madrid ten days later, on April 28, and was in Rome on 1 May 1948.

Nihil Obstat

On the flight to Rome, Macial struck up conversation with a Venezuelan priest, Father Luis Rotondaro, who offered to pay for his stay at Villa San Francesco, a boarding house for clergy run by a congregation from Germany.

Marcial kept busy but made little progress during his first few days in Rome, which fluctuated between high hopes and repeated disappointments. He met with different members of the Curia. Cardinal Nicola Canali and Cardinal Federico Tedeschini offered support and did their best to have doors opened to him. The Holy Office had no objections to the canonical establishment of his group, but the decision did not lie with them; Marcial had to wait for the Congregation for Religious to make a decision in its next plenary meeting. In the meantime, this Vatican body received a letter from a priest in Comillas asking that the approval be postponed *sine die*[9] on account of the founder's youth and inexperience. The sub-secretary of the Congregation for Religious, Father Arcadio Larraona Navarro CMF, informed Marcial that nothing more could be done for the moment, and that he should come back when the institute was bigger and more securely established financially. Despite all his efforts and prayers, it appeared that everything would end here. *Sine die*: an "indeterminate" amount of time—that could easily become "infinite." It might even mean never.

---

[8] Pius XII, *Discourse*, from Luigi Bizzarri, *Pio XII, il Principe di Dio*. Transcription.
[9] That is, postponed until an undetermined date ("without date")

Days passed, and Marcial heard no news. The young founder wandered the streets, sad and discouraged. He went to St. Peter's Basilica and dropped to his knees at one of the side altars. He felt weak and alone. He poured out his heart to God, and new strength, peace and consolation invaded his soul. The visit boosted his confidence, giving him courage to carry on. Once again, he could not doubt God's love, and the words of Psalm 37 came to mind: "Commit your way to the Lord; trust in God and he will act."

Marcial was kneeling before the altar of Our Lady of Perpetual Help.[10] When he looked up and saw her image, he was convinced that if he was there, it was because Mary wanted to offer him her motherly assistance. He pleaded that she do everything possible—even if it took a miracle—so that they would receive the *nihil obstat* they needed so badly. He placed everything in her hands, and left the basilica with his peace of mind renewed.

There was nothing left for him to do in Rome, and he decided to go back to Cóbreces. He stopped by the offices of the Congregation for Religious next morning to say farewell, and was told that Cardinal Luigi Lavitrano had agreed to grant him the *nihil obstat*! Marcial left the office with the document in hand. It was May 25. He rushed back to St. Peter's, his heart bursting with gratitude, and thanked Mary for such an immense favor.[11]

And an immense favor it was: the Holy See had given Bishop Espino y Silva the go-ahead to set Marcial's congregation on its feet. The bishop of Cuernavaca could now establish the congregation as an official entity within the Church. The canonical establishment would bring the Missionaries of the Sacred Heart out of a state of ecclesial nothingness into existence; it would be, in effect, their birthday within the Church.

---

[10] This image of Our Lady of Perpetual Help in St. Peter's Basílica is also known as the "Gregorian Virgin," since it is located above the altar containing St. Gregory of Nazianzus' relics.

[11] Each year the entire Legionary community in Rome goes to the altar to express their gratitude anew.

Mary was once again perceived to be accepting a motherly role for the congregation that would soon be born. Years later, Father Maciel gratefully asserted, "I owe so much to Mary!"[12]

Of the many favors that he attributes to her intercession, this was one of the greatest.

Stumbling Block

The novices and apostolics in Cóbreces had been praying intensely and offering their small daily sacrifices for the success of the founder's trip. Their happiness was indescribable when they received his telegram: "Approval granted. Tell Father Rector and Rodrigo. Best wishes. Marcial."[13] The news was received with enthusiasm, and congratulations poured in from seminarians, professors and superiors. The university seminarians who wished to join the group saw the way opening up before them. One of the professors who had previously expressed misgivings about the new congregation repeated the famous words: "Rome has spoken, the case is closed."[14] He never criticized the Mexican congregation again, nor did he allow others to speak badly of them in his presence. But the news did not please everyone.

Once back in Cóbreces, Marcial gave a detailed account of his recent adventures in Rome to the apostolics and novices. The boys sat enthralled, hardly blinking, as they were told of the unexpected intervention of providence and Mary's motherly protection. It was as if they were watching a good movie— or taking part in one. They were listening to the history of their family, and recognized that it was also part of the living history of the Church.

Marcial spent only a few short days in Cóbreces, then quickly left for Cuernavaca to deliver the *nihil obstat* to Bishop Espino y Silva and set a date for the ceremony of the canonical

---

[12] Marcial Maciel, *Letter to the Legionaries* . . . (Chicago, 20 December 1982—Rome, 29 May 1988)

[13] Marcial Maciel, *Telegram* (Rome, 25 May 1948)

[14] The original phrase runs: *Roma locuta, causa finita.* cf. Gustavo Izquierdo LC, *Written Testimony* (no date)

establishment. Something told him that everything should be done as soon as possible.

When he arrived in Mexico, Monsignor Gregorio Araiza informed him that some grave allegations had reached the office of the archbishop of Mexico, and told him to speak to his own bishop without delay. Bishop Espino y Silva confirmed the news: Father Lucio Rodrigo in Comillas accused Marcial of being a liar and of pressuring the boys and their consciences by forbidding them to go to confession with any priest other than himself. Father Rodrigo claimed to have received the information from Father Sergio Ramírez, a newly ordained Mexican who had only recently joined the Missionaries, and who had been left in charge of the boys during some of Marcial's recent absences. So contradictory did Bishop Espino y Silva find these affirmations to the extraordinarily positive reports written by the same priest only three months earlier, that he insisted a defense be sent to Rome as soon as possible. He asked Marcial to gather proofs of his innocence.

Deeply grieved, Marcial set out to obtain sworn testimonies for his bishop from all the people alluded to in the report. Three apostolics who had left the congregation and returned home testified that they had never been forced to go to confession with the founder. They had never been forced to stay. They had never been coerced or put under any kind of pressure. In fact, in the years when there were still few priests in the congregation, Father Maciel always ensured that confessors from the diocesan clergy or other congregations were available to hear confessions. Father Cristóforo Fernández explains:

> From the time we were in the apostolic school in the '40s . . . Nuestro Padre always provided outside confessors, on both an ordinary and extraordinary basis.
>
> I remember, too, that the bus that dropped us off at the university for classes each morning [in Rome], also brought us to a church run by Theatine priests, San Andrea de la Valle, one afternoon a week so that whoever wanted to could go to confession with any of the several

priests who heard confessions there at that hour. Due to his frequent trips and a host of responsibilities, Nuestro Padre was not an ordinary confessor for the communities, but occasionally, every now and again, we'd see him go down to the confessional. When he did, we wanted to take advantage of the opportunity, and considered ourselves privileged if we were able to have confession with him. I did so a number of times; not as many times as I would have liked.[15]

For Father Fernández, going to confession with the founder took on a special spiritual intensity. He says that he "better perceived the presence of God, loving and merciful," and the advice hit home more deeply:

What characterized his counsels, I think, was that they were all focused on and permeated by love of God, love of neighbor, finesse and uprightness of conscience, generosity, and authenticity in our self-surrender . . . His pieces of advice—and more generally, the spirituality of Nuestro Padre that I've known since I was a boy—have always been distinguished by being rooted in the love of God and neighbor. He tried to draw us towards God by presenting a loving God to our hearts. He spoke to us a lot about the [Sacred] Heart of Jesus, and fostered that devotion among us, up-dating the concept and terms.

For him, Jesus Christ was everything. He transmitted deep intensity when he spoke of him, when he explained passages of the Gospel. It was a divine Christ, certainly; but also a very human Christ, very much within man's grasp as his example and model . . .[16]

Father Maciel's priestly heart has not changed over the years, and the same ideas continue to characterize his thoughts and words:

---

[15] Cristóforo Fernández LC, *Written testimony* (9 January 2002)
[16] *ibid*

God is with you. It doesn't matter if you've made blunders or still have flaws. If weakness and ignorance have led you along roads that are not those of love, don't be anxious. He understands your weaknesses better than you do. All you have to do is turn your eyes to him and say: "Forgive me. I let you down, but I love you, and want to continue loving you with all my heart—not just until death, but for all eternity." The Lord forgets our failures as quick as a flash of lightning that appears and disappears in the blink of an eye. Besides being all love, he is all understanding, all tenderness, all pardon. He forgives you everything if you honestly try to seek him out.[17]

The boys' habitual confessor in Comillas was Father Luis Yagüe OCR, abbot of the nearby Cistercian monastery in Cóbreces. Bishop Espino y Silva asked him to confirm the fact in writing, and to send him his impressions of the founder and his Missionaries. The abbot wasted no time in responding. Other bishops and priests wrote letters, and even the archbishop's office of New York sent a message to emphatically refute the accusations leveled against Marcial. Bishop Luis Guízar Barragán of Saltillo knew the Mexican priest whom Father Rodrigo had mentioned as the source of some of the accusations, and testified that he was an individual who suffered from a form of psychosis.

In 2003, Jesús Colina asked Marcial Maciel how he reacted to these accusations:

Above all, what was hardest for me to understand was the fact that the accusations came from good people who thought they were acting in the interests of God's glory by accusing me in that fashion. Under such circumstances, with the help of God's grace I tried never to judge people's intentions, which may have been good. I have also tried sincerely never to harbor the least

---

[17] Marcial Maciel LC (11 February 1996)

grudge. Whenever the case called for it, I simply took steps to make the facts known. When this wasn't necessary, I preferred to let it pass and not waste time defending myself, because I believe we ought to dedicate our lives to positive things, working for the Church and for God's Kingdom in souls.[18]

He adds, a few sentences later:

That is not to say that human nature doesn't feel the weight of these hard blows, because, humanly speaking, they are very difficult to take. But all of this reminds us that the Church is made up of men, and men will have their errors and limitations, their failings and sins; in spite of this the Church is the universal sacrament of salvation. That is why, quite simply, I can acknowledge that these calumnies and persecutions never made me bitter, or did the least damage to my faith in the Church. On the contrary, they have helped me to be more deeply united to the mystery of Christ. . . . The disciple follows the footsteps of the Master, and if you want to be faithful, then sooner or later the time will come for you to be a sign of contradiction.[19]

Canonical Establishment

Bishop Espino y Silva and Marcial agreed that the canonical establishment would take place on 29 June 1948, the Solemnity of Saints Peter and Paul.

As Marcial was celebrating Mass on Sunday, June 13, something kept flashing through his mind, an idea so forceful that he could not ignore it: *Today!* The canonical establishment — do it today. It was unrelenting, and each time he tried to brush the idea aside, it only returned with greater intensity. *It has to be today!* The experience reminded him of the day he received the call to found a new group of priests; a type of

---

[18] Jesús Colina, *Christ is my Life . . .* , p. 47
[19] *ibid.*

interior motion that filled his mind and moved his will to do what God asked of him. He felt that a message this strong and clear must be from the Holy Spirit, urging him to act. Today. Today, today, *today* . . .

If God wanted it, there was no time to waste. After Mass, he left Mexico City for Cuernavaca to see if he could persuade the bishop to celebrate the canonical establishment that very day. How could he explain what had happened to him during Mass, and convey how urgent and insistent the matter was? Marcial mentioned that a friend and benefactor of the group was about to travel to Europe. He would not be able to attend the canonical establishment on the 29th, but could do so if Bishop Alfonso Espino y Silva moved the date forward. The bishop had no problem with the plan, but reminded him that it was not easy to draw up the official document: it would have to be in Latin, and had to be written by a canon lawyer.

"Your Excellency, if Monsignor Gregorio Araiza were willing to write up the paper, could you do it today?"

"Why yes, of course: if Monsignor Araiza prepares the document, I'd be happy to."

Marcial immediately returned to Mexico, and found Monsignor Araiza in bed with a fever of 102°.

"What's wrong?" asked Monsignor Araiza when he saw him.

"Monsignor, I'm sorry to bother you, but something came up, and . . . "[20]

Marcial explained what they needed, and Araiza got out of bed. They went to Monsignor Araiza's office together in the cathedral complex, and the elderly man typed out the appropriate canonical formula for establishing a religious congregation under the auspices of a diocese. When he finished, Monsignor Araiza put on his overcoat and said, "Let's go. I want to be there, too."[21] He had followed the progress of the group

---

[20] cf. Marcial Maciel LC (January 1992)
[21] *ibid*

closely, ever since the days when the young founder was a seminarian studying by night and begging for alms by day. He remembered the small handful of boys. There were now more than 60 apostolics at the Pacelli Estate, and another 40 in Spain: in just seven years, the work had blossomed. Today the congregation would be born in the bishop's residence in Cuernavaca, and Monsignor Araiza did not want to miss it.

They stopped by the Pacelli Estate to pick up Father Luis Ferrera, Brother Alfredo Torres and Brother Rafael Cuena, and for the second time that day, Marcial was off to Cuernavaca. Mr. Luis Barroso and Mother Concepción Solís of the Sisters of the Incarnate Word were invited.

At about 8 p.m., Bishop Alfonso Espino y Silva signed the document, and the "Missionaries of the Sacred Heart and of the Virgin of Sorrows" became a religious order of diocesan right.[22]

Marcial then knelt before the bishop and took the religious vows of poverty, chastity and obedience: the first Legionary of Christ. Bishop Alfonso named him superior general, and he, in turn, received the vows of brothers Torres and Cuena.

Regarding the title of the congregation, Marcial would continue to give it thought. Two or three years later, he chose a name that seemed better to reflect the dynamic apostolic spirit of men dedicated to expending themselves at the service of Christ and the Church: the "Legionaries of Christ." When the Holy See granted the congregation its Decree of Praise seven-

---

[22] cf. Alfonso Espino y Silva, *Decreto de Erección Canónica de la congregación de los Misionarios del Sagrado Corazón y de la Virgen de los Dolores* (Cuernavaca, 12 June 1948). The certificate for the Canonical Establishment of the congregation signed by Bishop Espino y Silva is dated 12 June 1948. Father Maciel affirms that the ceremony took place on Sunday, June 13, and this is corroborated not only by the Legion's constant tradition, but also by the fact that the certificates of religious profession bear the date 13 June 1948. The entry in the community journal (*Diary of the Juniorate in Cóbreces, 1947–1951*) for June 13 states that the rector of the apostolic school in Tlalpan had called and said that at 4 p.m. the congregation would be founded. The discrepancy, therefore, is likely due to a simple error on the part of Monsignor Araiza, given his state of health.

teen years later in 1965, both names appeared in the document and were used interchangeably. The Vatican approved the definitive name, "Legionaries of Christ," in 1996.[23]

It soon became obvious why the Holy Spirit had insisted. Only a day or two later, Marcial received an urgent call from the bishop's office, and he left for Cuernavaca straight away. Bishop Espino y Silva showed him a letter from the Sacred Congregation for Religious revoking the *nihil obstat* and ordering the bishop not to proceed with the canonical establishment. The letter reached the post office box by Saturday, June 12, but since the priest who normally sorted the bishop's mail spent his Saturdays on pastoral visits, the letter had not reached the bishop's hands until Monday, June 14. It was too late: the congregation already existed juridically, and the document Bishop Espino y Silva had signed on Sunday retained its validity. Hence, if the Congregation for Religious wanted to suppress the newborn work, they would have to use a different process.

Disband the Legion?

For Marcial, 1948 was a year of physical suffering and inner grief.

When Marcial returned to Spain, the rector at Comillas regretfully informed him that the Missionaries could no longer study there. The university council had reached the decision knowing that some bishops might be disconcerted to see seminarians from their dioceses joining a religious congregation. This decision, however, was not put into effect immediately, as the apostolic nuncio to Spain, Bishop Gaetano Cicognani, intervened on behalf of the Missionaries of the Sacred Heart during the summer. They were consequently allowed to stay for another school year.

Marcial's health was fragile, but he continued to carry out his responsibilities. An overwhelming workload and the emo-

---

[23] Eduardo Cardinal Martínez Somalo, *Decree*, Protocol n. R. 111–2/96 (Vatican, 27 July 1996). Cardinal Martínez Somalo wrote as Prefect of the Congregation for Institutes of Consecrated Life and Societies of Apostolic Life.

tional stress of the first half of the year had left him physically exhausted. Nevertheless, he dedicated himself to the formation of his Missionaries, being like a true father for them. He took an active interest in their schoolwork, their spiritual progress and their health, making sure there was always food on the table. Whenever he was in Cóbreces, he would watch their games, accompany them on their outings, and organize surprise trips to the beach. He dedicated large blocks of time to give them spiritual talks, tell them stories, and speak with them about the future of the congregation. He would let them in on the latest news, and help them broaden their horizons and enhance their desire to spend their lives for Christ and souls. The young men responded with full trust and oneness of spirit. They wanted him to know that, even when he had to be away, he could count on them and on their faithfulness—for they too had freely dedicated themselves to the same ideal.

Marcial took another blow midway through September, and it hit him hard. Very hard. He received a letter in Cóbreces from Bishop Espino y Silva, saying that the Holy See had issued the dreaded decree to dissolve the congregation. The bishop told him that he would have to start thinking of sending the boys to some other seminary in Mexico, and resolve what was to be done with the congregation's assets. Marcial was bewildered and shaken:

> I really didn't know what to do. I didn't have anyone to talk to. I didn't know whom to write, and my only refuge was God, Jesus in the Eucharist. I poured out my sorrows to him, talking with him and asking him to enlighten me.[24]

Marcial said nothing to the boys about this problem. He spent nearly two months in bleak loneliness. He looked inside to discover God's will, speaking with the Holy Spirit, asking him what he should do, and begging for light. His prayer was answered on the feast of Christ the King.

---

[24] Marcial Maciel LC (January 1992)

That day, during Mass, I received a light from God. It was so simple. Why not go to Rome? Why not talk with the cardinal prefect for Religious and ask his permission to bring eight, ten, twelve young men to a seminary in Rome? Once ordained, they could reestablish the Congregation of the Missionaries of the Sacred Heart.[25]

He didn't care who got the congregation on its feet. It could be him, it could be anyone else—he could join it later as just another Missionary. What mattered was that the mission God had entrusted to him went forward; what mattered was that God's designs were carried out.

It was a soothing thought, and Marcial looked for the first opportunity to go to Rome. He could finally do so on December 1.

In Rome, Father Maciel once again took up lodging at Villa San Francesco, and soon discovered that the prefect of the Congregation for Religious, Cardinal Luigi Lavitrano, lived in the very same boarding house: precisely the man Marcial needed to see! Since he and the cardinal had never actually met, Marcial's Venezuelan friend, Father Rotondaro, introduced him to Fra Girolamo, the cardinal's personal secretary,[26] and his appointment was set a few days later.

Marcial began by thanking Cardinal Lavitrano for having granted the *nihil obstat*, and told him that although he regretted that the congregation had been dissolved so quickly, he willingly accepted the Congregation for Religious' decision. Cardinal Lavitrano listened to the young priest's story with astonishment. Marcial said that he had come to Rome to ask the cardinal for a special favor. "Tell me what I can do for you," replied the cardinal.[27]

---

[25] Marcial Maciel LC (January 1992)

[26] Johann Roeger, FFSC (1901–1987), member of the Franciscan Brothers of the Holy Cross of Waldbrietbach (*Insitutum Fratrum Franciscalium a Santa Croce loci Waldbreitbach*). Fra Girolamo ("Brother Jerome"), as he was called, returned to Germany in 1952. He was general superior of the "German Franciscans" from 1964–1976 and 1980–1982. "Villa San Francesco" was the institute's headquarters.

[27] cf. Marcial Maciel LC (January 1992)

Marcial explained his idea: a few of the young men could come to study in Rome until they were ordained priests; Marcial would look for the money to support them. One or all of them—whatever the Holy See deemed best—could then restart the congregation; and he would happily join them as just another religious.

"Father, I think you've been misinformed," replied the cardinal when he had finished. "The congregation of the Missionaries of the Sacred Heart was approved and therefore established canonically with my consent. I did not authorize its dissolution, nor do I know of any meeting in which its dissolution was decided."[28]

The cardinal told him that the canonical establishment signed on June 13 retained its validity, and asked him to stay in Rome for a few days while he reviewed the case in his office. He encouraged Marcial to keep calm and press forward with his work.

They met several times over the next few days, and Cardinal Lavitrano confirmed that the letter asking for the dissolution had been sent to Cuernavaca without his authorization: its contents therefore were to be considered null and void. The Missionaries of the Sacred Heart enjoyed regular juridical status. Until his death in 1950, Cardinal Lavitrano would defend the congregation unconditionally.

Rome on the horizon

During their conversations, Cardinal Lavitrano advised Father Maciel to build a center in Rome. Marcial had no financial resources, but he felt he could count on God's assistance—and on Mary's, too. He became sure of this when he realized that the interview, which had brought him so much consolation and hope, had taken place on a Marian feast day[29]. It was

---

[28] Marcial Maciel LC (January 1992)

[29] The conversation with Cardinal Lavitrano appears to have taken place on December 12, feast of Our Lady of Guadalupe, although Father Maciel cannot vouch for the date. Perhaps his uncertainty stems from the fact that another

yet another instance of Mary making her presence felt when he and the congregation needed her assistance.

Marcial had dreamed of having a center in Rome from the beginning. After the feast of Christ the King in Cóbreces, when he had received the idea of sending a small group to Rome, the desire had grown even stronger. But Cardinal Lavitrano's invitation was decisive. God wanted it: they would come to Rome.

Rome meant being close to the Holy Father. Even today the founder wants Legionaries to be formed in Rome, close to the Pope. He wants them to deepen their faith in Christ's Vicar, and love him as their father and shepherd. He wants them to delve into and love the teachings of the Church's magisterium. Doctrinal fidelity and unconditional, loving adherence to Peter's successor are essential traits of the Legionary spirit and charism.

Rome beckoned. The move from Comillas to Rome would mark a new stage in the congregation's life.

Marian feast day also falls within the first half of December: the Immaculate Conception (December 8).

Pope Paul VI offered the Legionaries of Christ his affection and unconditional support throughout his pontificate. He granted the congregration its Decree of Praise in 1965. In this 1969 photo, Pope Paul VI receives Father Maciel and his family members in a private audience to commemorate the founder's 25th anniversary of priestly ordination. "Mamá Maurita," Father Maciel's mother, appears at right.

The Anáhuac University of Mexico, founded in 1964, was the Legion of Christ's first post-secondary educational institute. It moved to its definitive campus, pictured here, in 1968.

In June 1983, upon the altar of Our Lady of Guadalupe parish and in the presence of Father Maciel and the other Legionaries of Christ present in Rome, Cardinal Eduardo Pironio, Prefect of the Congregation for Religious and Secular Institutes, signed the decree granting definitive approval to the Legion of Christ's Constitutions.

*There are now **Mano Amiga** schools for underprivileged children in Argentina, Chile, Colombia, El Salvador, Mexico and Venezuela.*

Bishop Jorge Bernal LC exercising his pastoral ministry in the Cancún-Chetumal prelature, where 20% of the Legionary of Christ priests stationed in Mexico take part in pastoral work.

Since the prelature of Chetumal was established in 1970, Legionary missionaries have built 343 churches and oratories, 18 schools, 2 universities, medical dispensaries and residential complexes for those who are left homeless by the hurricanes that frequently ravage the Caribbean, as well as a wide range of other undertakings.

Participants in the 3ʳᵈ International gathering of Full-Time Evangelizers and School of the Faith catechists on pilgrimage to Our Lady of Guadalupe Shrine in Mexico City, from 29 January–1 February 2000.

A young missionary giving a catechism lesson on the foothills of Orizaba's Peak during Holy Week 2003. Here Father Maciel did missionary work during vacations in his first years as a seminarian (1936–1937). Responding to the needs of this region's rural communities, the Legion of Christ is constructing the Rafael Guízar y Valencia *Missionary Center*

XI

God Draws Up the Route
1949–1955

A center in Rome

In December 1948, Cardinal Luigi Lavitrano gave Marcial a business card of the Castelli construction company, which had done some important jobs for the Vatican in the times of Pius XI. Marcial arranged to meet Leone Castelli, the owner. He explained how Cardinal Lavitrano had invited his congregation to set up a house in Rome, and explained his financial limitations. The contractor offered to sell him 20,000 m² of property on Via Aurelia, at a dollar a square meter.

God would have to help out, because he didn't have a lot of money, or even a little money. He had no money.

He signed the contract.

That night, praying and wondering how he would find the wherewithal to purchase the property, it occurred to him to call Mrs. Delfina Castorena de Muñoz, from Zacatecas, in Mexico. She turned out to be willing to write him a check for the whole amount. In a matter of days, Castelli had the blueprints ready. Marcial looked them over with the architect Gianni Mazzocca, and signed the building contract before returning to Spain to spend Christmas 1948 with his young men. Marcial didn't have a red cent for the construction itself, but he reached a trustful conclusion: if God had put him up to this business, God would lend him a hand. For his part, he was determined to spare no effort to second God's plans, no matter how taxing it might be on him. It would be up to him to look for help; it will be up to God to provide it.

Marcial had also received some assistance from his friend, Father Rotondaro, before leaving Rome. He provided Father

Maciel with two letters of recommendation: one for Father Alfonso Alfonso, dean of the Cathedral of Caracas, Venezuela, and one for Miss Ana Cecilia Branger, a spinster living in Valencia, Venezuela. After Christmas, Marcial left Cóbreces and crossed the Atlantic. First he went to Mexico, where he had to talk over some issues with Father Luis Ferreira, the rector of the minor seminary. He then made an exhausting trek through several Mexican dioceses looking for vocations, and visited a number of benefactors and friends. Marcial told them about the opportunity that had come up in Rome, and explained what the congregation would need to finance the building project. Although he received some help, it was not nearly enough. He departed for Venezuela.

Venezuela

Archbishop Lucas Guillermo Castillo Hernández of Caracas gave him a kind welcome, and opened up many doors to him in the nation's capital. Father Alfonso Alfonso introduced him to a woman named Adriana de Valeri, and thanks to her he met several other women who promised him $30-dollar monthly stipends for a number of his Missionaries. Adriana de Valeri offered to gather the contributions, and send him the total each month. Nevertheless, the main reason for his trip—to find enough money to pay for the building project in Rome—was still pending.

He traveled to the city of Valencia, Venezuela, and presented Father Rotondaro's letter to Miss Ana Cecilia Branger. She offered him a donation that would help offset some of the construction costs. It was a generous amount, and he was thankful as he made his way back to Caracas, but he knew that he still had a long way to go.

That evening he was surprised to receive a call from Miss Branger. She said that with all the haste of the visit, she had been rather nervous and had not been able to think things through. "Could you drop by again, Father? I'd like to speak with you." Back in Valencia the next day, Father Maciel was told over lunch why she had asked him to return. He remembers the gist of her conversation:

Father, I've been thinking about your work, and I wanted to offer a little more help with building your seminary in Rome. My parents were French, I love France—I know that when your congregation goes there, France will be blessed, just as Venezuela will when the Lord brings you here. I want to do everything I can for this work to build Christ's Kingdom. I have a house in Cannes, on the French Riviera. You might find it useful as a Novitiate or formation house. I'll give it to you, furniture and all. It is a very beautiful house—two houses, actually: one is smaller . . . I lived a good part of my childhood there. . . ."

As Marcial was leaving, Miss Branger handed the surprised founder the deeds to the two houses, along with a letter for her representative in France, the parish priest in Cannes. "If you want," she added, "you can also sell the houses to build your college in Rome. Later on we'll provide for when you begin in France."[1]

Marcial could hardly believe what had taken place. He had just received a very considerable endowment, and knew that God was behind it all. "I was elated when I left," he says, "and also extremely grateful to God."[2]

After two long months of absence, Marcial returned to Spain, and reached Cóbreces on the night of 20 February 1949. Over the next few days, he dedicated long stretches of time to the apostolics and novices, telling them about his recent adventures in Mexico and the Caribbean. Of course, they had not lost track of each other over this period.

Thousands of letters

As founder, Father Maciel's priority was that of forming his future Legionaries. Circumstances suggested a simple, providential way of doing so, despite his forced absences: letter-writing. This is how he explains it:

---

[1] cf. Marcial Maciel LC (January 1992)
[2] *ibid*

> Since I had to travel to raise money, leaving them in Spain or Rome, I was obviously always concerned about how each of them was doing. I wrote them, and then waited for a reply. I was attentive to see who answered and who didn't; if one of the members of the community didn't write back, I'd write him again, so that he'd let me know how things were going. . . .
>
> I wanted to give them a bit of encouragement and spiritual guidance through these letters.[3]

Father Maciel's letters, notes, and postcards number in the thousands, and the postmarks offer a fascinating record of his travels. Written on planes, in airports or waiting rooms, in the silence of chapels—even from a hospital bed—Marcial poured spirituality onto each page, consciously shaping the charism of the Legion and the future Regnum Christi movement, line by line. The founder's letters reveal the figure of a priest, a spiritual father, a son of the Church and a friend of Christ. Colorful, poignant words paint paragraphs that are simultaneously full of gentleness and charged with energetic power. They have a sincere, unassuming tone. Whether smiling or weeping, the author shines through them.

Father Carlos Mora LC recalls:

> If you were behaving yourself and Nuestro Padre wrote, you'd open it joyfully, and read it over and over again. The same goes for when Nuestro Padre, from wherever he might be, pointed out something you needed to work on, because—I don't know how Nuestro Padre realized it, being thousands of miles away—the letters always had exactly the advice you needed. So, logically, they pulled you out of your difficulty and set you back on the right track. . . . they now form part of an admirable store we have as Legionaries."[4]

---

[3] Marcial Maciel LC (1 January 1998)
[4] Carlos Mora LC (1 January 1998)

Father Maciel wrote with the awareness that he was a priest called to love and forgive, and a father who had to prayerfully instruct, correct, and encourage his sons. Responding to a Legionary's question, he once admitted that he sent letters to as many Legionaries as he could, writing "on cards, scraps of paper, the pages of a note-book, whatever was available." When a priest commented that his recent letters seem much more formal than they used to be, Father Maciel replied:

> Father here says that now the letters are all so formal. Those are the ones that are transcribed, since I basically continue with the notebook and the loose pages that I have on hand or happen to come across: that's what I use to write. Afterwards I give everything to the priest who writes them up on the typewriter or computer, and sends them out by mail . . . [5]

His letter-writing tradition continues. Many Legionaries receive personal letters from him each year, as do hundreds of men, women, teenagers and children, whether they belong to the Regnum Christi movement or not: lay people, nuns, priests and bishops, people from all over the world, and from many social standings.

Exhausting Work

Marcial was in Mexico and Venezuela again during June and July 1949. This time Father Luis Ferreira traveled from Mexico to Cóbreces to look after the novices and apostolics, as he had already done on some previous occasion.

Father Maciel had been working hard in Venezuela. Worn out, weak, and feeling ill, he had lain down for a quick rest when he suddenly suffered a heart attack.

> I lost movement in my arms, and couldn't speak. I knew right away what was happening, and began praying to

---

[5] Marcial Maciel LC (1 January 1998)

our Lord and to the Blessed Virgin, asking them to help me die well. A few minutes later, I managed to ring the front desk and explain what condition I was in. A doctor came immediately. I will be going to the hospital this afternoon.

He was probably not in the mood for writing after a brush with death, but he began a letter to an apostolic that ended up being extremely long. It was as if they were speaking face-to-face:

I am writing from bed . . . To take advantage of my time, to find comfort in my solitude, and to avoid delaying a few words of encouragement to help you continue along the way of perfection, I will begin to answer the points of your letter . . . [6]

Approximately a week had passed when he again wrote from Caracas, having just visited Mérida in the Andes. His health had given way once more:

I was sure they'd bury my bones there. I had a terrible time, especially on Sunday evening: I thought that I wouldn't wake up next morning. Thanks be to God, Father Paparoni was in the hotel and he very charitably took care of me. At 12 midnight I had a fever of 104°F, and only at 4 a.m. did the sharp pain in my intestines go away, thanks to some tablets I took. I rested from 4 until 7 a.m., and then, against the will of every inch of this poor body (it "dragged itself" rather than "walked") I left for Caracas. My luck was so bad that there was no direct flight, and the trip took six hours instead of two, stopping at Barquisimeto . . . , Maiquetía, San Felipe, and La Guaira. From there I got a ride, and an hour later succeeded in reaching Caracas."[7]

[6] Marcial Maciel, *Letter to an apostolic* (Caracas, Venezuela, 15 July 1949)
[7] Marcial Maciel, *Letter to a religious* (Caracas, Venezuela, July 1949)

His workload was intense, his cares were many, and his frail state of health was often further aggravated by lack of sleep. In 2001, Father Maciel and some of the very first Legionaries had the chance to return to Comillas. They recalled the times they had spent together there, and took advantage to greet Elías Iglesias Valdizán, whom Marcial had hired to drive the Wawa, their bus, and to help out with sundry chores in Cóbreces. Elías stated:

> Father always had delicate health, always, always. The other day when I saw him, I was taken aback. . . . After fifty years not seeing someone who was always so frail, and now to see him stand so tall . . . I wouldn't have imagined it, and that's the truth. I thought he'd be older, and more wrinkled from having worked that much. He worked so much . . . even when he was asleep, that man's mind was working. . . .
>
> Is it possible not to have good memories of someone who was always so kind? From the time his foot touched Spanish soil, he was flat-out kind. The thing is that goodness just flowed out of him . . . A very generous person, very hard-working, involved in everything, always attentive to the needs of the apostolics, the novices, the cook, the driver: to everything—when he had the time. Because Father traveled a lot.
>
> Just as soon as he'd arrive back at Cóbreces, they had everything prepared to let him rest . . . but half-an-hour or an hour later he'd already be rushing about, seeing to the monastery building, to the lads, to everything, everything, everything. . . . He was a very busy priest, with a very strong sense of responsibility for what he had brought over from Mexico."[8]

During 1949 and 1950, Marcial split his time between life in Cóbreces and trips to finance the construction then under-

---

[8] Elías Iglesias (26 September 2001)

way in Rome. As always, the founder counted on his co-founders to help him keep the different undertakings going. He entrusted the supervision of the building project in Rome to some of his young religious in the Juniorate; they took the duty in turns. Just like the founder, hands-on experience would teach them how to work. They learned well. Legionaries of Christ are encouraged to use their freedom and creativity, and they know they can count on their superiors' trust, support, and advice.

The Move to Rome

Life in Cóbreces was a model of unpunctuated serenity and happiness. A few new vocations joined them from Comillas.[9] New groups of apostolics arrived from Mexico.

Father Francisco Javier Baeza had been transferred to a new post, and in July 1950 the university's new rector, Father Pablo Pardo, under pressure from some of his priests, confirmed that the group would no longer be allowed to attend classes with them. Providentially, the house in Rome was almost finished by that time. When the new school year began, Marcial hired teachers to give the apostolics classes in Cóbreces, and he took the novices, juniors, and those who would begin to study philosophy and theology with him to Rome. They would attend classes at the Gregorian University.

Marcial had acquired enough money to pay for the construction of the house on Via Aurelia. The materials used were far from the best, and since he didn't have the funds to pay for the front entrance porch, he decided that the house would simply have to do without it. The architect, Mazzocca, protested that a building without a stately front entrance was a pitiable thing, ugly and (therefore) unthinkable.[10] He succeeded in convincing the company to build it for Father Maciel free of charge.

---

[9] By the time they moved to Rome, the number of seminarians from Comillas who joined Marcial's group had not exceeded 15.
[10] cf. Marcial Maciel LC (8 October 2002)

An abundance of large windows meant that the college was well-lit. Its lines were simple, it was functional, and there were no nooks or crannies. Marcial believed that even architecture could contribute to the formation of his men. Luminosity and cleanliness inside, well-groomed gardens outside: these aspects are part of the building style adopted by Father Maciel.

Marcial planned their move while in Cóbreces, since they had some friends and acquaintances in Spain who would be able to lend them a hand. The community took along whatever might help them live through their first few months in Rome: the building was finished, but unfurnished. As Father Marcial explained to a later generation of Legionaries,

> They had given me three pigs on credit. We killed them and boiled them, stewing the meat and putting it into big glass jars . . . . We portioned out the meat, cut it into smaller pieces, put it in the lard, and sealed the jars. We brought it all along with us on the bus, and it provided us something to eat during our first few months in Rome. They gave me credit on 5-kilogram (11 lb) tins of tuna as well, here in Santander. When the Second World War ended, no one had anything in Italy. So I'd sell tins to the stores, and they gave me a good price for them; with that I would buy bread . . . [11]

Since they would have no money to buy things in Italy, they asked Santiago, the carpenter of Comillas, to make all their furniture: tables, chairs, shelves for the library . . . everything except beds. Santiago generously volunteered to accompany them to Rome to assemble all the furniture there. Father Maciel says that they "slowly paid it off with donations"[12] that they received.

In Rome, they each had a crate for a chair and another for a desk. They slept on the floor. For cooking, Leone Castelli donated them a small stove with two burners. They used tin

---

[11] Marcial Maciel LC (22 September 2001)
[12] *ibid*

plates and knives and forks on loan from Father Isaiah's or-
phanage in Primavalle until they managed to scrape together
enough money to purchase their own. They planted a veg-
etable garden, built a cowshed, and soon added a chicken
coop. Once again they experienced the poverty that had characterized their existence when the group, living in the basement of 39 Turín Street, consisted of Marcial and thirteen
adolescents.

Ten years had passed quickly: from 39 Turín Street to their
first house at 21 Victoria, and from there to 10 and 12 Madero
Street, in Mexico City; the move to Comillas; from Comillas to
Cóbreces; and now, towards the end of 1950, the opening of a
major seminary and novitiate in Rome.[13] The congregation had
already received official recognition on the diocesan level.
Marcial was 30.

An 81-year-old Father Maciel would marvel at how God's
hand had guided the new foundation:

> The important thing here is to see how marvelously God
> brings about the fulfillment of his work, step by step,
> through the instrument he had chosen . . . It wasn't
> chance that brought us to Comillas: God doesn't do
> things by accident. We went to Comillas because that was
> in God's plans, and because he . . . wanted us to be at the
> heart of the Church promptly, as soon as possible, quickly;
> close to his Vicar on earth. We didn't know this; I didn't
> understand—I didn't even dream of it. But he did. . . .
>
> Without my having considered it or sought it out, God
> provided the circumstances for us to have our novitiate
> and center for philosophy and theology in Rome by the
> end of 1950 . . . It is something that seemed natural at the
> time, things that "just had to be done", that had to be
> done quickly: there was no real pondering involved. But
> now, with the passing of time, looking back, you can see
> something tremendously profound, tremendously mys-

[13] The building now serves as the general directorate of the Legion of Christ and
the Regnum Christi Movement.

terious, something tremendously wise, something that only someone like God could have imagined and brought to completion in that way, within that time-frame.[14]

From 1950–1955, the congregation developed constantly and swiftly. In 1952, the first Legionary priests from Comillas were ordained: José María Escribano, Faustino Pardo, Antonio Lagoa, Rafael Arumí, and Gregorio López. They would offer the founder much-needed assistance. In Mexico, the apostolic school in Tlalpan was growing so quickly that it was necessary to put up a new building on the Pacelli Estate with a capacity for 200 students, a project completed when Santiago Galas and Gastón Azcárraga generously offered to foot the bill between them. The Trappist monks in Cóbreces once again had need of the facilities of the Quiroz Institute, and so the apostolics in Spain, under their recently-ordained rector, Father Gregorio López LC, needed to find a new place to live before 1 October 1952. After several weeks of unfruitful searching, at the end of September the Legion of Christ finally found and rented an old closed-down hotel with hot springs in the town of Ontaneda, in Santander, Spain. They would purchase the property between 1953 and 1954 with the help of a Venezuelan woman, Mrs. Josefina Gómez de Delfino.[15] In April 1952, Mr. Manuel Santos—a native of Monterrey, Mexico, and founding President of the Bank of Monterrey (*Banco Regiomontano*)—told Father Maciel on a visit through Rome that he would cover the costs of building a new Legionary novitiate in Salamanca, Spain. The cornerstone was laid on 11 February 1953, but construction was interrupted for several years after Manuel Santos' unexpected death. Meanwhile, in Rome, work was still being done on the house: there was furniture to be bought, a sacristy to be prepared, and grounds to be landscaped.

Marcial traveled to Spain, Mexico, Cuba and Venezuela to look for benefactors who could help him pay for the center in Rome. Although his health fluctuated between "poor" and

[14] Marcial Maciel LC (Fall 2001)
[15] The building continues to function as a Legionary apostolic school.

"poorer", it was up to him to feed, clothe, and educate his Legionary family in Mexico, Spain, and Rome. Nevertheless, he dedicated the best of himself to help form his men in the four spheres of a Legionary's preparation—spiritual, social, apostolic, and intellectual—down to the smallest details. Given that Father Maciel was away so often, such painstaking formation would have been impossible without the dependable, loyal help of his first priests: Antonio Lagoa was the superior of the major seminary in Rome, Rafael Arumí took care of the novices, and Gregorio López ran the apostolic school in Ontaneda. Father Luis Ferreira continued his work in Tlalpan.

When he arrived at any Legionary center, especially Rome, he would resume his responsibilities as a former, and attend his religious in spiritual direction whenever they requested it. That meant he usually ended up seeing everyone.

After years of experience forming priests and attending seminarians in spiritual direction, Father Maciel would be able to describe every last particular of priestly formation—the general principles as well as their concrete applications—with the precision and care of an artist. He would explain their apostolic goals and the concrete way they ought to go about their apostolic work. He would do the same, some years later, when it came to the Regnum Christi lay movement. He looked at how they were living the small details of religious life to help them gauge their personal progress: it is all too easy to do things haphazardly.

In this sense, formation in the Legion or Regnum Christi is like a mosaic, constructed piece by piece, color by color, stone by stone. It implies time, constancy, and patience. The more carefully the small pieces are put in place, the more commendable the final product. And since men and women who consecrate their lives to God are called to imitate Christ—the most perfect person who ever existed, who "reveals man to man"[16]—even the little things make a difference. Each day, stone by stone, consecrated men and women try to forge

---

[16] Vatican II, Pastoral Constitution on the Church in the Modern World *Gaudium et Spes,* 22

virtue, temper their wills, and form their personality with the help of God's grace, learning what it means to pray and to preach the Gospel.

To convey the fruit of his experience, Father Maciel has left a great deal in writing. The Legionaries of Christ have their Constitutions, and there are a wide variety of Regnum Christi manuals that deal not only with general ideas, but also with all the particulars of formation, spirituality, pedagogy and apostolic work.

The Legion's first apostolic project . . .

At the beginning of 1954, the Legion of Christ numbered 272: 167 apostolics, 33 candidates, 30 novices, and 42 religious with vows, 8 of whom were priests. The time had come to start working apostolically.

Rome June 1951: the doorbell rings at Via Aurelia 677.[17] A lady from Monterrey, Mexico, would like to see Father Maciel. After a short wait, she introduces herself: *Father Maciel, my name is Flora Barragán de Garza.*

Flora Barragan had lost her husband not long before, and acting upon his wishes now wanted to dedicate part of the inheritance to setting up a new project for the Church. Taking advantage of a school-trip organized by her daughter's school,[18] she had come to Rome, and sent the Pope a letter asking what type of organization he suggest she fund. Interviewed some time later, Mrs. Barragán narrates what happened:

> I told him that I had mulled over several ideas, and asked what would be best for people, for souls. A few days later a letter signed by Montini . . . arrived, in which he told me that the three projects I had suggested were all very good ways to serve God, but that the best would be to help priests, since many souls are saved through their work, and the Church really needs their guidance. So I immediately decided . . . to settle every-

---

[17] In 1951, the Legionary center's street number was Via Aurelia 643.
[18] It was a pilgrimage arranged for the canonization of Saint María Mazzarello.

thing before leaving Rome, not returning to Mexico without carrying out the Holy Father's advice . . . [19]

The future Pope Paul VI, Monsignor Giovanni Battista Montini, knew how eager the young Mexican founder was to begin serving the Church. He suggested she give her donation to the Legionaries.

After Flora Barragán's visit, Father Maciel spent time thinking and praying, trying to decide how to make their love for the Church a concrete reality, according to the charism that God wanted for the Legion. What shape would the Legion's first apostolic work take? Build a parish? Run a school? Whatever they did, he wanted to help bishops and diocesan priests in their work... and so he finally decided that they would complement parish work in the field of education: teaching children, forming catechists, strengthening Christian families. They would build a school.

Years later, Father Maciel would say:

> I was very interested in the opportunity to bring the Gospel to the greatest possible number of children, teenagers and young people. We would . . . create centers where we could continue to evangelize the middle-aged, mature adults, and the elderly. To succeed in establishing Christ's Kingdom, to succeed in evangelizing, we would have to set up schools, universities, family centers and various institutes offering moral, medical, and other kinds of professional help to different groups: families with psychological problems or troubled parent-child relationships; engaged couples and newlyweds; married couples . . . ; and those who were approaching the end of their lives. Another crucial part of our apostolic activity would be the preparation of lay Catholics capable of spreading the Gospel, schools to teach the Faith, and schools for training catechists."

---

[19] Flora Barragán (1986)

He ran various ideas by Monsignor Montini, Archbishop Luis María Martínez, and Bishop Espino y Silva, and they all agreed with the choice of starting a school. Once again, there were obstacles. As soon as news of his plans got out, several influential people and even some clergy began to discredit the founder and his activities, trying to persuade Flora Barragán to change her mind. They alleged that the Legion was not yet approved by the Church, and that Father Maciel was a liar who was just after her money. Bishop Luis Guízar Barragán of Saltillo refuted the rumors, showing his support for Marcial and the Legionaries. He explained to Flora that the congregation enjoyed full juridical standing on the diocesan level (the first step for every newly-founded congregation), and that it would become a congregation of "pontifical right" once it received the Vatican's "Decree of Praise," something that would take another several years.

Marcial asked Father Faustino Pardo LC to supervise the school's construction, and together they dedicated weeks on end to carefully plan, direct, and supervise the Legion of Christ's first educational undertaking, its first apostolic venture. The Cumbres school of Mexico City opened its doors in February 1954, and Father Pardo was the school's first principal.

Father Samuel Lemus recalls an encounter he witnessed between Mrs. Flora Barragán[20] and the newly-elected "Monsignor Montini": Pope Paul VI.

> When Mrs. Flora Barragán came to consult with Pope Pius XII to see what to do, he sent her to see Monsignor Montini, and Monsignor Montini directed her to Father

---

[20] Mrs. Flora Barragán died on 6 January 2002. At Father Maciel's request, the community Mass was celebrated for her the next day in all of the houses of the Legion of Christ and consecrated Regnum Christi members. The note on the bulletin board read: "Commend in your prayers the eternal rest of the soul of Mrs. Flora Barragán, who died yesterday. Mrs. Flora was one of the principal benefactors of the Legion and the Movement, particularly in the decade of the fifties. Her help in founding the Cumbres Institute of Mexico City was decisive."

Maciel. [Years later, she] came with a group of people from Monterrey, and Father Maciel arranged an audience for them with Pope Paul VI. And at one point the monsignor who always accompanied the Pope . . . presents Mrs. Flora to him and says: "The founder of the Cumbres school of the Legionaries of Christ, in Mexico." And then Pope Montini says: "No . . . *I'm* its founder." . . . I heard this from his very lips.[21]

Today, almost fifty years since that first school, the Legion of Christ runs 194 institutes dedicated to education, from kindergarten to university level.

. . . and a church in Rome

Although Father Maciel was constantly on the go, he continued to cherish a dream: to build a church dedicated to the Blessed Virgin Mary before he died. In 1954, therefore, when Pope Pius XII, through his vicar for Rome, Cardinal Micara, entrusted him with the construction of a church in Rome dedicated to Our Lady of Guadalupe, patroness of Mexico and of Latin America, Marcial willingly accepted the invitation. It would be built on a property adjacent to the Legion of Christ's college, at Via Aurelia 675.

Marcial set about looking for economic assistance, confident that the Mexican people would respond well and supply everything needed. Pope Pius XII blessed the cornerstone in 1955.

---

[21] Father Samuel Lemus (17 October 2003)

XII

The Great Blessing
1956–1959

The first few exhausting months of 1956 had fled by quickly. From the beginning of January until mid-April, Marcial had been in Mexico. He returned to Rome on April 14. Then a quick trip to Spain at the end of May and another to Mexico at the end of June. On July 9 he was back in Rome with news about the Cumbres school.

At the end of July he went to Ontaneda, Spain, with the juniors, philosophers and theologians for their summer break, interrupting this period only to go see the novices in Rome for a few days in August, and to check up on the construction of Our Lady of Guadalupe church.

The Legion's own vows

Since the brothers didn't have classes in Spain, Marcial took advantage to give a more in-depth explanation of various aspects of the Congregation's charism[1] through conferences, spiritual talks and long after-meal reflections, as well as conversing with smaller groups of brothers or attending individual religious in spiritual direction.

They spent a great deal of time speaking about the Legion's own vows. In a long, single-subject letter written in Ontaneda, Spain, on 15 September 1956, Marcial mentions the

---

[1] In Church terminology, *charism* means a special gift that God gives to someone for the good of the whole community (cf. 1 Cor 12:4–31, especially verse 7: *To each is given the manifestation of the Spirit for the common good*). When speaking of religious congregations or similar groups, *charism* is a term that refers to its distinctive spiritual and apostolic profile, the whole set of customs and ideals that identify it as a unique "family" within the Church.

vows, their significance and their importance, and offers a theological foundation.

Legionaries take the congregation's own vows along with the standard religious vows of poverty, chastity, and obedience. Father Maciel explains:

> Besides these three vows we have a vow of charity and a vow of humility. The vow of charity is meant to safeguard and respect to the maximum our brothers in the congregation—especially our superiors—in our words and attitudes. With this vow a religious commits himself not to criticize a superior's actions in front of someone who is not in a position to resolve a given problem or conflict. But he is invited, if he thinks it appropriate, to express his views about a superior's governance to those who can fix the problem. [2]

Father Maciel clarified that the vow does not encroach on freedom of expression, but rather gives it an effectual outlet:

> We only ask that the criticism not be made in the presence of those who are powerless to resolve possible conflicts. In this way we foster the spirit of charity and unity among our religious, which is the very backbone of our spirituality, and hence we call it the vow of charity. [3]

The second vow particular to the Legion is called the "vow of humility". Its aim is to help remind Legionaries that, like Christ, they should serve others, and not wait to be served by them. The vow consists in simply doing God's will, without falling prey to ambition.

> We avoid desiring and procuring for ourselves positions of responsibility; and we are joyful in whatever work obedience entrusts to us. We call it the vow of humility because this attitude of service takes constant mastery of our natural passion to be important, to stand out, and to

---

[2] Jesús Colina, *Christ is my Life . . .* , p. 98
[3] *ibid*, pp. 98–99

attain positions through intrigue and playing dirty, as is unfortunately common in other institutions in civil, social, professional or political life.[4]

A new ordeal

Their vacation in Spain came to an end, and in the evening of 30 September 1956, the bus with Father Maciel, the juniors, philosophers and theologians pulled into the driveway of Via Aurelia 677 in Rome. Father Rafael Arumí LC, the novice instructor and general procurator of the Congregation, was there to greet them, having stayed in Rome with the novices over the summer.

"Nuestro Padre, I need to have a word with you," said Father Arumí. "I have some bad news."

While the brothers were unloading the bus, Marcial accompanied Father Arumí to the adjacent property, where the church of Our Lady of Guadalupe was under construction.

"What's the matter, Father?"

"Nuestro Padre," replied a distressed Father Arumí, "you've been stripped of the faculty to exercise authority in the Legion. The rector of the apostolic school in Tlalpan has been named vicar general with faculties to govern. You're still the general superior, but without governing rights."

"But . . . Why?"

"I just don't know . . . "[5]

Marcial spent the night in prayer. As on previous occasions when misfortune had struck, he repeated simple heartfelt phrases: "Jesus, I believe in you; Jesus, I hope in you; Jesus, I trust in you; Jesus Christ: help me. Jesus Christ, give me strength."[6]

A few days later Monsignor Donati, a friend at the Congregation for Religious, informed him that a document containing a very serious accusation had arrived from Mexico,

---

[4] Jesús Colina, *Christ is my Life . . .* , p. 99

[5] cf. Marcial Maciel LC (January 1992)

[6] *ibid*

signed by several people. Besides reformulating some of the calumnies made in 1948, it accused him of being a drug addict.

Marcial went to speak with Cardinal Giuseppe Pizzardo, prefect of the Sacred Congregation for Seminaries and Universities, asking for advice. Pizzardo had proved a steadfast friend ever since Marcial first came to Rome in 1946.

The cardinal recommended that he bear this new trial with patience. Since one of the allegations was that Father Maciel was addicted to morphine and was or ought to be hospitalized, Cardinal Pizzardo suggested that Marcial do the rounds of the Vatican: visiting key people, dropping in on acquaintances and friends, and going to diverse Congregations of the Roman Curia (including the Congregation for Religious). They could judge for themselves if the man standing before their eyes was someone sunk in the vice of substance abuse and in need of treatment—or if it was the same Marcial they had always known, master of his faculties. Marcial took the cardinal's advice. He was healthy, and everyone saw it.

Cardinal Pizzardo also counseled Marcial to get a checkup ahead of time with two doctors he could recommend. The personal physician of Pius XII, Doctor Galleazzi Lisi, and cardiologist Luigi Condorelli both come to Via Aurelia at the beginning of October to examine the founder, and wrote up their reports.[7] Both categorically denied the existence of any trace of drugs. They found nothing that might indicate an addiction.

Around the same time, the Sacred Congregation for Religious named an apostolic visitator to the Legionary houses, Father Anastasio of the Holy Rosary Ballestrero.[8] He spoke with Father Maciel, conveying the order to sign himself into a hos-

---

[7] *Medical certificates:* Doctor Riccardo Galleazzi Lisi (no date), Doctor Luigi Condorelli (5 October 1956)

[8] Anastasio Alberto Ballestrero was ordained bishop (Bari, Italy) on 2 February 1974, named archbishop of Turin on 1 August 1977, and made a cardinal on 30 June 1979. He died on 21 June 1998. Father Anastasio was to be aided in his duties as visitator by Father Benjamin of the Child Jesus. However, the Suez Canal crisis erupted at this time, and they were dissuaded from traveling to Mexico to visit the Legionary houses there. The Prefect of the Congregation for Religious, Cardinal Valerio Valeri, named new visitators several months later, in July 1957.

pital for detoxification. Furthermore, he explained to Marcial that he was not to communicate with his Legionaries without authorization from his superiors in the Congregation for Religious, and once released from the clinic, he was to continue working to sustain the congregation, since, even though he had been divested of his right to govern, the responsibility for the congregation's upkeep fell to him.

Late in the afternoon of 3 October 1956, Marcial said a few words of farewell to the community before his imminent departure. He explained, in a voice choked by tears, how all religious congregations undergo moments of trial and painful purification in the course of their histories, and that God abundantly blesses them afterwards. This hour had now arrived for the Legion. He would have to leave them for now.

Marcial had always taught them that obedience should not be "blind", but fully conscious, freely willed, and rooted in faith and love, just like Christ obeying God the Father. *Father, if it is possible, let this cup pass from me; yet not my will, but your will, be done!* (*Mt* 26:39). Now it was up to him to show them an example of what it meant to obey, embracing the redemptive cross at Christ's side. He said:

> I want you to never forget that you have a father who will also be joyfully giving his life for you, wherever they send him, wherever obedience places him . . . May the Lord keep us united in spirit, and may you do honorably by your Legion.
>
> Remember what constitutes the heart of the Legion. Do not allow my departure to destroy your spirit of faith and charity.[9]

He was admitted to the Villa Linda Clinic in Rome on October 5. Five days later, the clinic doctors issued their own medical certificate saying that there was no reason for him to be there.[10] Marcial, however, could not leave the clinic without

---

[9] Marcial Maciel LC, *Farewell words to the community of Rome* (3 October 1956). Transcription.
[10] Enrico Gambini, *Medical Certificate* (Rome, 10 October 1956)

his superiors' authorization, and he stayed there for 20 days. Cardinals visited him each week, accompanying him as a sign of their friendship and offering him a word of encouragement. Several Legionaries got permission from his Vatican-appointed superiors to call him by phone or pay him a visit. Marcial was grief-striken. He had weighed 85 kg (187 lbs) when he walked into Villa Linda. When he was dismissed a few weeks later, he weighed 58 kg (128 lbs).

Reasons

But who? And why? To set the record straight against erroneous versions that might circulate, an overview of the problem follows. Out of Christian charity, we have striven to withhold names of those who are still alive or who have only recently passed away.

Bishop Alfonso Espino y Silva was no longer in Cuernavaca: he had been transferred to the archdiocese of Monterrey in 1951. Bishop Sergio Méndez Arceo was appointed to lead the diocese of Cuernavaca in 1952. The criticism of some long-time opponents of the congregation succeeded in sowing bad seed among a small number of religious. One, a Spaniard who had entered the Legion as a theology student, driven by ambition to exercise authority within the congregation, spearheaded a campaign of denigration against the founder. He got the priest assigned to help Marcial by the Archdiocese of Morelia entangled in his schemes, so that his signature also appeared on the 1956 document signed by the bishop of Cuernavaca, an abbot named Lemercier,[11] and some additional ecclesiastic or other. The document was sent to Rome, and contained the accusations that will be mentioned shortly. The Legion's detractors and the signatories of the letter worked insistently to sway an official at the Sacred Congregation for Religious. Influenced by their efforts, he ended up complicat-

---

[11] During the 1950s Dom Gregorio Lemercier was abbot of the experimental monastery "Santa María de la Resurrección" in Cuernavaca, Mexico.

ing and delaying the solution to a problem that was clearly recognized as a grave injustice against Marcial.

Father Maciel never received formal written notification regarding the document's contents from the Congregation for Religious.[12] Everything was done by word of mouth. All Marcial knew was what Father Rafael Arumí (general procurator) and Father Antonio Lagoa (rector of the Legion's college in Rome) told him. Their information was ratified, both then and in later years, by what friends and members of the Roman Curia, particularly Cardinal Pizzardo, Cardinal Cicognani and Monsignor Giuseppe di Meglio,[13] told them or other Legionaries.

The document accused Marcial of insufficient ecclesiastical formation. It alleged he governed and formed his young religious like a despot. It accused him of being incompetent to run the finances of the congregation (this seems to have been based on his having "stolen" a sizable sum of money from Flora Barragán, benefactor of the Cumbres school and life-long friend of the Legion, to use it for a charitable work of apostolate). It also accused Marcial of insubordination to legitimate superiors—even though his legitimate superior, Cardinal Clemente Micara, vicar for Rome, esteemed the young congregation and its founder.[14]

Drug addiction, however, was the most serious allegation, and triggered his being sent to a clinic. For those who had seen the founder's style and pace of life for themselves—constantly dedicated to work and to the seminarians, and carried out with profound austerity and integrity—the accusation struck them

---

[12] The Legionaries of Christ were never shown the document, and still do not have a copy for their Archive.

[13] They were not the only ones.

[14] Cardinal Clemente Micara manifested this publicly by presiding at the inauguration ceremony of Our Lady of Guadalupe parish in Rome on 12 December 1958, and by signing the document—as direct superior of the congregation, when the Sacred Congregation for Religious delegated the solution of the problem to him—which fully restored to the founder his governing functions. He confirmed Father Maciel's status as general superior of the Legionaries of Christ on 6 February 1959.

as an evident calumny. A drug addict could never maintain his rhythm. The letters of priests, bishops and benefactors, in the years both before and afterwards, attested to his moral stature and would leave no room for doubt.

First-hand appraisals

The following paragraphs have been excerpted from a long letter that Luis Barroso and Santiago Galas sent to Cardinal Giuseppe Pizzardo on 14 July 1957:

> By accident, but through a trustworthy channel, the sad, lamentable news has reached us that Father Maciel has been divested of and suspended from exercising his faculties as Superior.
>
> For us, who know this priest from his youth and since he began his endeavor—helping him with considerable sums of money to bring it about—we consider it a duty of conscience to come before your Eminence to explain our opinion regarding this woeful situation.
>
> Our contact with Father Maciel and his project has been constant and close in every sense: religious, intellectual and social. His unblemished conduct and immense capacity for work caused an admirable impression. Your Eminence, this is why we associated ourselves with him from the very start, and were so eager to help such a good priest, offering him as much moral and economic help as possible, so that he could set up the Legionaries of Christ . . .
>
> Seeing that our effort has borne marvelous fruit in the hands of Father Maciel brings us satisfaction. Your Eminence, in 15 years he has created one of the most distinguished educational institutes in the Mexican Republic, with a capacity for 2,000 students; he is constructing the national Church [for Mexico] in Rome because the Holy Father asked him to do so; he has set up four large seminaries in Mexico and Europe, and has approximately 400 young men who have decided to consecrate their lives to the service of the Church. With the excellent for-

mation he imparts, they constitute an authentic guarantee for the defense of our Religion.

But, your Eminence, what do we see? In the moment when our hopes increase, when excellent fruits begin to appear, cultivated by this worthy, holy priest's complete self-giving, new difficulties arise that threaten to destroy or obstruct his undertaking.

We cherish the hope, however, that now as on other occasions, the . . . justice characterizing the Holy See will shine forth again, and that after investigating the motives that produced this deplorable situation—surely wrought by evil tongues—the Reverend Father Maciel will be reinstated in his functions as Superior, posthaste.

To put it simply, you Eminence, we have formed such a high opinion of this priest that we deem it to be a certain case of defamation eager to do its nefarious work. This is our conclusion. Here is a priest judged to be outstanding by society and principally by those of us who have dealt with him closely and have been able to appreciate his exceptional virtues: how could he have so long concealed an evil that merits such a severe punishment, namely, that of removing him from the administration of a project that he has set up at the cost of such great sacrifices?

Before closing, we can assure Your Eminence that this letter could easily have been signed by all the people in this country who have helped with his project; but we considered it more prudent not to give publicity to this situation.[15]

Many other lay people and ecclesiastical figures who knew the Legion and the founder from first-hand experience wrote similar letters to the Holy Office and the Sacred Congregation for Religious. Monsignor Polidoro van Vlierberghe,

---

[15] Santiago Galas Arce and Luis Barroso, *Letter to Giuseppe Cardinal Pizzardo* (Mexico City, 14 July 1957)

who had been asked to report on the situation, wrote to Luigi Raimondi, apostolic delegate to Mexico, in 1958, to share his impressions of the Legionaries of Christ:

> The formation that Reverend Father Maciel instills in his members, as I was able to verify, adjusts itself to the instructions published in pontifical documents. These religious profoundly edify all those who have dealt with and lived with them, myself included. Composed, modest, self-sacrificing, joyful, very well-mannered; selfless in their practice of exquisite, impartial, Christian charity; with a fervent Eucharistic life and supernatural spirit; who love the venerable person of the Pope and overflow with zeal for the salvation of souls and for the critical interests of the Church. They constitute a very special group even in the intellectual field, as can be deduced from the splendid results habitually crowning their studies in the Gregorian University. It [their formation] is producing magnificent fruits."[16]

The Legionaries hadn't changed.

"There reigns among them great unity and fraternal charity," Father Oñate had written years earlier in his report on the apostolic school of Tlalpan, advising Bishop Francisco González Arias to go ahead and petition a nihil obstat for the nascent congregation.

Several Mexican bishops who would stay with the Legionary community on Via Aurelia 677 for months during Vatican II would testify to their unity and charity.[17] Bishop Ernesto Corripio Ahumada, then bishop of Tampico, wrote:

> Thank you for your expressions of attention, your Christian manners, and the examples of virtue I've received in this house. I ask Jesus to inflame with his love, more

---

[16] Polidoro van Vlierberghe OFM, *Letter to the apostolic delegate in Mexico, Luigi Raimondi* (1958)

[17] During the diverse sessions of the Council, the Legionaries of Christ offered lodging to approximately half of the Mexican bishops of the time.

and more each day: the most Reverend Father Founder, his priests the "Legionaries", and all the young men who are preparing themselves to increase the number of those who constitute this institute, from which God and the Church hope so much.[18]

Bishop Samuel Ruiz, then bishop of Chiapas, added:

We would never have imagined that within the significant framework of an Ecumenical Council we would be able to savor once again . . . this delicacy: the Legionaries of Christ's customary charity and well-mannered demeanor. Now we realize your name (which speaks of battles and privations) implies a promising hope of renewal in our country and everywhere your presence has begun to be felt. This organized battalion is a lively force through which the saving influence of the . . . Council will reach the world. God protect you and temper you for your battles for Christ!"[19]

Cardinal John Joseph Wright, Prefect of the Congregation for the Clergy, capsulized his impression of the Legionary community in Rome with the following idea, paraphrasing a classic Italian song: "Legionary: you are an empire of harmony."[20]

Ever since January 1941, many people who get to know Legionaries of Christ are surprised at their formation, and express admiration for the happy serenity on display in their words, behavior and bearing. In September 2002, Bishop Victor-Hugo Palma, coadjutor bishop of Escuintla and General Secretary of the Episcopal Conference of Guatemala, stayed at the Legionary's college in Rome for several weeks, one of the

---

[18] Ernesto Corripio Ahumada, bishop of Tampico, *Handwritten note* (Rome, 9 December 1962)

[19] Samuel Ruiz, bishop of Chiapas, *Handwritten note* (Rome, 8 December 1962)

[20] John Joseph Cardinal Wright, Prefect of the Congregation for the Clergy, *Handwritten note* (6 February 1970). After an evening spent with the Legionary family, the cardinal wrote: *Tu sei l'impero dell'armonia. Legionario di Cristo! Legionario di Cristo! Grazie per una serata indimenticabile!* [You are the empire of harmony. Legionary of Christ! Legionary of Christ! Thank you for an unforgettable evening].

many prelates taking part in a course for new bishops organized by the Congregation for Bishops.[21] In a letter to Father Álvaro Corcuera LC, the college's rector, he wrote, "I've come across the testimony of lives consecrated with dedication and love, but also with profound joy at the service of the Church."[22] Spiritual joy cannot flourish apart from inner freedom, deep personal conviction, and a sincere effort to form sound habits.

"Too lax"

Another accusation of 1956 would be almost laughable if the context had not been so dramatic. It alleged that Father Maciel lived and taught his seminarians to live a concept of discipline that was "too lax" and "too American."[23] To refute the allegation in the simplest of ways, it would have been enough to read a copy of the Legionaries' detailed daily schedule, or watch them doing manual work, or see the implications of their poverty. They have no possessions to call their own, and each room (then and now) has only what is strictly necessary: a bed, a desk, chair and lamp, a kneeler, a closet for suit and cassock, and a crucifix on the wall: nothing else.

The criticism concerning the "relaxed discipline" of the Legion and the founder was based on certain undeniable facts. Whenever Legionaries left their house, they wore a black suit and clergyman collar instead of the traditional cassock. They went swimming in bathing suits,[24] something considered scandalous. Vatican II's guidelines regarding the renewal of priestly life merely confirmed the life-style already practiced within the Legion, a way of living the priesthood considered

---

[21] Since 2001, the annual course for new bishops has been held at the Legion of Christ's Center for Higher Studies, Rome.

[22] Víctor Hugo Palma, coadjutor bishop of Escuintla, Guatemala, and General Secretary of the Guatemalan Bishop's Conference, Letter to Father Álvaro Corcuera LC (25 September 2002)

[23] Pardon the expression. At the time, certain ecclesial circles, especially in Europe, used the term to designate an extremely easy, comfortable way of life.

[24] With pick and shovel, the Legionaries had dug a swimming pool at their house on Via Aurelia in 1952.

"normal" by the Church today. The accusations against them did not spring from any Church teaching of the time, but rather from a mentality that was accustomed to certain ways of doing things, and tended to overemphasize externals: it was more of a cultural question than a religious one. Today the pendulum has swung to the opposite extreme, and priests once labeled "too lax" are now criticized for being "too conservative." And the Legionaries simply continue following their path, as they did then, at the Church's pace.

Banished

At the end of October 1956, once he had been released from the clinic, Marcial received new instructions. He had to leave Rome until further notice. Spain was his land of exile. He settled down in Madrid.

Ever since the Missionaries of the Sacred Heart's spell in Comillas, Father Maciel had been able to count on strong friendships at the nunciature. The papal nuncio, Gaetano Cicognani, had been a friend to Marcial from the time Bishop Espino y Silva sent him proofs of the founder's innocence in answer to the accusations of 1948. Cicognani had since been named cardinal, and transferred to Rome. The new nuncio in Madrid, Bishop Ildebrando Antoniutti, also held the founder and his congregation in deep esteem.

"Bishop Antoniutti was very fatherly, very good, very charitable towards me," Father Maciel explains,

> because, without saying anything, in the period when he saw me in such a sorry, broken state, he'd drop in to see me, or invite me to visit him once, twice or three times a week . . . . To take my thoughts off my problems, he'd ask me to accompany him on his evening walks. He'd invite me to have lunch with him at the nunciature from time to time. All of these were signs of an extraordinary charity.[25]

---

[25] Marcial Maciel LC (January 1992)

Marcial has always had many friends among the clergy, the Legion's benefactors, and Legionaries. Nevertheless, he has always reserved a particularly grateful memory for Monsignor Diego Bugallo, from Galicia, Spain. "Don" Bugallo was a big, intelligent, trustworthy man. He was auditor and advisor to the Spanish nunciature, and along with Cardinal Ildebrando Antoniutti, he offered Father Maciel his unconditional friendship. "When it wasn't the nuncio," Father Maciel says, "it was Don Diego—it seems that they had the watchword not to leave me alone for too long."[26]

Like Cardinal Ildebrando, Monsignor Diego made sure Marcial took care of himself:

> Don Diego had me over at his home for lunch, and I would spend the afternoon there. He'd invite me to go and walk. I'd have a quick something for dinner at his house, and then I'd return to the hotel. Don Diego was aware of what was going on; he didn't ask me any questions, he just told me to trust a lot, and not to worry.[27]
>
> Don Diego would take it upon himself to see that I ate . . . There I began to find my feet again, as best as I could, and I recovered as fully as the circumstances permitted.[28]

Monsignor Bugallo was not a fair-weather friend: he was not afraid to give his word or to stand up for Marcial in his hardships. He was willing to risk his career and his reputation by maintaining and cultivating a friendship with someone then considered by many as a person best to be avoided: blighted, a priest of disrepute, perhaps an apostate, and certainly a failure. If in Madrid Marcial "found his feet" again, it was largely due to friends like these.

There was something gnawing at Macial's mind during his first weeks in Madrid, a set of considerations that he just couldn't shake: "Not being able to reconcile what was going on

---

[26] *ibid*
[27] Marcial Maciel LC (1 October 2002)
[28] Marcial Maciel LC (January 1992)

with human logic, or with simple human justice and Catholic morality."[29]

Of this period, Father Maciel would say:

> I'd struggle to find an answer, and kept turning things over and over in my head: "Why has this happened? Why? There's no reason for it." I couldn't find a reason why people would act like that. It was incoherence. It was not moral. It was a type of nightmare I had there . . .
>
> "Christianity" without love? It's a farce. It's a stage prop. It may be nice-looking or whatever else you want to say about it . . . as a human institution, but without love, well, does it mean anything at all?[30]

Those were the thoughts going through his head at the time: the importance of love, the fact of our Redemption. "I did not start to mistrust the Church or my Faith," he says. He did not begin to mistrust anything "except man."[31]

This inner unrest persisted until December. As he was praying in a church on Silva road,[32] he had an experience similar to the one he had had in Cóbreces on the feast of Christ the King in 1948.[33] He received

> a simple light from God: "don't struggle to understand everything with human reasoning alone. Climb onto the roof, and try to understand it 'from the shingles on up,' looking up to heaven . . .Stop worrying about it: it's just . . . man, with his freedom. And that's not the essence of the Church. Our Faith hasn't changed. Christ's doctrine hasn't changed. So keep pressing forward."[34]

---

[29] Marcial Maciel LC (January 1992) and Marcial Maciel LC (1 October 2002)
[30] Marcial Maciel LC (January 1992)
[31] *ibid*
[32] A church belonging to a Spanish religious order founded in 1218 by St Pedro Nolasco called the *mercedarios* (Order of Our Lady of Mercy).
[33] He is referring to the impulse of the Holy Spirit that gave him the idea of going to Rome to speak with Cardinal Luigi Lavitrano, and brought him inner light and peace.
[34] Marcial Maciel LC (January 1992) and *idem* (1 October 2002)

People devoid of love: that was the problem. People who use their freedom wrongly. The problem was not Christ, nor the Church. The problem was with some who called themselves Catholic, but who had never understood or put into practice the essence of Christ's message. On the other hand, how many hundreds and thousands of the Church's children transform their corner of the world into a foretaste of heaven each day! One thinks, for example, of Mother Theresa of Calcutta's Sisters of Mercy. They transform their world by the power of love.

The commandment of love is at the center of the Gospel. "If as priests, religious, or plain Christians we do not live this commandment, we are outside the gospel, we are 'playacting' Christianity," replied Father Maciel when asked to define the essence of the Legion of Christ's charism. He added:

> I don't understand Christianity any other way except as the sincere, authentic love for our brothers and sisters in imitation of Christ. Everything else—piety, devotions, ceremonies, rites, processions, and so forth—are forms of prayer, and if you do them with a sincere heart, they please God; but without charity they are meaningless because the spirit of charity is the backbone of the gospel message.[35]

Of all the inner griefs the calumnies occasioned him, one was especially painful for Father Maciel: the sad letdown of seeing that some of the Legionaries he had formed from their early teenage years, even from the time of foundation itself, had let themselves become entangled in the proceedings of 1956–59, and later on, in others that were similar or even worse.

"These disappointments are extremely powerful, extremely hard, extremely painful," Father Maciel once explained, "I believe they can only be compared . . . to the pain, the hurt that fathers or mothers feel when they lose one of their children, when death snatches a child away . . . "[36]

---

[35] Jesús Colina, *Christ is my Life . . .* , p. 67
[36] Marcial Maciel LC (Fall 2001)

Everyone knows many of the founders of religious orders: Francis of Assisi, Theresa of Avila, Ignatius of Loyola, John Baptist de la Salle, Alphonsus Liguori, Anthony Maria Claret, Jeanne Jugan, Don Bosco . . . and the list could go on. They share a common denominator: they were purified in the furnace of defamation, they were persecuted, and they were misunderstood. In their lives, in the wake of such pain, love came out victorious. *Unless a grain of wheat falls in the earth and die . . .* (*Jn* 12:24). Their incorporeal blood was shed, and it produced abundant fruit for the Church: Franciscans, Discalced Carmelites, Jesuits, Brothers of the Christian Schools, Redemptorists, Missionary Sons of the Immaculate Heart of Mary, Little Sisters of the Poor, Salesians . . . . The fruitfulness of another seed is already visible in the contemplation of the Legion of Christ and Regnum Christi:

> The small seed which the divine sower planted in the soil of a few young hearts is now a flourishing tree (cf. Mt 13: 32), [with] many priests, consecrated persons and lay people whose ideal is to devote their lives to spreading Christ's kingdom in the world.[37]

As an expression of his gratitude towards God, Marcial would later name this period of trial "The Great Blessing." He was also able to discover the trace of charity and love that suffering left in its wake.

> I think that just as the sun helps trees to grow, making them fragrant and fruitful . . . suffering helps people mature, makes them stronger. Spiritually speaking: because their spirit is nourished. And humanly speaking: it makes them much humbler, gentler, and kindhearted. They understand others, and understand how to help others.[38]

---

[37] John Paul II, *Words to the Legionaries of Christ and members of Regnum Christi . . .* (Vatican, 4 January 2001). Transcription.
[38] Marcial Maciel LC (Fall 2001)

Marcial was speaking from experience. On more than one occasion he has mentioned that, during those unending weeks in Madrid, his joy and relaxation consisted in rising early and accompanying the laborers on the bus on their way to work. He would listen to them and speak with them about their concerns. He would visit the poorer districts. Walking down the streets and speaking with so many people in Vallecas (a neighborhood of Madrid), it seemed he was back in the Rinconada district among "his" poor in Cotija. Here too, he had next to nothing to give them, but he offered them a kind word and helped them as much as he could. Remembering his experiences in Vallecas, Marcial exclaimed that it was a shame that human beings are so limited and can do so little. "If only God would let us multiply ourselves! . . . there are so many good things to be done . . . Even with all the limitations, you do what you can . . . "[39]

Father Maciel often laments not having been able to do more. It will be up to future generations to judge whether Marcial has been able to multiply himself and do good—an extraordinary amount of good—to tens of thousands of people, especially among the poor and those most in need.

At the beginning of 1957, during his exile in Madrid, Marcial wrote a collection of existential verses addressed to God that have been published in Spanish as the *Salterio de mis días* ("A Psalter of my Days"). They are pages of poetry and prayer, offering a glimpse into Marcial's mind and heart:

I forgive them all, Lord:
all of them, and everything . . .
I received freely, and freely do I want to give.
And since I want to give freely,
I wish to give not only to those who give,
but also to those who take things away from me.
And I want to love, and I love my enemies.
And I want to do good, Lord,
to those who detest me.
And I bless those, Lord, who curse me.

[39] Marcial Maciel LC (6 September 2002)

And, Lord, not a day has passed
when I ceased to pray
for those who slander me and persecute me.
Because you did not create the world only for those
who would love you,
but also for those who would crucify you. . . .

They brought me to the gates of death
because I did not know how to hate.
And from the gates of death I return,
And still I have not learned to hate.[40]

If goodness and kindness take the shape of pardon when tribulation strikes, they are not just nice words or empty masquerading.

Looking for solutions

Cardinal Gaetano Cicognani, ex-nuncio in Madrid, was now a member of the Sacred Congregation for Religious. He repeatedly asked for status reports on the Legion of Christ's situation and the plight of Father Maciel, but received no straight answers.

The apostolic visitator, Father Anastasio of the Holy Rosary Ballestrero, thought that the whole situation would be resolved by Christmas 1956, and had in fact told the cardinals as much. But 1957 arrived, and the state of affairs remained unchanged.

Given the impasse, the cardinals who wanted to help Father Maciel and his congregation used their influence to have a trusted priest nominated to the post of sub-secretary in the Congregation for Religious: Pietro Palazzini.[41] Cardinal Cicognani demanded to be given constant updates. He wanted

---

[40] Marcial Maciel LC, *Salterio de mis días*, Ediciones CES, Roma, VII
[41] Pietro Palazzini, a moral theologian, was born in 1912 in Piobbico, Italy. He was ordained in 1934, named sub-secretary of the Congregation for Religious at the beginning of 1957, and promoted to Secretary in 1958. He became archbishop of Caesarea in Cappadocia in 1962, and made cardinal in 1973. He later served as Prefect of the Congregation for the Causes of Saints (1980–1988).

to put an end to the evasive answers and half-truths, and as a member of the Congregation for Religious, he had every right to receive complete information. "I was in Rome at the time, and I remember that word spread that it had been Cardinal Cicognani who had moved things to promote a new sub-secretary at the Congregation for Religious,"[42] says Father Javier Tena LC, who for many years served at the Roman parish of Our Lady of Guadalupe.

> I heard that the cardinal was somewhat upset at not having been clearly informed about issues under his competence. Years later I learned from other sources—it may have been through Monsignor José [Giuseppe] di Meglio—that it had to do with the issue of our congregation."[43]

Marcial's orders were to continue taking care of the congregation's finances and administration. He was deprived of the possibility to guide the congregation he founded. He was separated him from his spiritual sons. He found his honor in tatters. But they had him beg.

By 1957 the congregation numbered some 70 professed religious, not counting novices and minor seminarians. They all needed to be clothed and fed: no easy task, considering Father Maciel's physical and emotional state. The assignment was further complicated by his banishment to Spain, and the fact that there were serious question marks after his name and doubts regarding the future of the congregation itself. Given these circumstances, the attitude of unconditional support displayed by the Legion of Christ's benefactors during this period was all the more admirable.[44]

---

[42] Javier Tena LC, *Written testimony* (Rome, 3 January 2004)
[43] *ibid*
[44] Even if it is not possible to include a full list of benefactors, special mention must be made of Mr. and Mrs. Luis Barroso (Mexico City), Mr. and Mrs. Santiago Galas (Mexico City), and benefactors from Monterrey: Mr. and Mrs. Salvador Sada-Gómez, Mr. and Mrs. Jorge Sada-Gómez, Mr. and Mrs. Ignacio Santos, and Mrs. Flora Barragán de Garza.

Giovanni Battista Montini, by then archbishop of Milan, continued to support Marcial and encouraged him not to lose hope. His friends in Rome, the cardinals Giuseppe Pizzardo, Clemente Micara, Giovanni Piazza, Federico Tedeschini, and especially Gaetano Cicognani, tried to accelerate the resolution of the congregation's problems. Cardinal Pizzardo filled him in on the latest news every two weeks or so. Unfortunately, they were able to do next to nothing. The Holy Father Pius XII had fallen gravely ill, and the cardinals were unable to ask him to intervene. If the Pope had known what was happening, things may have turned out differently: but no news ever reached him.

Through Monsignor Palazzini, the new sub-secretary for Religious, the cardinals learned that the situation was actually getting worse. The official at the Congregation for Religious who had accepted the accusations sent from Mexico at face value was doing his best to have Father Maciel's congregation dissolved. Cardinal Gaetano Cicognani, who by that time had gathered sufficient proofs to expose the injustice of the allegations, intervened in the summer of 1957. He approached the Prefect of the Congregation for Religious, Cardinal Valerio Valeri, who stepped in to prevent the congregation's dissolution, ensuring that truth prevailed.

Gaetano Cicognani also requested that new apostolic visitators be named for the congregation. At the beginning of July, Cardinal Valeri appointed two men known for their prudence to the post. They were untainted by prejudice and did their best to discover how things really stood. Monsignor Alfredo Bontempi, rector of the Roman Nepomucene College, was asked to investigate the Legionaries of Christ in the Eternal City, and Monsignor Polidoro van Vlierberghe,[45] a Belgian Franciscan, was appointed to carry out the apostolic visitation of their houses in Mexico and Spain.[46]

---

[45] Bishop Polidoro van Vlierberghe is now emeritus bishop of Illapel, Chile.

[46] Valerio Cardinal Valeri, Prefect of the Sacred Congregation of Religious, *Letter naming visitator Alfredo Bontempi* (Vatican, 10 July 1957); cf. Luigi Raimondi, apostolic delegate in Mexico, Letter to Polidoro Van Vlierberghe (Mexico City, 17 September 1957). In this letter, Raimondi mentions that the Sacred Congregation for Religious had appointed van Vlierberghe at the same time, on 10 July 1957.

Bontempi and van Vlierberghe personally interviewed the Legionary religious under oath: priests and seminarians, all of them of majority age. The aim of these interviews was to obtain an objective account of the founder's personality, life and behavior, and to have the information needed to evaluate the life and development of the congregation. The questions were open-ended, formulated in such a way as to encourage the religious to express themselves with absolute freedom on anything that they might perceive to be wrong with the congregation or, above all, with the founder's conduct, whether or not it had anything to do with the accusations against Father Maciel, accusations of which most of the religious knew nothing. During the interviews, the Legionary priests and seminarians spoke about what they saw, what they thought, what they felt, and how they lived.

Bontempi and van Vlierberghe were unanimous in their conclusion: *a grave injustice is being committed.* Not only did they send favorable reports to the Holy See; while doing all they could to speed up a solution to the harsh trial being borne by the congregation and its founder, they also tried to lighten their burden, giving Marcial and the religious authorization to communicate, and offering them all words of encouragement and moral support. Both of the apostolic visitators would maintain a sincere friendship with Father Maciel and the Legionaries of Christ for the rest of their lives.

Many bishops, priests, and benefactors from Mexico and Spain continued to write letters defending and expressing support for Father Maciel and the Legion.

During these years, the Legionaries of Christ had remained faithful, firmly united among themselves and firmly united to the founder in spirit. The few who had created rifts slowly abandoned the congregation of their own accord. Others, a small number of religious who had not totally communed with the Legion, would do the same some years later. Still others, good and faithful sons, suffered the effects of this mighty blow—the forging of the congregation, those years when the future remained uncertain—and would also leave.

Those who remained, the majority, were willing to accompany their founder to the very end. If the congregation were dissolved, they were ready to begin with him all over again.

Marcial continued to provide for the apostolics and religious in Tlalpan, Ontaneda and Rome. In 1956 he re-commenced work on the future Legionary novitiate in Salamanca, Spain. He also dedicated himself to fund-raise for the construction of Our Lady of Guadalupe in Rome. The greater part of the Mexican bishops let him take up a special collection for this project among the faithful of their respective dioceses. Father Jorge Ruiz, a priest from the diocese of Queretaro, offered to help preach in several dioceses for this purpose. Mexicans are incapable of denying anything to Our Lady of Guadalupe, their "beloved Virgin of Tepeyac", and with a great deal of sacrifice they succeeded in covering the costs of her new basilica in Rome. Those who could give more gave more: some pledged a monthly contribution until construction was finished. Those who could give less perhaps gave only once, perhaps only a small amount, but they gave their donation with an abundance of affection, digging deep into their almost-empty pockets. Poor fingers reached out to offer the Virgin of Guadalupe a token of their love.

It was 1958, and two years had passed since Marcial had been banished from Rome. Although the reports of the apostolic visitators were positive, within the Congregation for Religious the same official continued to place obstacles in the way of a solution. His influence on the Prefect was considerable, and Cardinal Valerio Valeri did not quite manage to bring Father Maciel's banishment to an end. Cardinal Gaetano Cicognani knew the Legion well since 1948, and had been keeping in touch with the procurator of the Legion, Father Rafael Arumí, throughout this whole period of hardship. At the end of the summer of 1958, he decided to go to the cardinal Prefect for Religious for a second time. During the conversation he noted that, with the situation at its current state, it was evident that a grave transgression was being perpetrated against Father Maciel and his community. He said that he would be willing to ask for the convocation of a Plenary Session of cardinals with the sole aim of analyzing Father Maciel's case, and so put an end to the problem once and for all.

"For the sake of charity, please don't do it,"[47] said Valeri.

"No, I won't do it for the sake of charity," replied Cicognani. "If I do, it will be for the sake of justice."[48]

Cardinal Valeri promised to resolve the problem himself.

Exile's fruits

The minor Roman basilica of "Our Lady of Guadalupe and Saint Philip, Martyr" at Via Aurelia 675 was dedicated on 12 December 1958. It was a solemn, joyful ceremony. Cardinal Clemente Micara, Vicar for Rome, was the main celebrant, and he was joined by Cardinals Gaetano Cicognani, Giuseppe Pizzardo, Federico Tedeschini, and the archbishop of Guadalajara, José Garibi y Rivera, who three days later would be made Mexico's first cardinal.

The generosity and sacrifice of many Mexican people had made the new church possible, and Marcial now knew that another of his dreams, that of opening a church dedicated to Mary, had been fulfilled. He knew—but he wasn't there to see it for himself. The ban preventing him from entering Rome still stood (even though the new visitators had, at least, granted him complete freedom of movement to other cities and countries, and allowed him to communicate with his Legionaries). He spent December 1958 in Salamanca, Spain, attending to all the last-minute details for the novices who would soon come to live in the new novitiate. Bishop Ildebrando Antoniutti had inaugurated the building in September 1958, another fruit of Marcial's sacrifice and hard work throughout those years of tribulation. If he had built a new church in Rome and a new novitiate in Spain, it had not been for his own sake. It wasn't

---

[47] In Italian, *per carità* ("for charity's sake", "out of charity") is simply an elegant way of saying: "please." However, in order to faithfully capture the interplay between Cardinal Valeri's plea and Cardinal Cicognani's response, it has been rendered with the unusual (but more literal) translation: "for the sake of charity."

[48] cf. Rafael Arumí Blancafort LC (1 January 1998)

simply for the good of his congregation. It was for the good of the Church. In the face of persecutions, calumnies and exile, it was his faith, hope, and a constantly renewed love for Christ and the Church that allowed Father Maciel to press onwards.

Cardinal Federico Tedeschini had asked him: "Why do you continue building this novitiate, if you might very well end up being expelled from the congregation, or if it might be disbanded?"

"I figured," says Father Maciel, "that if our situation failed to right itself, at least the building would be there for the Church to use. That's why I kept going forward with the project."[49]

Today the Legion of Christ has houses in 19 countries, where Legionaries from 34 nationalities live and carry out their diverse pastoral ministries. Ordained priests number almost 600. The congregation runs nine novitiates in as many countries, and the Novitiate and Juniorate in Salamanca forms more than 200 novices and juniors each year. They are priestly vocations, vocations for the Church. Once again, a seed crushed by suffering and cast into the furrow has borne an abundant harvest, through love.

---

[49] Jesús Colina, *Christ is my Life . . .* , p. 58

XIII

At the Church's Pace 1959–1979

Easter 1959

Cardinal Valerio Valeri, prefect of the Congregation for Religious, was completely satisfied with the reports that the apostolic visitators filed concerning the Legionaries of Christ and their founder. Father Maciel's congregation depended on the diocese of Rome since 1952, and so in the closing months of 1958 Cardinal Valeri delegated the final resolution of the case to Cardinal Clemente Micara, Vicar of Rome.[1] It is Cardinal Micara's signature, therefore, that appears on the decree of 6 February 1959 reinstating Marcial Maciel as superior general of the Legionaries of Christ.[2]

Several days later, Monsignor Giuseppe di Meglio[3] decided to share the good news with several of the Legion of Christ's Mexican friends and benefactors whom he knew. He explained what the conclusion of this painful trial meant, and described the effect it had had in Rome. In a letter to Salvador Sada Gómez written on stationary of the Holy Office and dated 22 February 1959, he explained:

---

[1] On 17 October 1952 Cardinal Clemente Micara, Vicar of Rome, granted approval for the Legion of Christ to move its general directorate to Rome. The Congregation for Religious granted the corresponding permission on December 23 of the same year (No. 5458–52).

[2] Clemente Cardinal Micara, Vicar of Rome, *Decree* (6 February 1959)

[3] In February 1959, Monsignor Giuseppe di Meglio worked in the revision of publications at the Sacred Congregation of the Holy Office. He was personal secretary to Cardinal Giuseppe Pizzardo, Prefect of the Sacred Congregation of Seminaries and Universities, and Secretary of the Sacred Congregation of the Holy Office until 12 October 1959.

You are well aware of the distressing problem that afflicted our esteemed Father [Maciel] and his admirable endeavor for some time now. I now hurry to inform you that the problem has been satisfactorily resolved once and for all by the Holy See. His Eminence Cardinal Micara, general vicar of His Holiness, issued a decree by which the Holy See confirms Father Maciel as general superior of the institute of the Legionaries of Christ.

By this action, the Holy See publicly and officially recognizes the absolute, complete innocence of this esteemed priest in relation to the campaign of accusations leveled against him over the past two years. His Eminence considered it opportune to meet with the Legionaries of Christ, underlining the juridical importance of the Holy See's Decree and its deepest meaning.

The official and definitive declaration of Father Maciel's innocence was received with utmost satisfaction by the cardinals of the Roman Curia who have manifested constant, unconditional esteem and support since the beginnings of the institute, and especially during this more intense period of beleaguerment . . . The Legionaries of Christ's integrity and spirit of humility were a primary factor in the triumph of truth and justice. They have come through this harsh ordeal with even higher prestige in the Roman Curia and in the most relevant university centers of the Eternal City. Nevertheless, the road Father Maciel must travel is still arduous and difficult. Defamation and calumny have done their work, creating in some a hostile attitude that is totally unjustified, but which our esteemed Father Maciel will have to continue bearing with the same great valor and sacrifice that he has displayed until now.[4]

After the cold Roman winter, spring arrived with a smile, and for the Legionaries of Christ on Via Aurelia, the joy of Easter

---

[4] Msgr. Giuseppe Di Meglio, *Letter to Mr. Salvador Sada Gómez* (Vatican, 22 February 1959)

came early. Marcial returned to Rome on Holy Saturday, 28 March 1959. On Easter Monday Marcial led the community on a pilgrimage to the altar of the Gregorian Virgin in St. Peter's for a Mass of thanksgiving. He had spent two-and-a-half lengthy years far from the Holy Father, far from his Legionary family, and far from this image of Mary. She had offered him solace and support during this entire period, and it was a way of saying "Mother: thank you!"

Marcial wanted to thank the cardinals who had helped, resolutely defended, and accompanied him from afar with their words of support and hope as soon as possible. After several days in Rome, Marcial paid a visit to Cardinal Federico Tedeschini. When the cardinal saw him, he was taken aback and visibly moved. He paused in his doorway, threw open his arms and exclaimed: "Lazarus! Come forth!" The cardinal then strode forward and offered him a fatherly embrace.

How often his friends had feared Marcial would not come through this ordeal! He returned to Rome like someone who had survived a shipwreck. He was physically weaker but spiritually stronger. His heart was recovering from wounds and deep grief, and only forgiveness had been able to staunch the bleeding. "Lazarus, come forth!" Marcial emerged from the tomb of exile: he was alive once more.

On various occasions Father Maciel has spoken of what he calls the "innermost death"[5] of those who are made the object of gossip, slander, and defamation. Among the many sins against love that a human being can commit, this one, he explains to his Legionaries, is comparable to murder:

> A human being has two kinds of lives, his physical life, and his innermost life: his honor, his reputation. When a person attacks a human being with a weapon, taking his life and killing him, this person is called a criminal. He

---

[5] The Spanish *muerte moral* has been rendered "innermost" and not "moral" death. Here the Spanish moral is used as in the English phrase "they have our moral support." Likewise, in the following quotation *vida moral* has been rendered "innermost life."

knows it, and everyone else knows it. In the moral order, there are many criminals who destroy the lives of others, without considering themselves as such . . .

When a man's physical life is taken away, death itself frees him from all suffering and hardship; but when man is stripped of his reputation—the inherent right given to him by God of enjoying others' respect—he is condemned by calumnies to be a living corpse; he is subjected to a suffering that is much, much harder to bear and withstand.[6]

These words, spoken in 1992, were based on more than just the two-and-a-half years of exile. With time, slander originally spoken in private began to spread. New falsehoods looked for new ways to shock public opinion. It is the high price that the Legionaries of Christ pay even today for striving to remain faithful to the Magisterium of the Church and for cultivating a deep filial love for the person of the Holy Father.

Even before the Great Blessing Marcial had recommended the habit of speaking well of others as a concrete expression of authentic Christian charity. Afterwards, however, he preached this virtue even more insistently. During one of the darkest months of his exile, as was explained in chapter 12, Marcial had written that, despite having been subjected to slander and scorn, there had never been any room for hatred in his heart:

They brought me to the gates of death
Because I did not know how to hate.
And from the gates of death I return,
And I still have not learned to hate.[7]

"You can't measure what it means to receive a grace of this magnitude from God," Marcial commented when asked about these lines many years later.

---

[6] Marcial Maciel LC (January 1992) and *idem* (19 September 2002)
[7] Marcial Maciel LC, *Salterio de mis días . . .* , 9

Not knowing how to hate, or how to bear a grudge, and being able to treat the very people who caused me all of this damage honestly and kindly . . . I was able to go on living with great interior peace. It is an undeserved, incalculable grace to have gone on, to have lived and to continue living without the slightest flicker or the slightest feeling of hatred or bitterness or malice towards anyone, whether inside the congregation or out. Not then. Not later. Not now. It is a grace that lets you live in advance what is, I believe, the closest thing to the vision of God and the best slice of heaven that you can live on earth: serenity. Perhaps if you asked me what my attitude and my state of mind were in the face of all of these difficulties all life long, I would answer that my attitude has been, and continues to be, one of serenity. I am infinitely grateful to the Lord for that.[8]

The Legionaries of Christ would celebrate the 50th Anniversary of their founding on 3 January 1991. Pope John Paul II ordained 60 Legionaries of Christ in St. Peter's Basilica. Thousands of friends and members of Regnum Christi and the Legion of Christ came to Rome for days of celebration and intense joy. For Father Maciel in particular, they were days of spiritual comfort, and he gave thanks to God for all of the blessings he had received over the years. On the afternoon of January 4, Father Evaristo Sada came across Father Maciel walking alone with a thoughtful expression on his face.

"Nuestro Padre, do you mind if I accompany you?"

"Come along."

After a while, Marcial interrupted his thoughts and broke the silence with a heartfelt exclamation:

"How I'd like to see So-and-so right now, and So-and-so, and all the rest" (naming the former Legionaries who had caused his exile and the sufferings he endured during the Great Blessing) "to see them now, give them a strong embrace

---

[8] Marcial Maciel LC (January 1992)

and say, 'It was nothing . . . soon we'll see each other in heaven!'"[9]

Marcial named the period 1956–1959 The Great Blessing since, from whatever angle he looked at it, it seemed that God had brought about only good things from it. When he came back from exile, the founder saw his Legionaries united, happy and enthusiastic. After years of hardship, they had not swerved. They had been faithful, and had grown and matured in their love for God and their awareness of their mission within the Church. With their founder back at home and once again at the helm, the Legion of Christ could lift its sails.

Springtime

The Holy Spirit is like a wind that knows exactly where to blow. For years, the Church and all the sectors of its life had been preparing for a joyful explosion of light, a renewing fire, a kaleidoscope of color, an outburst of evangelization for the world: the springtime of the Church that the *Papa buono*, John XXIII, had proclaimed in January 1959. Two months before Marcial's return, in fact, the Roman Pontiff had made a surprising announcement. There was to be a second Vatican Council.

Marcial resumed his intense schedule as soon as he got back to Rome in 1959, principally dedicating himself to the Legionaries. Although he was often in Rome, he would periodically visit the novitiate in Salamanca, the Legionaries at the Cumbres school of Mexico City, and the apostolic schools of Ontaneda and Tlalpan.

> I always considered everything else simply a means, something accidental. The really important thing for the institute was its men and their formation: spiritual, human, intellectual and social. That is why I always paid attention to all these aspects and was always working. In the formation centers, I would normally work about 20 to 21 hours a day.[10]

---

[9] cf. Evaristo Sada LC (21 January 2002)
[10] Marcial Maciel LC (January 1992)

The number of Legionary apostolates began to climb, and vocations increased. In 1959, Marcial was busy developing the apostolic movement Regnum Christi. In 1962 the Legion opened a novitiate in Ireland. The Pan-American Cultural Center in Mexico City began in 1963. Classes in the Anahuac University, directed by Father Faustino Pardo LC, started in 1964 on a provisional campus in Mexico City. The Legion would receive its much-desired *Decretum Laudis* in 1965. This year also saw the Legion's first house in Madrid (run by Father Alfredo Torres LC) and a novitiate in Woodmont, Connecticut. The *Irish Institute* school was started in Mexico City in 1966, and the same year and in the same city, the first *Mano Amiga* school would open, offering subsidized education to underprivileged students. Ireland's *Dublin Oak Academy* and the *Irish Institute* of Monterrey, Mexico, were inaugurated in 1968. The climb continues to this day.

The Legion of Christ's dedication to apostolic work swelled after the Great Blessing ended in 1959. Since the foundation in 1941 Marcial had been preparing his Legionaries for the mission. In the fifties the first men had been ordained and the first work of apostolate had opened its doors. The Legionaries could now get down to work. Their apostolates would be clear manifestations of their charism: love for Christ, love for the Church, love for souls.

Each of the apostolates mentioned towards the end of this chapter would be like a melody that could be played again and again in other parts of the world. In many cases, harmonies— other apostolates of a similar nature—would quickly follow. Both the Church and the Legion were being moved along rapidly by the Holy Spirit.

The charism of Christian love

Even as a child, Marcial began to discover in the person of Jesus Christ, true God and true Man, the sole object of his love, his model and inspiration, the center of his life and the very reason for his existence. It would not be difficult for him, therefore, to decide upon Regnum Christi's spirituality. That question had already been answered when he had founded the novitiate on 25 March 1946 and determined that the spiritual life of his Legionaries must always be centered on Christ. Jesus Christ, God's-Love-made-manifest: this is the essence of Christianity.

Again, Father Maciel explained the thoughts that went through his head when he first heard the call to found the Legion in this way:

> It seemed impossible to me that there were souls in this world who did not know Christ, souls who could not enjoy the beauty of his love, the sweetness of his love, the serenity and confidence that his love inspires. And so, without knowing everything that I was committing myself to, I responded to the Lord that I would do everything he wanted . . . [11]

Marcial understands the Christian vocation, received in baptism, as a sharing in Christ's mission and an active participation in the urgent task of evangelization entrusted to the Church. God's love was made visible when Christ took on flesh and died on the cross to save humanity, and life is the time that men and women are given to respond to his Divine Love with love. Hence, evangelization is a question of experiencing the irresistible attraction and beauty of God's love, and letting this love overflow to others.

For Marcial, Christianity implies a profound personal relationship with a real, living, human, divine Jesus Christ, a sincere friendship that is expressed in concrete signs of love.

> Christ's entire life was a sustained, supreme act of self-giving to his Father and to men out of love. . . .
>
> So, when you want to know if you really and truly love, look at Christ crucified. If your love is like his, that is, total self-giving with concrete deeds, then your love is authentic, and you are real Christians. It might well be that you don't have lots of feelings and emotions, that at times your love stands on the rock of a faith stripped

---

[11] Marcial Maciel LC (1980s)

of all human consolation, but it is love because there is giving and commitment.[12]

Marcial understood this early in life. He had thought about it up on the hill overlooking Cotija. He had seen it in the example of his saintly uncle, Bishop Rafael Guízar. It had been deeply impressed on his heart by the death of his friend José Sánchez del Río. He had not only heard the Gospel on Mamá Maurita's lips, but had seen it at work every day in her actions, as she generously helped others.

> I know of no other way to love or to be a Christian because this is the way he [Christ] followed. My mother often said: "A painless Gospel is no Gospel." This is, then, the Gospel I learned from my childhood, the one the Cristero martyrs taught me, and so many others who in silence live and lived their love for God and their neighbor to a heroic degree.[13]

For Marcial, a practical man, "faith" must be accepted, lived, and shared with others. Nothing better can be offered to others than Christ's love, source of profound peace and happiness for all people. This is why the Legion of Christ and the Regnum Christi Movement are essentially "apostolic" in nature. For Father Maciel, every apostolic project must spring from love: love that means "self-giving," love that is necessarily expansive and outgoing, love that seeks what is best for others. When this love fills the human heart, it spills over and floods its surroundings, making everything fruitful.

"Believe in love!!! Believe in love!!," wrote Marcial from Cotija on 8 September 1986:

> From when I was young I found that the Letters of Saint John strongly insist on God's love for man: *In caritate perpetua dilexit te*[14] (*Jer* 31:3). I nourished myself on this

---

[12] Marcial Maciel LC, *Lenten Letter to all Regnum Christi members* (Rome, 1 March 2003)

[13] *ibid*

[14] "I have loved you with an everlasting love."

thought and took joy in it, and I decided that in my life
I must not teach about the God of terror and justice but
the God of love. The God who loves us, the God we
must love, and the God for whose sake we must love
our brothers and sisters as we love ourselves.[15]

Vatican Council II

The second Vatican council was a grace-filled period for
the Church, when the Holy Spirit poured new light and vital-
ity into the hearts of the bishops called together by Peter's successor. They sought to give a precise and detailed account of
the Church's nature and mission in the difficult circumstances
of the modern world. "What a grand occurrence this Council
is!," exclaimed Paul VI when he opened the fourth and final
session of Vatican II in the fall of 1965. He added:

> It must also be taken into account—oh, diligently bear it
> in mind!—that in this assembly we are not alone: Christ
> is with us; in his name we have been gathered (cf. *Mt*
> 18:20), and he is present, accompanying us on our jour-
> ney through this earthly life (cf. *Mt* 28:20).[16]

Analyzing the mystery of the Church and its relationship
to the modern world, Vatican Council II ushered in a vivifying
renewal of the Church's life. Father Maciel states that during
the Council

> the Church was able to grow in self-awareness, in
> knowledge of the treasure of God's Word, in dialogue
> with the world, whose joys and sorrows the Church
> shares. . . . There were no changes in doctrine; there was
> a desire to better understand today's world and be
> understood by it.[17]

[15] Marcial Maciel LC, *Letter* . . . (Chicago, 20 December 1982–Rome, 29 May 1988)
[16] Paul VI, Discourse to open the Fourth Session of Vatican II, *"Credidimus caritati
—Caritas Christi urget nos,"* 14 September 1965, in *Insegnamenti di Paolo VI,* vol. 3
(1965), Vatican City, 1966, p. 461. Translated from the Latin.
[17] Jesús Colina, *Christ is My Life* . . . , p. 53

The dogmatic constitution *Lumen Gentium* (21 November 1964) saw the Church from a new perspective, and served as a point of reference for the whole Ecumenical Council. The constitution *Gaudium et Spes* (7 December 1965) gave pastoral guidelines that promised to bear much fruit.

The renewal reached diocesan priests directly: there were two documents addressed straight to them. *Optatam Totius* (28 October 1965) dealt with priestly formation, and *Presbyterorum Ordinis* (7 December 1965) concerned itself with their ministry and life. The Council laid the foundation for a new way of living out the priesthood. The movement for priestly renewal, driven forward by the documents and norms of John XXIII and Paul VI, reached an acme in John Paul II's Pontificate with the apostolic exhortation *Pastores Dabo Vobis* (25 March 1992). Translated as "I will give you shepherds after my own heart" (*Jer* 3:15), it offers an overview of everything having to do with priests' formation and life in the Church's present circumstances.

The fresh breeze that entered the Church had a tremendous impact on parish life. The liturgical reform, initiated under Pius XII, culminated with a constitution on the Sacred Liturgy entitled *Sacrosanctum Concilium* (4 December 1963). While various documents of the Holy See invited parish priests to go out to their parishioners wherever they worked or gathered, and to strike up conversation with those who were far from the Faith, the Church also promoted a greater involvement of lay people in parish life: carrying out certain functions in liturgical celebrations, invigorating parish life, and being examples of Christian living in their own environment. It reminded lay people that their mission consisted in sanctifying the world. The Council appealed to the laity in a particular way through the documents *Lumen Gentium* and *Apostolicam Actuositatem* (18 November 1965). It urged them to become aware of their mission in the Church, to participate actively, and to build her up by living their baptismal consecration to the full.

After he returned from exile, Marcial dedicated several years to forge, delimit and launch the idea of working with lay people through the Regnum Christi Movement. He could not know that the Holy Spirit was hard at work in the hearts of many other future founders, and would soon inspire a new understanding of the role of the laity in the Council. The fact is that myriad new lay groups and associations and movements of different kinds were soon to spring into existence.

Many things were going on in the Church during the 1960s. Kiko Argüello (Vallecas, Madrid) was beginning the Neocatechumemal Way. Andrea Riccardi began what would eventually become the Community of Sant'Egidio in the shantytowns of Primavalle on the outskirts of Rome, at the service of the poor. Monsignor Luigi Giussani was working with his "Student Youth" group, and coined the expression that would give his movement its name: "Communion and Liberation." Patti Mansfield, one of the leaders of the Charismatic Renewal, had a powerful experience of the Holy Spirit at a weekend retreat at Duquesne University in Pittsburgh, Penn. José María Escrivá opened the ELIS Center of Opus Dei just outside Rome to form young professionals. Josef Kentenich returned from his long exile in Milwaukee and dedicated the last three years of his life to consolidating the international Schönstatt Movement. Chiara Lubich had been vigorously promoting the Focolare Movement for several years.[18] And this list is not exhaustive.

In his homily for Pentecost on 31 May 1998, John Paul II would say:

> The movements and new communities, providential expressions of the new springtime brought forth by the Spirit with the Second Vatican Council, announce the power of God's love which in overcoming divisions and barriers of every kind, renews the face of the earth to build the civilization of love.[19]

---

[18] cf. Manuel María Bru Alonso, *Testigos del Espíritu. Los nuevos líderes católicos: movimientos y comunidades*, Madrid, EDIBESA, 1998. This book offers an overview of some of the new ecclesial realities within the Church.
[19] John Paul II, Homily: Pentecost Sunday (31 May 1998)

Charity's Hour

John XXIII, the Pope known for his love of peace and openness to dialog, passed away on 3 June 1963; it would be up to his successor to guide the Council and bring its work to completion. The world awaited the wisp of white smoke that signals the election of a new Pontiff, and on 21 June 1963, the next Pope had been elected: Cardinal Giovanni Battista Montini, archbishop of Milan, who would shepherd the Church under the name of Pope Paul VI. He had been a friend of Father Maciel's since 1946, when the young founder had first presented the congregation's constitutions to Pope Pius XII and was told to go and ask him for advice. During Marcial's successive trips to Rome, Montini had helped Marcial organize the contents of the constitutions of the "Missionaries of the Sacred Heart;" he had been instrumental in the opening of the Cumbres school in Mexico City in 1951; and as archbishop of Milan, he had offered Marcial encouragement during the difficult years of the Great Blessing. Marcial considered Paul VI a good father, a faithful friend, and an authentic shepherd. Once elevated to the Chair of Saint Peter, Marcial venerated him above all as Jesus Christ's Vicar on earth.

On 6 August 1964, with Vatican II still underway, Paul VI published his first Encyclical, entitled *Ecclesiam Suam.* He wrote:

> We must love and serve the Church as it is, wisely seeking to understand its history and to discover with humility the will of God who guides and assists it, even when He permits human weakness to eclipse the splendor of its countenance and the holiness of its activity. It is precisely this holiness and splendor which we are endeavoring to discover and promote.[20]

Asking what mission the Holy Spirit was entrusting to the Church at that moment in history, the Pope responded:

---

[20] Paul VI, Encyclical Letter *Ecclesiam suam* (6 August 1964), 47

We are convinced that charity should today assume its rightful, foremost position in the scale of religious and moral values—and not just in theory, but in the practice of the Christian life. And this applies not only to the charity we show toward God who has poured out the abundance of His love upon us, but also to the charity which we in turn should lavish on our brothers, the whole human race. Charity is the key to everything. It sets all to rights. There is nothing which charity cannot achieve and renew. Charity "bears all things, believes all things, hopes all things, endures all things" (1 *Cor* 13:7). Who is there among us who does not realize this? And since we realize it, is not this the time to put it into practice?[21]

Paul VI acknowledged that the Church's mission implies a grave responsibility, and recognized the Church's limitations, human shortcomings, and the failings of its own members. But he underlined that the fruitfulness of evangelization does not spring from human effort or favorable circumstances, but from God's action to bring his saving plan to fulfillment. The Church has a message for everyone.[22]

The Church can regard no one as excluded from its motherly embrace, no one as outside the scope of its motherly care It has no enemies except those who wish to make themselves such. Its catholicity is no idle boast. It was not for nothing that it received its mission to foster love, unity and peace among men.[23]

According to the Pope, the Church would emerge from Vatican II invigorated for centuries to come, with a renewed awareness of its fundamental mission. A new period must begin: a period marked by genuine Christian love, by charity.

---

[21] Paul VI, *Ecclesiam suam* (6 August 1964), 56
[22] *ibid*, 95
[23] *ibid*, 94

The Legionaries and post-Vatican II

When Paul VI brought the Council to a close on 8 December 1965 with a solemn Eucharistic concelebration, the seed of the Church's renewal — the *aggiornamento* Pope John XXIII had so fervently desired — had been sown. In the years that followed, there would be seasons of rain and sun, and the seed would grow and produce new foliage and fruit.

As Marcial saw it, the Council was a time of grace. He was able to follow the Council's working closely since approximately half of the Mexican bishops were guests at the Legion's headquarters in Rome throughout the four Sessions. He knew that Councils like Vatican II were always followed by a delicate phase of acceptance and implementation. He shared the Pope's sorrow as he contemplated how certain mistaken interpretations of the Council buffeted the Church. There were diverse currents of thought, and they differed greatly in their interpretation of the Council's documents and the implementation of its norms.

The Church's deep roots would not be shaken, but the gale would strip many branches of their leaves and fruit. The Council wanted to help the Church influence the contemporary world more incisively; some were reticent about the new direction being taken. Others interpreted *aggiornamento* as an invitation to disregard liturgical norms and priestly or religious discipline. There were liturgical abuses, and many lay people's faith was damaged. The disorientation affected a broad stratum of priestly and religious life as well, resulting in numerous desertions. The post-conciliar period would witness a vocation crisis and a progressive abandonment of the sacraments, and the customs of traditionally Christian societies would be subjected to aggressive trends of secularization.

During and after the Council, Father Maciel always asked his religious to remain serene, and to maintain total adherence to the Council, exactly as it was explained and applied by the Holy Father. He often repeated to them this simple thought: *We will walk at the Church's pace: not a step ahead, not a step behind.*

Marcial chose this route as a consequence of his faith in the faculties given to Peter and his successors by Christ, and it was an option that bestowed unity and peace upon the congregation during those turbulent years. He succeeded in preventing a vocational hemorrhage within the Legion of Christ. Vocations increased.

The Decree of Praise

Cardinal Ildebrando Antoniutti, apostolic nuncio in Spain during the difficult years of the Great Blessing and a good friend of Father Maciel, had been appointed Prefect of the Congregation for Religious on 26 July 1963. One day in February 1965, while Father Maciel was busy with his work to get the Regnum Christi movement on its feet, he received an unexpected piece of good news. The Legion of Christ would become a congregation of pontifical right within the Church!

On 6 February 1965 Cardinal Antoniutti signed the *Decretum Laudis*, the Vatican's "Decree of Praise," on behalf of the Holy Father, and the next day, February 7, he visited the Legionaries on Via Aurelia in person to officially present the document to them.

"Gaudium magnum nuntio vobis!"[24] With these words, as applause filled the very room where Marcial had bid his Legionaries farewell on his way to exile less than ten years earlier, Cardinal Antoniutti announced that they had received definitive recognition by the Holy See. The cardinal congratulated them:

> You received diocesan recognition . . . Later, you had the good fortune to be recognized as an Institute of diocesan right in the very diocese of the Pope, in Rome. Yesterday, at the end of a meeting at the Congregation for Religious that studied the entire history of your institute, its phases of development and its Constitutions,

---

[24] A phrase traditionally used to announce the election of a new pope. It echoes the angel's words to the shepherds: *I bring you tidings of great joy.*

we decided to give you the Decree of Praise. So you are now included among the institutes of pontifical right.

The Holy See recognizes that your institute has done good work in the field of the Church's apostolate. The official recognition is proof of confidence in you. And, sending you as Legionaries of Christ . . . the Holy See is certain that you will prepare yourselves each day with greater attention, with greater diligence, and with more generous enthusiasm to offer yourselves to serve Christ and to be true soldiers for Christ: "Labora sicut bonus miles Christi Iesu."[25] That is the meaning of this decree. The Holy Father well knows how much you have done up until now.

A moment ago, I told your very beloved and esteemed Superior General, "You have also passed through some trials and some difficulties. This always happens in human projects. It is a proof of the Lord's affection, fondness, and love." The Holy See's official recognition should also be interpreted as a sincere and heartfelt thank-you to your Father General for all that he has done in the course of his life. It is not only a manifestation of gratitude for all that he has done until now, it is also a stimulus and a push . . . [26]

The Legionaries accompanied Cardinal Antoniutti to the chapel to sing a joyous, thankful "Magnificat"[27] together. Once the cardinal had departed, they excitedly gathered around to congratulate their founder. The first ones to do so were Father Alfredo Torres, Father Antonio Lagoa, and the other priests.

The Pope's representative had just spoken words of recognition, encouragement and thanks: Marcial now turned his eyes to his spiritual sons standing around him. The Church was blessing them. It was confirming their vocation and mission,

---

[25] "Work as good soldiers of Christ."
[26] Ildebrando Cardinal Antoniutti (7 February 1965)
[27] Mary's song of praise to God that begins: "My soul magnifies the Lord" (cf. *Lk* 1:46–55)

and they could scarcely contain their joy. Some had joined the Legion in 21 Victoria, others at 12 Madero Street or at the Pacelli Estate, and others had entered in Comillas or Ontaneda. He called to mind the Legionaries in other countries as well: he would phone each and every Legionary house before the day was over. They had all trekked a long journey at his side. They had assisted him with faith and persevered through the storms that the Legion had had to weather. The founding of the Legion of Christ and the growth of its apostolic works would not have been possible without them. He knew that he could count on them and that they would continue to serve the Church as faithful cofounders. A single, heartfelt phrase escaped his lips, all the more poignant when one considers how greatly he had longed for the Church's approval. "Thank you for being faithful," he said. "For me, that is worth more than a hundred Decrees of Praise."

Mail poured in over the next few months as many of those who had walked alongside Marcial at some stage of his journey sent him telegrams and letters. From many far-off places, friends shared his joy and sent him warm words of congratulations.

While still a young seminarian, Marcial had carried out mission work in Córdoba, Veracruz, with Father Ignacio Lehonor Arroyo, the zealous priest who had since been named bishop of Tuxpan. "This Pontifical recognition," he wrote, "is nothing other than a reward from God, a gesture of Jesus' love for your community."[28] There were also heartfelt, fatherly words from many elderly bishops who had accompanied and supported him during the first years of founding. Manuel Martín del Campo, bishop of León, wrote:

> Sooner or later, through his Vicar on earth, Jesus Christ our Lord had to manifest his express desire in a still more evident way: that his Legionaries go out to the whole world spreading his message of love and peace.

---

[28] Ignacio Lehonor Arroyo, bishop of Tuxpan, *Letter to Father Marcial Maciel LC* (17 March 1965)

. . . God knows that if I was able to contribute in some small way to this enterprise, it was because everything was obviously in order. . . . The eternal words of the Gospel spontaneously come to my mind at this moment: *Nisi granum frumenti*[29]. . . ![30]

Bishop José del Valle of Tabasco admitted that his joy was all the greater when he remembered, with agreeable surprise, how many difficulties Marcial had had to overcome to see his plans fulfilled. He was glad to see how the "hand of divine providence gently, progressively opened the way up before you, until he crowned all of your work with the felicitous *Decretum Laudis* of the Holy Father for your Congregation."[31]

Father Maciel received letters from friends both old and new, and not only from clerics, but from lay people as well. There was the humble joy of Alberto Martín Artajo, who had granted him 32 scholarships as Spain's Minister for External Affairs . . .

I congratulate you and your congregation for the "Decretum Laudis" granted to you by the Holy Father. It fills me with joy, almost as if it were something that had to do with me personally, since I can say I saw the enterprise being born—although the devotion you convey exaggerates the importance of the help I gave you at the beginning. In any case, I assure you . . . that your mementos and prayers generously recompense whatever I did, great or little.[32]

. . . and the exuberant Spanish enthusiasm of an old friend, Santiago Galas:

Alleluia! A due reward for the Congregation and for your total, life-long self-surrender to organize this enter-

---

[29] "Unless the grain of wheat . . . " (Jn 12:24)

[30] Manuel Martín del Campo, bishop of León, *Letter to Father Marcial Maciel LC* (26 February 1965)

[31] José del Valle, bishop of Tabasco. *Letter to Father Marcial Maciel LC* (25 February 1965)

[32] Alberto Martín Artajo. *Letter to Father Marcial Maciel LC* (9 March 1965)

prise. The most surprising successes of its progress have been paid by the toll of the most desperate sufferings, that cannot be borne but with God's assistance. . . . [We] sing with you, Father Maciel: Alleluia![33]

Among the letters of cardinals, nuncios, archbishops, bishops, parish priests, benefactors, friends and family members, several letters had special sentimental value: those of the ecclesial Superiors—true fathers for the congregation—who had made it all possible. Archbishop Alfonso Espino y Silva of Monterrey wrote:

I send my sincerest, most effusive, wholehearted congratulations to you and the other priests and brothers for this immense grace that the Lord has granted you, an event that acquires a transcendental importance for the life of the institute. It gives you citizenship among the religious institutes of the Universal Church, and places you under direct dependence to the Supreme Pontiff. I rejoice deep inside, participating in the joy that must flood your heart upon seeing this undertaking—into which you have put your whole life and infused your whole spirit—firmly consolidated. I remember that memorable afternoon in Cuernavaca with delight, when I took part, with my insignificant contribution, in giving juridical life to the institute.[34]

Bishop Polidoro van Vlierberghe, ex-apostolic visitator to the congregation and friend of the Legion's for life, sent a reply from Chile when he received the good news:[35]

The Lord has finally rewarded you for so many years of toil and suffering; he has finally heard the petitions of so many people who have prayed for this intention. Isn't it

---

[33] Santiago and Edmé Galas and their son Marcelo, *Message to Father Marcial Maciel LC* (1965)

[34] Alfonso Espino y Silva, archbishop of Monterrey, *Letter to Marcial Maciel LC* (8 March 1965)

[35] Polidoro van Vlierberghe, OFM, apostolic administrator of Illapel, Chile, *Letter to Father Marcial Maciel LC* (16 February 1965)

true, dear Father, that to suffer everything you've suffered was worth it, to obtain such a singular favor? You cannot imagine, Reverend Father, how much joy this splendid news provoked in me. I immediately went to the Blessed Sacrament to pray a fervent "Te Deum" and a hymn of thanksgiving for such a great blessing. I am certain that the great friends of the institute—Archbishop [Luis María] Martínez, Cardinal Gaetano Cicognani, Monsignor [Alfredo] Bontempi—were overjoyed to still be alive! How happy your benefactors and friends will be: Mr. [Santiago] Galas, Mrs. Flora [Barragán], Mrs. Josefina [Gómez de Delfino], the Santos brothers [Ignacio and Manuel], Don Diego [Bugallo], Don Ángel Morta, and so many others.

Now a new stage of increasing prosperity will undoubtedly begin; everyone will be invigorated by renewed enthusiasm to continue working for the great Legionary ideals, summed up in your 'Thy Kingdom Come!'"[36]

Cardinal Clemente Micara, as the Pope's vicar for Rome, was a superior for the congregation; he had also supported the Legion in crucial moments of its history. He wrote:

The highest recognition attributed to the Legionaries of Christ by the Holy See through the *Decretum Laudis* is a cause of lively satisfaction and great joy in which I also wholeheartedly partake. This hour of consolation has been prepared by the entire institute's generous sacrifices and persevering fidelity to the mission to which it is consecrated. For my part, I rejoice at having been able to offer my humble but always heartfelt and willing assistance—as good providence has allowed me to do—to accelerate [the arrival of] this admirable day, which crowns and rewards an entire past and offers encouragement for the future.[37]

---

[36] The letter uses the initials "A.R.T." for the Latin *Adveniat Regnum Tuum!*
[37] Clemente Cardinal Micara, Vicar of Rome, *Letter to Father Marcial Maciel LC* (Rome, 11 February 1965)

Only after a year had passed was Marcial able to put into words what that day had meant for him:

> Twenty-something years struggling ... believing and hoping against all hope, and to see God's hand in the person of the Supreme Pontiff, his representative on earth, saying: "Here is my blessing upon your life and efforts. You were on the right track all along, this was your calling." Put yourselves in my place and [you will] see that it was something ineffable, an incomparable joy. If I had been given all the honors and riches in the world, it would probably have left me indifferent. But when the Pope, the Vicar of Christ, says to me: "I thank you for this on God's behalf and I confirm that you are on the path of truth, fulfilling God's Will," for a priest there can be nothing greater, nothing more consoling or sublime in this world. It fills my soul with happiness and it prepares me and strengthens me to continue fighting.[38]

By granting the *Decretum Laudis* to the Legion of Christ, the Holy Father, Christ's Vicar, blessed 24 fatiguing yet luminous and spirited years of history. He recognized in this congregation the unmistakable imprint of God's love, wishing to draw close to humanity once again through a new charism in the Church.

The apostolic movement "Regnum Christi"

In 1959, Father Rafael Arumí LC was appointed superior of the Novitiate in Salamanca, Spain, to continue his work of forming novices.[39] Father Maciel met with him there that same year to draw up a systematic outline of how the Legion of Christ

---

[38] Marcial Maciel LC (1966)
[39] The novices had moved to Salamanca in December 1958. Carlos Mora LC, not yet a priest, was the interim superior. Father Arumí went to Salamanca once Father Maciel returned to Rome.

would serve the lay faithful. Of course, the idea of working with lay men and women was not something new to Marcial.

On 19 June 1936, as a teenage seminarian in Atzca-potzalco, Marcial had received the interior "motion" to found a group of priests. Their mission would be to dedicate their lives wholeheartedly to preaching the Gospel: "missionary priests who would live the Gospel thoroughly, love Christ with all their strength, be missionaries of that love, and preach Christ's new commandment of love among all people."[40]

Ten years later, in July 1946, the 26-year-old Marcial had visited Rome and Madrid during his first trip to Europe. He saw both Rome and Spain recovering from war and fighting against hunger, chaos and misery. He was saddened to see churches stand empty, and observed disenchantment, indifference, and the reflection of bitter nihilistic pessimism etched in the faces of many. Europe was incubating deep personal unease and stark existentialism, and its social unrest was feeding Marxist-socialist ideas of class consciousness. At 11 p.m. on 2 July 1946, in Spain, Marcial wrote a long letter to the young men who would come to Comillas two months later to begin their studies:

> When I think of the world waning and dying because it does not know Christ, when I think of the utter chaos into which this restless, blind humanity is tumbling for lack of Christ, when I contemplate ruin and barrenness in so many good souls for lack of Christ, . . . when I meet up with the strength of youth withered and torn apart in the very springtime of life for lack of Christ, I cannot hold back the cries of my heart. I want to multiply myself, divide myself, so as to write, preach and teach Christ. And from the very depths of my being, from the very spirit of my spirit, bursts forth this single resounding cry: My life for Christ![41]

---

[40] Jesús Colina, *Christ is My Life . . .* , p. 17
[41] Marcial Maciel LC, *Letter to the novices* (Madrid, 2 July 1946)

The first intuition of the 1930s made clear *what* had to be done. Marcial's experiences in 1940s had helped provide more reasons *why,* and in the 1950s, apostolic work had gotten underway. But a question remained: *how?* How would he "multiply himself" and "divide himself" so to tell as many people as possible about Christ and his love?

With God's help, the answer would gradually take shape in Marcial's mind. He saw that, in a world often hostile to the Gospel and the Church, lay men and women would be able to bring the Good News to places where a priest could not go. Although it would be years before Marcial had clearly delineated and defined the structure of the apostolic movement Regnum Christi, that did not prevent him from getting started. That was his style. He had learned to found by founding. He would learn to set up a Movement by setting up a Movement.

The internal difficulties of the 1950s had prevented the Legion of Christ from fully developing Marcial's apostolic intuitions, but at last, on the threshold of the 1960s, the Holy Spirit seemed to be telling him: "Working with lay people? The time is now!"

After the initial planning session with Father Arumí in 1959, Marcial and a number of Legionary priests would work together throughout the '60s to plan the movement and set it in motion. Membership? Regnum Christi would be open to men and women, young people and grown-ups, single or married. Diocesan priests, too, could take part. Spirituality? Nothing new. They would all benefit from the same spirituality, the one the apostolics at 39 Turín Street had already heard the founder describe from the very beginning: personal love for Christ, for the Blessed Virgin Mary, for the Pope and for the Church, and a deep love for souls that would drive them to work untiringly for people's genuine happiness, in time and in eternity. Formation? It would have to be sound, deep and lead to mature personalities. It would have to embrace every aspect of the human person: character and intellect, body and spirit. It would have to take into account Christianity's social and apostolic nature. Activity? To the degree of their possibilities, they would carry out effective, wide-reaching apostolates, so as to offer real answers to the urgent needs of the world and of the Church. It would have to help build up the universal Church in the particular circumstances of each diocese and region.

Marcial considers the Regnum Christi movement as something to be offered to all Catholics; some will feel called to it. He sees it as a way to help men and women live their baptismal commitments to be holy and to actively work to spread the Gospel. Faith and love have to become the driving force behind members' daily lives, not only on the personal, family and parish level, but also in their professional and social spheres.

As in many other groups raised up by the Holy Spirit throughout the Church's twenty centuries of history, God would give a certain number of Regnum Christi members a specific vocation. These men and women would consecrate their entire lives to loving Christ and serving the Church, and offer God all their talents, time, and the love of their hearts. Lay consecrated Regnum Christi members live their team life together as a family, dedicate themselves to prayer and apostolic activity, and live the evangelical counsels so as to imitate the life-style of Jesus Christ and his Blessed Mother.[42]

During the early 1960s, the Legionary priests who worked at the Cumbres school in Mexico City started offering formation and apostolic activities to groups of teenagers and college students. On 15 March 1963, Archbishop Darío Miranda of Mexico City established the first Pan-American Cultural Center in Tlalpan in the diocese of Mexico City. Although ownership had changed hands several times, the center was located on the very property where the houses of 10 and 12 Madero Street had once stood. It was a center for study and reflection,[43] a house where spiritual retreats could be offered to people of

---

[42] The branch of the Movement for consecrated women came into existence in Mexico City on 8 December 1969, and their first formation center was established in Dublin, Ireland, several weeks later. The first house for the consecrated men opened in Madrid in 1972.

[43] The Legion of Christ currently has 17 centers for reflection and study in various American and European countries. In these centers groups of business leaders might get together, for example, to deepen their knowledge of the Church's social doctrine and to look for concrete ways to apply it in their businesses.

all walks of life: bishops, diocesan priests, men and women religious, lay men, women and youth.[44]

A number of Cumbres school alumni—many of them students at the new Anáhuac University—embraced the ideal that Regnum Christi presented to them with enthusiasm. They saw it as a calling, a concrete way to develop their Christian vocation. They would soon organize teams with their friends from the Cumbres, the Anáhuac, and other Mexican colleges and universities, giving rise to Regnum Christi centers for spiritual and human formation and diverse youth activities in the cities of Mexico and Monterrey. Simultaneously, in Madrid, Father Alfredo Torres LC began to form the first groups of young Spanish Regnum Christi members.[45]

Father Maciel had no desire to found two different institutes, one "religious", the other "lay". He wanted a single "family" sharing a single spirit and charism. The Legion of Christ and Regnum Christi were to be one reality, each taking part in diverse apostolic projects. The Legionaries of Christ would serve as a type of backbone to the Movement, supporting its apostolic activities and impelling them forward. They would offer what priests can offer: sacraments, spiritual guidance, and formation. Lay people, as their numbers increased, would be able to help transmit their own experiences and formation to newcomers, and launch projects of evangelization together with the Legionaries of Christ. Here was a way to contribute something to the vast, urgent mission of the Church.

On 2 March 2002, Pope John Paul II wrote to Father Maciel:

> In this regard, I see that not only the professed religious of the Congregation but also members of the

---

[44] The first spiritual exercises in the Pan-American Cultural Institute were preached to a group of 17 Mexican bishops, 16–22 February 1964.

[45] In November 1964, during a lunch at the congregation's general directorate in Rome, the Holy See's nuncio for Spain, Bishop Antonio Riberi, suggested to Archbishop Casimiro Morcillo of Madrid that he bring the Legionaries of Christ to his diocese. The archbishop turned and invited Father Maciel to open a house and begin working apostolically in Spain's capital. Father Alfredo Torres LC went to Madrid in February 1965.

diocesan clergy and lay faithful participate in your
spirit through the Regnum Christi Movement. To help
them live this charism in many diverse situations of life,
they receive guidance, help, counsel and encouragement in their apostolic drive from the Legionaries. . . .
Thus Legionaries have a special commitment toward
those who are closest to them, helping them to live their
baptismal commitments ever more intensely . . . according to their specific vocation, and to progress steadily
towards the holiness to which everyone is called (cf.
Lumen Gentium, 39–42): fostering a spirituality based on
Christ, promoting an intense sacramental life and unity
of mind and heart with Peter's Successor and the Pastors
of each local Church, and encouraging the practice of
spiritual direction and other means of formation.

This close association also entails sharing Legionaries' characteristic apostolic zeal. Thus Regnum Christi
will effectively take part in building the civilization of
love and justice—through numerous endeavors dedicated to education, to supporting the family, to aiding
those most in need or to the use of the mass media to
spread the Christian spirit—finding its inspiration in
the spirit of the Gospel and its guidance in the teachings of the Church.[46]

Mano Amiga

*The first Mano Amigo school for underprivileged children
opened in 1966, a year after Vatican II ended.*

From the very start, many parents of Cumbres students,
friends and benefactors got involved in apostolates and works
of Christian charity that the Legionaries of Christ proposed to
them. In particular, they began to set up and support the first
Mano Amigo (Helping Hand) school in Mexico City. The same

---

[46] John Paul II, *Letter to the Most Reverend Father Marcial Maciel Degollado* (Vatican,
2 March 2002)

thing would happen with the parents of students in the Irish Institutes of Mexico and Monterrey.

The first of many *Mano Amiga* schools was inaugurated in June 1966 by Cardinal Carlo Confalonieri[47] at San Antonio de Zomeyucan in Mexico City. These schools, under the direction of the Legion of Christ and Regnum Christi, offer subsidized education in the poorest and marginalized zones of large urban centers. Their aim is threefold: to educate less fortunate children, to promote the human, cultural, and spiritual development of their families, and to contribute to the progress of their communities. For this reason, the schools do not limit themselves to their primary goal of teaching and educating. The *Mano Amiga* network currently carries out a wide range of initiatives to serve society: training workshops in new technology for working men and women, medical attention for adults and children, monthly food and clothing drives for the poor, courses in self-betterment and human development for parents, marriage preparation classes, career discernment, one-on-one counseling to help form spiritual and human values, education in the Faith, catechesis, and sacramental attention.

Anáhuac University

The Legion of Christ finished constructing its first university in 1968.

Already in 1947–1948, Elías Iglesias Valdizán, the driver of the Wawa in Cóbreces, had admired 28-year-old Marcial's capacity for work. For those who knew him in the 1960s, it seemed that Father Maciel's energy increased with age.

For Marcial, founding the first Legionary university implied a gigantic effort. Every step was a battle: he had to locate a suitable plot of land, purchase it, obtain the necessary permissions from both Church and government, and form the board.[48]

---

[47] The head of the Holy See's Sacred Consistorial Congregation (now the "Congregation for Bishops")

[48] Santiago Galas Arce chaired the Board, whose members were chosen from the world of Mexican business and finance: people such as Manuel Espinoza

There were obstacles, and opposition was never absent. To find an architect, he set up a first-rate project committee that organized an urban planning and architecture competition:[49] the winner was architect Imanol Ordorika. Last but not least, the facilities themselves had to be built. The gargantuan task was completed in just six years. Blueprints were drawn up in 1962, and the definitive campus opened its doors in 1968.

Marcial opened four schools during the same period, and established two novitiates in countries where the Legionaries had never worked before: Ireland and the United States. Work was begun on a university residence in Madrid: the *Hispano Mexicano Don Santiago Galas*. Marcial would later say that he did his best to carry out what God had asked of him:

> You really can't believe that all of this would come about by accident, or that it was achieved—or is achievable— by someone like me without God's intervention, without his providence.
>
> The action of God is so rapid and the lessons of these events were so powerful, that . . . I had no time to think, "Oh! Now I'll be well regarded, they'll think that I'm really something . . . ." There is no time for that.
>
> I think that this also is one of the . . . blessings that accompany occurrences of this type. Without realizing how, they keep things in perspective and put us in our proper place: God's instruments, who lend themselves to God the Creator so that he, the one who is able to do all these things, can bring them about through us. It leaves no time for becoming bigheaded before God, before others, or in our own eyes. I think that this is an invaluable blessing.[50]

Yglesias, Claudio Zapata, Pablo Díez, Gastón Azcárraga Vidaurreta, Adolfo Autrey Dávila, Justo F. Fernández, Eugenio Garza Sada y Roberto Garza Sada.
[49] The panel included architects of national and international renown: Henry L. Wright (New York), Pedro Ramírez Vásquez (one of the best architects in Mexican history), Héctor Mestre, Vicente Medel (representing Mexico's National College of Architects), and the engineer José Villanueva (Chief of the Urban Planning Office, Mexico City). A number of experts in Pedagogy completed the panel.
[50] Marcial Maciel LC (Fall 2001)

The Anáhuac University was the first of the 22 Catholic institutions for university studies and specialization that the Legionaries currently operate in Mexico, the Americas and Europe, including Francisco de Vitoria University in Madrid and Regina Apostolorum Pontifical University in Rome.

The Family

The first apostolates for the family began in 1968.

As students were busy rebelling in Paris and *Humanae Vitae* hit the press,[51] Regnum Christi inaugurated its first FAME[52] center for the family in Mexico City. It was the spontaneous, cordial response of Marcial, the Legionaries and the first members of Regnum Christi to Pope Paul VI's concern regarding life-, marriage- and family-related issues.

FAME was the Movement's first apostolate to address the pastoral needs of families, and its aim was to promote family values in culture and society, in the moral and ethical fields. It provides marriage preparation courses and offers guidance on themes such as married life, the difficult task of running a household, the raising and education of children, and how to form a rich personality and a stable family life founded on common beliefs.

It helps couples live their married life in a happy, balanced way, and allows them to lend a hand to other families at the same time.[53]

---

[51] Pope Paul VI published the Encyclical Letter Humanae Vitae on 25 July 1968.

[52] Two syllables, a short form of the full title: *Familia Mexicana*

[53] Other Legionary apostolates dedicated to the helping the family include *Familia Unida* in Chile, *Family Life in America* ("Familia") in the USA and DIF (*Desarrollo Integral de la Familia*) in Spain. On 13 May 1981 the Holy Father founded the *John Paul II Institute for Marriage and the Family* with the Lateran Pontifical University, to form researchers, teachers and professionals capable of promoting, defending and spreading family values in today's society. There are extensions in Australia, Austria, Benin, India, Ireland, Spain, and USA, and in 1992 the Legion of Christ helped open three centers in Mexico (Mexico City, Guadalajara, and Monterrey), each offering university-level licentiates and a master's degree in Family Sciences, recognized by Mexico's Ministry for Public Education.

Like every Regnum Christi apostolate, FAME and other family-related initiatives spring from a sincere love for the Church and the desire to serve her in a concrete way. As Father Maciel wrote in a letter dated 25 December 1966:

> It is a real, objective love for the Church—just as it is and just as Christ has wanted it to be—not an idealistic, subjective love for a Church according to our fancy. It is a love that meditates on her in faith, accepts her in obedience, expands her in apostolate and makes her holy in our lives."[54]

After living at the Legion of Christ's Center for Higher Studies in Rome for several weeks during a course for new bishops called *Pilgrimage to St. Peter's Tomb* (organized by the Congregation for Bishops), Spanish Bishop Amadeo Rodríguez Magro of Plasencia wrote to the Legionary house's rector:

> Thank you very much for the love towards the Church that we perceived, [for the Church as] personified in each bishop who participated in this course.
>
> Our experience was that in all the "details"—your attentiveness included even the smallest details — the point of reference was the Church and, of course, Jesus, always so present in the very atmosphere one breathes in this house.[55]

And Bishop Marco Eugênio Galrão Leite de Almeida, from the diocese of Estância, Brazil, said:

> Your testimony of faith, of joyfulness in your religious consecration, of availability and service to the Church, of fidelity to the Magisterium, of brotherliness, in short, of holiness, made a deep impression on me, and gave me the joy of feeling that, in the chaos in which we find

---

[54] Marcial Maciel LC, *Letter to the Legionaries of Christ* (25 December 1966)
[55] Amadeo Rodríguez Magro, bishop of Plasencia, Spain, *Letter to Álvaro Corcuera LC* (1 November 2003)

ourselves, God always sustains "a small remnant" that remains faithful to him . . .[56]

Father Maciel concluded his 1966 Christmas letter stating that love and adherence to the Church must translate into two things. First, internal unity based on doctrinal fidelity, walking in the Pope's footsteps. Second, apostolic renewal: an audacious response to the Church's most pressing needs, making use of modern means and technology to bring Christ to those who do not know him or whose knowledge of him is only partial.[57]

Young People

The Youth Sections of Regnum Christi experienced strong growth in the 1970s. ECYD was created.

The Legion of Christ held its first Extraordinary General Chapter in autumn 1968. It gave the Regnum Christi movement a definitive impulse, and called for the development and launching of an international organization for adolescents, which evolved into what is now called ECYD (Education, Culture and Youth Development).[58] When the General Chapter concluded on 16 October 1969, the Legionaries of Christ would turn their attention to forming lay adults and young people, encouraging them to take active part in the Church's mission. This work quickly bore fruit.

Regnum Christi wants to help its teenage members to be coherent young people, living their Catholic Faith and transmitting their love for Christ enthusiastically. Young people are encouraged to be protagonists in a continually changing society, capable of perceiving, analyzing and taking on new challenges with maturity and responsibility. They generously commit themselves to the demanding task given to today's young

---

[56] Marco Eugênio Galrão Leite de Almeida, bishop of Estância, Brasil, *Letter to Father Alvaro Corcuera* (2 October 2003)

[57] cf. Marcial Maciel LC, *Letter to the Legionaries . . .* (25 December 1966)

[58] This is the English adaptation of the Spanish acronym for *Educación, Cultura y Deporte*.

people: that of building up the world of tomorrow, a world of love, justice and peace.

Father Álvaro Corcuera LC, current rector of the Legionaries' Center for Higher Studies in Rome, remembers a meeting that several of the first ECYD members had with Father Maciel a few months after ECYD's creation:

> In 1971, a group of [students from Mexico] . . . were spending some time in Dublin, Ireland. ECYD had just barely started. One day, Nuestro Padre called five of us to meet with him. We were all about 13 or 14 years old. . . .
>
> I remember very clearly that Nuestro Padre spoke to us about the greatest gift that we had received in our lives, which was the Faith. He spoke to us about what other children and young people our age did for non-Christian ideals. Looking at each one of us as Christ must have looked at his apostles, he asked if we were willing to give ourselves to Christ in the same way. He encouraged us and urged us to live in keeping with our Catholic Faith, to be more than just "Sunday" Christians, to always live out the call to be apostles of Jesus Christ with maturity and total self-giving. He told us that ECYD was not a club, but rather a means to live out our baptism to the full.
>
> We could not remain satisfied with what had been given to us, because the Church needed authentic Christians, convinced of their faith and their love for Christ. But I remember very well that the fundamental framework, and the principle motivation, was the idea of friendship with Christ. He would say, "Are you really a *friend* of Christ?" And then he would speak about everything that he, Christ, had done be faithful to his friendship with us.[59]

In the mind of Father Maciel and the Legionaries who dedicated themselves to youth work, ECYD youth clubs could

---

[59] Álvaro Corcuera, L.C, *Written testimony* (10 April 2000)

offer a wide variety of activities: from competitive sports, camps and excursions to debates, competitions, cultural activities and healthy recreation; from spiritual retreats, conventions and seminars to formative talks on current events. Above all, however, ECYD meant getting involved in a broad range of apostolates, especially popular missions of evangelization and works of Christian charity among those most in need.

As time went on, they noticed that the initiative to undertake new projects came from the young people themselves. Over the years, ECYD and young Regnum Christi members have planned and created projects, associations, NGOs and foundations (both confessional and non-confessional) to benefit teenagers and young adults. This was the case with both *Gente Nueva* in Mexico and IUVE in Europe, organizations dedicated to promoting human values among young people.

The network of clubs and youth centers extends across 4 continents and reaches more than 25 countries.

Mayan Missions

The Legion began to work in the missions in 1970.

In 1970, when Pope Paul VI created the mission territory of Chetumal and entrusted it to the Legionaries of Christ, Father Maciel offered the Holy Father the services of Father Jorge Bernal, the first Legionary priest to be ordained from the founding group of apostolics and, consequently, someone whom he had formed from adolescence on. Jorge Bernal would become the first Legionary bishop. He arrived as apostolic administrator of the Prelature of Chetumal with a handful of Legionary missionaries on 21 November 1970.[60]

Located on the southeast of the Yucatan Peninsula in Mexico, the mission region covers more than 51,580 square

---

[60] Jorge Bernal Vargas LC was ordained in Lourdes, France, on 15 September 1957. Pope Paul VI appointed him apostolic administrator of the Prelature of Chetumal on 16 July 1970. He was named Prelate of Chetumal on 7 December 1973, and consecrated bishop on 19 March 1974. On 8 December 1997, his title was changed to Prelate of "Cancún-Chetumal."

kilometers of jungle along the Caribbean coast. The breath-taking territory—inhabited predominantly by people of Maya origin—had suffered religious neglect since the time of colonial evangelization, and particularly since the 18th century, due to a shortage of priests and a series of local wars (the "caste wars"). A group of priests with exemplary pastoral zeal had attended the needs of the region with unflagging generosity in the preceding decades, but they were so few in number that they could not cover the whole territory. It was here that the Legion of Christ began its missionary work among the rural and indigenous communities.

"With a missionary spirit, and accompanied by my brother Legionaries, we have witnessed an amazing change," says Bishop Bernal:

> Although it is in a remote corner, God has blessed us by making the whole State [of Quintana Roo] grow in an astonishing way . . . it is a privileged place because of the exuberance of its tropical forests, the beauty of its coastal waters, and above all because of the human warmth and hospitality of its inhabitants.[61]

There were only eight churches when the Legionaries arrived more than 30 years ago. At that time the region was sparsely populated by Mayan communities scattered throughout the low jungle and along the sandy coastline. The priests would search out the communities by jeep, on horseback or on foot, overcoming tiredness, heat, and enormous distances. Even though so many decades had passed without priests, the indigenous peoples had conserved some religious traditions of the Catholic Faith, but these had been fused to native ancestral rites. Little by little, the people learned to trust the missionaries who came to help them, teach catechism, and celebrate the sacraments, and they began to receive the missionaries with more faith and a greater thirst for God, opening to them the doors of their houses and hearts.

---

[61] Jorge Bernal LC, bishop Prelate of Cancún-Chetumal, *Written Testimony*, (no date)

Bishop Bernal's most memorable moments—and the ones he considers to have been most useful from a missionary's point of view—are those spent among the Mayan people.

> At the outset of my evangelizing work, I could go to see our brothers frequently on my pastoral visits. At the time, Quintana Roo had little more than 100,000 inhabitants. Now, with more than a million inhabitants,[62] many have . . . gone to the cities in search of work. But we have not stopped attending the villages, and I enjoy visiting the rural parishes.
>
> Those are the moments when I thank God for being able to come close to my brothers to praise and bless God our Father: he has given us his Son, Jesus Christ, to save us and to teach us to love God.[63]

The work of evangelization has borne fruit, and the region has grown and prospered in peace.

Forming "apostolically active" lay leaders

Mano Amiga opened the way for a whole gamut of works of Christian charity.[64] Although the primary apostolic focus of the Legion of Christ and Regnum Christi consists in forming leaders according to the Gospel in every sphere of society—intellectual, cultural, scientific, social, artistic, economic, religious, and so on—no forms of apostolate are excluded. The needs of the Church in each place and time determine the course of action to be taken, in coordination with the pastoral programs of each diocese.

Leadership, by definition, entails having an influence on others. For Father Maciel, the leadership exercised by Catholics

---

[62] In 2003 the mission territory had a population of 1,132,433

[63] Jorge Bernal LC, *Written Testimony* (no date)

[64] In the area of education, new projects like *Lazos* were begun to complement the work done in *Mano Amiga* schools. *Lazos* offers economic and material aid for educating children from low-income families. In 2002, 94 schools were affiliated with the program, and by June 2003, 109 schools had received aid benefiting 38,168 children. In 2003, *Lazos* sponsored 15,493 children, offered 500 job training courses, and provided 6,234 tutors.

in the world should be an authentically Christian type of leadership, uniting faith and action and imbued with the ardor of St. Paul the apostle who exclaimed "the love of Christ urges us on!" (2 *Cor* 5:14). Father Maciel believes that, moved by Christ's charity, Catholic leaders can exert a great deal of positive influence at home, in their social relationships, and within their professional surroundings through their example and apostolic action, thus enabling the message of Christ to reach the greatest number of people quickly and effectively.

Every person is a potential leader. To the degree that men or women open themselves up to God's grace and forge an authentic Christian personality, they become a reflection of Jesus Christ and true guides for others: strengthened by the power of God's grace and assisted by the Holy Spirit; supernatural in mind and magnanimous of heart; effective, realistic and tenacious, and convinced of how important it is to spread the Gospel. At the same time, the Holy Spirit needs the human "clay" to be prepared so he can sculpt it into Christ's image.

That is why Legionaries run a countless number of projects and initiatives offering lay men and women an integral formation: one that nourishes the spirit, educates the mind and forms character. Some projects are dedicated to teach the Faith and further a wider acceptance of Christian living, while others promote culture, research, and academic excellence. Human and Christian values are not fostered by conventions, seminars, and formative activities alone. They are also advanced through the media, art, and sports.

Once formed, lay people carry out apostolic activity in projects like these, choosing whenever possible to get involved in undertakings that respond to the urgent needs of the Church and the world in their countries. Hence, the poor and marginalized, immigrant and urban working-class communities, agricultural workers and indigenous peoples in rural areas receive frequent, special attention through works of Christian charity in countries where Regnum Christ and the Legion are present. They benefit from projects in sectors ranging from education and nutrition to health and housing. Charity is not only a question of offering handouts: it is conceived as providing all-around help to people in their material, human, and spiritual needs. In their apostolic action, Legionaries and Regnum Christi members seek to foster and promote the dignity of every person, helping them to become the chief proponents of their own development, and active players in the development of their families and communities.

To form the Christian consciousness of their students and sensitize them to the problems afflicting society, all Legionary schools include social work in their curriculum. Students visit orphanages or old age homes or lend a hand to those building their house. Others go on to help out in hospitals, give courses in hygiene or basic first aid, or offer training to agricultural workers on farming and ranching techniques. Even the students attending *Mano Amiga* schools participate in these programs, looking after those who stand in greater need than themselves, and making an effort to help their own communities make progress.

In 1974, the wives of some business leaders in the industrial city of Monterrey, Mexico, felt called to promote human values in the heart of working class families. They launched *Pro Superación Personal* (ANSPAC)[65] to help form well-balanced individuals through educational programs for adults. The courses are especially geared towards the wives of workmen in developing nations, and the workshops, given by the wives of business executives, are held in places close to where the majority of the employees live.[66]

Many *Pro Superación* alumni apply the formation they received by actively promoting Christian values in their own surroundings, and undertaking concrete forms of social commitment and Christian apostolate.

---

[65] "In Favor of Personal Betterment"
[66] *Asociación Nacional pro Superación Personal*, AC. A report from 2002 stated that 454 parishes and 338 businesses in 58 cities had benefited from the program, and that in approximately 3,000 centers some 80,000 women members have, since ANSPAC's foundation, completed the 4-year formation program. As of May 2003, more than 61,000 women were enrolled as active members in Mexico alone. The program *Pro Superación Personal* has started up in various South American countries and has been well received.

New Ways of Evangelizing

Numerous apostolic initiatives of evangelization sprang up in the '60s and '70s.

Marcial possesses two qualities proper to children: first, a capacity to live the present with great intensity, and second, an overflowing creativity. Father Maciel has commented that his mind is like a "laboratory of ideas": it is. He launches one idea after another and works tirelessly to see them finished. He is not alone in this task. During the '60s and '70s (and in the decades that followed) the Legionaries of Christ and Regnum Christi developed many of these ideas, converting them into concrete works of apostolate. Father Maciel often repeats that the fruitfulness of the Regnum Christi Movement's many apostolic activities is not just due to the talents and time of its members: the fecundity comes from God.

The mission territory of Chetumal constituted the Legion of Christ's first large-scale commitment to the task of evangelization, but others would follow. Two initiatives are worthy of special mention: door-to-door missions, and the training of professional catechists.

Mexico has a tradition of tolerance, and Catholics have lived peacefully side by side with their separated brethren for more than 200 years. Over the last few decades, however, it has been affected by the invasion of insistent, self-styled religious sects whose aim does not seem to be that of strengthening people's faith. At one point, a sect was preparing to canvas Father Maciel's hometown of Cotija. A group of young Regnum Christi members offered their services to Cotija's parish priest, and undertook a door-to-door mission of their own from 10–16 October 1986 to strengthen the people's Catholic Faith. They spoke to the people, forewarned them, and offered them essential catechesis so that they would have answers to defend their Faith. *Juventud Misionera* was born.[67]

---

[67] *Juventud Misionera* means "Missionary Youth". Its sister program in English speaking countries is *Youth for the Third Millennium,* founded in the United States in December of 1994.

Many bishops and parish priests took to the idea, and people hungry for a word about God were happy to receive the young Juventud Misionera missionaries. Young people had started off dedicating the odd weekend to offer preventive measures in communities with the greatest risk of losing the Faith, but their numbers soon began to multiply. Bishops began to send the young missionaries to lend a hand to parish priests in rural zones and among indigenous people where distances made it difficult for the priest to be there on any type of regular basis. The missionaries were also sent to urban neighborhoods suffering from poverty, violence or a lack of formation.

This was followed by an idea to carry out missionary work as a family, leading to the creation of *Familia Misionera.*[68] Parents and children go on missions together. At present, Juventud Misionera and Familia Misionera work with bishops and pastors around the world to promote the new evangelization through rural and urban missions.[69]

Evangelization requires the formation of catechists. Ever since his years as a seminarian, Marcial had observed the difficulties that parish priests have in getting the message of the Gospel across to their parishioners, especially in societies where the population is large or growing, or where the practice of the sacraments is scarce. The need was great then, it is even greater today. This is the reason behind Father Maciel's desire to form entire groups of lay people well-formed in Catholic doctrine who in turn can educate others in the Faith.

The idea crystallized at last in September of 1976 when the first center of the Pontifical *School of the Faith* opened in Mexico City. This pontifical catechetical institute was approved and

---

[68] The counterpart to Familia Misionera in English speaking countries is *Missionary Families for the Third Millennium*

[69] By 2003 its work had spread to 30 countries. During Holy Week of 2002, more than 50,000 missionaries participated in missions in 22 states of the Mexican Republic, while 15,000 missionaries participated in parallel missions in other American and European countries. These missions reached 3,141 communities, and the missionaries visited more than 950,000 people in their homes. During Holy Week of 2003, the number of missionaries in Mexico grew to 63,000, thanks to the work of *Juventud y Familia Misionera* and the Full-Time Evangelizers.

endorsed by the Prefect of the Congregation for the Clergy, Cardinal John Joseph Wright. It specializes in teaching catechesis to adults and aims at forming qualified catechists with degrees, true "teachers of the Faith" able to explain, defend, and communicate Catholic beliefs to the men and women of today. The School of the Faith uses the most up-to-date teaching methods and carries out its work in complete fidelity to the Magisterium of the Church, thus supporting the work of bishops, parish priests and pastoral agents in the local churches.[70]

The rapid spread of adult Regnum Christi groups, first in Mexico and later in other parts of the world, generated continual growth and the multiplication of apostolic undertakings. By the end of the 1970s, Marcial's desire to *multiply myself, divide myself, so as to write, teach, and preach Christ* was coming true.

The Legion of Christ was bearing its first fruits for the Church: Regnum Christi was active in the most diverse social spheres and fields of action. There was pastoral outreach to families, young people, women and men. There were missions and works of Christian charity promoting the human development of the underprivileged. There were centers to form catechists, spirituality centers for reflection and study, and free schooling for the poor through *Mano Amiga*. The Legion and Regnum Christi were running educational institutes from primary to university level. All of these works of apostolate got started in the two decades that followed the Great Blessing, and have continued to grow and spread.

Lay Regnum Christi members and their apostolic works were essentially missionary in nature, dedicated to spread the good news of God's love. In this, they were much like the young Polish Pope who, as a witness to hope, would soon come to Rome "from afar". He was a pilgrim and a pastor, and the whole world would be his mission territory.

---

[70] *The Schools of the Faith* (Escuelas de la Fe) network currently has 34 centers and 281 study groups. 10,465 students in Mexico, Guatemala, El Salvador, Venezuela, Brazil, Chile, Argentina, Colombia, the United States, and Italy are preparing to become catechists.

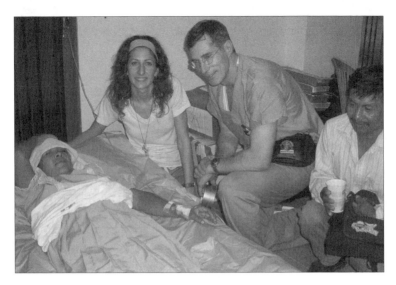

Dallas-based Helping Hands Medical Missions *came into existence in 1996. It arranges for volunteer doctors and nurses to offer medical services to the marginalized communities of Latin America. Over the course of its first seven years, medical missions have been organized in Brazil, the Dominican Republic, El Salvador, Guatemala, Mexico, and Venezuela, offering 45,300 consultations and more than 1,000 operations free of charge.*

Aerial view of a CIDECO community development project under construction in Santiago Nonualco, El Salvador

On 3 January 1991, the congregation's 50th anniversary, John Paul II ordained 60 Legionary priests in St. Peter's Basílica.

The Holy Father John Paul II offered another sign of his fatherly closeness and appreciation for the Legion by visiting what was then the Legionary of Christ's Center for Higher Studies in Rome, on 19 March 1998. The building now houses the International Pontifical College Maria Mater Ecclesiae, *for future seminary formators, at the service of diocesan bishops.*

Father Maciel participated in the Synod of Bishops dedicated to the formation of priests in October 1990. In October 1992, the Pope invited him to take part in the 4th General Latin-American Episcopal Conference in Santo Domingo. In 1994 he was named advisor to the Vatican Congregation for the Clergy, and invited to participate in the Synod on Religious Life. In the photo, Father Maciel taking part in the 1997 Extraordinary Assembly of the Synod of Bishops for America.

Regnum Christi's consecrated women carry out a wide range of apostolates, with special mention being made of those directed towards the formation of women. The fidelity of the first cofounders (pictured here in a 1991 photo taken in Rome) allowed a new style of consecration to be introduced to the Church. Top row: *Patricia Bannon, Graciela Magaña, Guadalupe Magaña, Margarita Estrada, María Carmen Perochena, Teresa Vaca.* Bottom row: *María Laura Moreno, Belén Sánchez de Ocaña, Elizabeth Cosgrave.*

Aerial view of the Pontifical Regina Apostolorum University and the Legionaries of Christ's Center for Higher Studies in Rome. Along with Faculties of Philosophy and Theology, the University opened the world's first Bioethics Faculty.

The Holy Father's Secretary of State, Cardinal Angelo Sodano, inaugurated the new facilities of the Pontifical Regina Apostolorum University on 31 December 2000.

Through specialized formation courses, the Center for Seminary Formators has offered its services to 860 formators from 383 dioceses in 85 countries. It has hosted 11 international summer courses, and of its 8 national programs, several have been dedicated to the young and flourishing Church in Africa: Ethiopia, Ghana, the Ivory Coast, and Tanzania. A group photo of the priests in Ghana who took part in a course directed by two Legionary priests.

XIV

Yesterday's Seed, Today's Harvest

On 6 August 1978, the news of Paul VI's death stirred the world. After the brief pontificate of John Paul I—one of the shortest in history—a new conclave elected a new Pope. He was a largely unknown, young Polish cardinal with a surprising background: an actor, writer and poet who was no stranger to hard work; an underground seminarian who became a parish priest; a lover of humanistic studies, a philosophy professor and a doctor in theology; a great mystic, yet one who loved skiing in the mountains and kayaking in the great outdoors.

It was natural, therefore, that much was initially said about his many human strong points. Nevertheless, it wasn't the attractive personality alone that would make the first 25 years of his pontificate so fruitful. As an orphan who had lost his father and mother early on, he anchored his heart in God, and placed himself in the hands of the Blessed Virgin Mary, his Mother. As a seminarian, he forged his vocation in a clandestine seminary, and in the fertile soil of persecution he sank deep roots of fidelity and perseverance. As a parish priest, he spoke with the people around him and showed them, especially the young, the timeless beauty of Christ, his mystery, his person, and his teachings. As bishop—and later as cardinal—he had his desk placed in the chapel, to be able to work for long hours in silence alongside Jesus Christ, present in the Eucharist. As Pope, his total dedication to the Church's mission has been a blend of daily prayer, love, work and suffering.

The cardinals who had been bold enough to elect a Slavic Pope in October 1978 knew that his election would signal the beginning of a new stage in the Church's life and its relation to the world. They were confident that John Paul II would interpret and propel the ecclesial renewal introduced by the Second Vatican Council. Their judgments proved true, even though many of them would probably say (if it were possible to ask them now) that the results surpassed their expectations.

On 17 October 2003, Father Maciel penned the following lines:

> Yesterday we had the pleasure of accompanying His Holiness John Paul II as he celebrated 25 years of Pontificate. What a marvelous example of supremely faithful surrender he has been and continues to be for us, day after day: no holding back, no cutbacks, no compromises. His love for Christ, the Church and souls is so immense and full that no obstacle, great or small, has been able to prevent him from carrying out the weighty mission the Lord gave him when he placed him at the head of the Catholic Church. Bullets, sickness, the wear and tear of the years: nothing has affected his love. Many admire his greatness—and he is a giant of the Faith— and admit that he is the most important, influential and commanding leader of recent times. Others continue to predict the fateful proximity of his departure (even if many sham prophets have gone ahead of him on the road to eternity).
>
> But no one denies that today John Paul II is, in fact, the world's supreme moral and spiritual point of reference, for believers and unbelievers alike. At the beginning of the millennium, humanity would not be the same if this radiant, serene light had not shone, emanating from the Pope's entire being: his word, his unreserved self-giving to the mission, his perfect existential coherence, his extremely profound life of faith and prayer, and—in an ever more intense way—the teaching authority of his own suffering, through which the Lord our God has chosen to closely associate him with Jesus Christ's cross.[1]

---

[1] Marcial Maciel LC, Letter to Angeles Conde (Roma, 17 October 2003)

John Paul II met the Legion of Christ, Regnum Christi and Father Maciel during his first trip to Mexico in January 1979, since several Legionaries and Regnum Christi members put themselves at the service of the then apostolic delegate in Mexico, Archbishop Girolamo Prigione. They helped him organize details of the trip and attend to the Holy Father during his stay at the apostolic delegation's residence.

John Paul II has frequently recalled his first encounter with the Blessed Virgin of Guadalupe, "the star of evangelization," and with the Mexican people, who are enthusiastic believers deeply in love with Our Lady of Guadalupe. It was a moment of grace that helped shape his pilgrim-like missionary pontificate. He felt especially called to live out Christ's command to "Go out to the whole world . . . " (cf. *Mt* 28:19, *Mk* 16:15). At that precise moment of history, Jesus would say to him, just as he had said to Peter, the first Pope: "Put out into the deep water and let down your nets for a catch!" (*Lk* 5:4).[2]

As a sign of esteem and gratitude for the assistance he received during the visit to Mexico, John Paul II invited Father Maciel, the community of the Legionaries of Christ and consecrated Regnum Christi members living in Rome to a Mass in the "Lourdes grotto" of the Vatican Gardens on 28 June 1979. He asked the founder to concelebrate. The Holy Father exhorted them to be like the "prudent man who built his house on rock," and expressed his "profound appreciation and gratitude" for the young people who had given him their "generous, enthusiastic assistance in the apostolic delegation."

As shepherd of the diocese of Rome, the Holy Father proposed visiting all the parishes of the Eternal City over the course of his pontificate. On 31 May 1970, as cardinal archbishop of Krakow, Karol Wojtyla had already celebrated Mass in Rome's Our Lady of Guadalupe parish with a group of Polish priests on pilgrimage. It would be one of the first parishes he visited as bishop of Rome. Some had suggested December 12 (Feast of

---

[2] By June 2003, the 83-year old Pontiff had already completed his 100th visit outside of Italy.

Our Lady of Guadalupe) as an appropriate day to visit, but the
Holy Father preferred the first anniversary of his pilgrimage to
the Virgin of Guadalupe's image in Mexico. On 27 January 1980,
therefore, John Paul II went to the parish at Via Aurelia 675, and
stayed for dinner with the Legionary community in what is
now the Legion's general directorate.

According to those who were present, the Pope was surprised to see how many and how young the Legionary religious were, and was interested when Father Maciel told him all
about the seminarians' formation and the charism of the
Legion and Regnum Christi. Before leaving, the Pope invited
the Legionary seminarians to "reproduce the image of Christ in
yourselves," and to "show it to others with a courageous, un-
divided heart."[3]

The Definitive Approval of the Constitutions

In 1983, the Sacred Congregation for Religious had
reached the last stage of revision before the Legion of Christ's
Constitutions could receive their final approval. Since the proposed Constitutions contained certain novel elements, the
authorities of the Sacred Congregation who had gathered on 31
May 1983 to discuss the issue decided that, if they wanted to
respect the founder's wishes, it was something that exceeded
their competence. In an audience with the Pope later that
morning, Cardinal Eduardo Pironio (Prefect of the Congregation for Religious) and Bishop Agustín Mayer OSB (Secretary)
submitted the Legion's Constitutions to the Pope. They asked
for a papal indult to approve them just as they had been written by the founder.

Because of the Holy Father's visit to Poland and Cardinal
Pironio's trip to the Holy Land, the news reached Father Maciel
after a twenty-odd day delay. On June 28, he was finally able to
jot down in his diary:[4]

[3] John Paul II (27 January 1980)
[4] Marcial Maciel LC transcribed this page from his diary in a *Letter addressed to all
religious and novices of the Legion of Christ* (Rome, 30 June 1983)

Today, at 10 p.m., Father Vérgez came to my office to tell me that Cardinal Pironio, Prefect of the Sacred Congregation for Religious, wanted to speak with me on the phone. At three minutes past ten . . . he put me through to him:

"Good evening, Father Maciel."

"Good evening, Your Eminence."

"I'm calling to let you know that a few moments ago I received an envelope from the Holy Father's personal secretary. It contains the document with the Pope's hand-written approval of the Constitutions; the Pope approves the Legion of Christ's Constitutions."

"Thank you very much, Your Eminence. I also thank God because he chose to associate you so closely with the history of the Legion of Christ."

"On the contrary," said the cardinal, "it is I who feel profoundly grateful to the Lord for this grace he is giving the Church through my unworthy person."

I invited him to give the news to the community. He wanted to bring the document in person. The decree will be signed tomorrow, the 29th, Solemnity of St. Peter and St. Paul. His Eminence will come to give them to us the next day, on Thursday, June 30th.[5]

The official announcement of the Constitution's approbation was made on 29 June 1983. It was a moment that Marcial had been looking forward to for almost 40 years. In a letter dated June 30, Father Maciel explained to Legionaries what the Pope's approval meant:

I ask the Lord and the Blessed Virgin that all those who have been called to lay the foundations of this undertaking will give thanks for the gift that has been given to

---

[5] Cardinal Eduardo Pironio wanted to sign the decree granting definitive approval to the Constitutions in the presence of Father Maciel and in the company of the Legionaries of Christ present in Rome. So, although the decree is dated 29 June 1983, the signing took place on 30 June 1983 on the altar of the parish of Our Lady of Guadalupe on Via Aurelia.

them—and through them, to the Church—by striving to prevent the Constitutions from ever becoming dead letter in their lives, or in the lives of their communities. On the contrary, may they [the Constitutions] be for everyone a source of prayer, personal growth in holiness, indefatigable zeal to establish Jesus Christ's Kingdom in the world, and final perseverance.[6]

First the man, then the saint

The first ordinary General Chapter of the Legion of Christ (10 October—30 November 1980) marked a new stage in the congregation's life: a period of institutionalization, consolidation, and growth. This was especially true in the area of vocations. The Legion of Christ did not suffer the vocation crisis that had affected ample sectors of the Church during the post-conciliar period, and its membership continued to grow rapidly and steadily. In 1987, a novitiate in Brazil was added to the novitiates that already existed in Spain, Ireland and the United States, and during the decade of the 1990s other novitiates would be opened in Canada, Colombia, Germany, Italy and Mexico.

As has been the case since founding, work and multiple occupations did not succeed in distracting Father Maciel from his number one priority: personal attention to and integral formation of the men and women entrusted to his care. Father Maciel has declared, on hundreds of occasions, that it is not the sum total of activities and projects that constitute the Legion of Christ and Regnum Christi. It is their members.

"You have a beautiful complex of buildings and a beautiful church, but your real treasures are your students," wrote Bishop Paul Chomnycky. "I was extremely impressed by their spirit of service, by their courtesy and helpfulness, by their discipline and by their genuine piety. You have the right to be very proud of them. They are obviously very, very well formed."[7]

---

[6] Marcial Maciel LC, *Letter addressed to all religious* . . . (Rome, 30 June 1983)

[7] Bishop Paul Chomnycky OSBM, apostolic exarch of Great Britain, faithful of the Eastern Rite (Ukrainian). *Letter to Father Álvaro Corcuera LC* (28 September 2002)

It is impossible to run apostolic projects without men, just as it is impossible to have apples without trees. But robust trees do not grow overnight: they mature and grow over a span of many years.

The preparation of a Legionary comprises several distinct periods of formation: novitiate, juniorate, philosophy, theology, and a period of apostolic internship. This means that a seminarian will usually spend from 13 to 15 years in the Legion before reaching ordination. Why? Angels don't knock on the novitiate's front door. Today's young men do. It takes time to help them form their consciences. It takes time to help them acquire a full range of interpersonal, human virtues: sincerity and loyalty, sturdiness and service, goodness and attentiveness in their dealings with others, coherence and simplicity, gentlemanliness, and the correct understanding of people's dignity, both their own and that of others. It takes time to form spiritual virtues such as humility, charity, and obedience, fortitude, prudence, and justice, and purity of body, heart, and soul. The world expects as much from a priest, and some need more time than others to attain psychological, human, spiritual, affective or and intellectual maturity. The goal is to offer well-formed, balanced men to the Church on their ordination day. Father Maciel explains it in this way:

> If it were only a matter of giving men a good intellectual preparation and a vague idea of what it is to be a Catholic priest, if it were only a matter of "churning out" priests, then priestly formation wouldn't have to take the time it does, and a Legionary's would seem very long. But if it's a matter of forming the man that God has chosen to be a priest in every aspect, and watching over him as he matures so that he becomes a priest after God's own heart, then we can't try to skip or rush through the stages of this evolution.[8]

This is the wisdom of someone who knows the value of patience.

---

[8] Jesús Colina, *Christ is My Life . . .* , p. 77

In their seminary years, students strive to increase their love for God, the Blessed Virgin Mary, the Church and humanity, and there is no other reason for investing so much time, effort or energy in the formation of young men. The goals are high and demanding, and an entire life is at stake.

After his stay at the Legionary college in Rome during the month of September 2002, Bishop Roger J. Foys of Covington, Kentucky, was struck by what he had seen: "It was a great blessing to see so many seminarians at various stages of their journey so on fire with the love of the Lord! . . . What a remarkable and uplifting display of faith in action!"[9] Many years earlier, in January 1974, Pope Paul VI addressed the following words to a group of newly ordained Legionary priests:

> You have been preparing yourselves for years, through prayer, study, and meditation, for the solemn moment of your definitive self-surrender to God and the Church, choosing Jesus as the one great goal of your youth and your entire life . . . You are "Legionaries", that is, not languid men, or men who just observe how things are going, but men who want to impress energy upon all things and give Christianity an expression that is characteristic to it: combativeness.[10]

Christian "combativeness": putting the Faith in action. For Legionaries and Regnum Christi members, living the Faith means actively searching for ways to make Christ known among today's men and women. This is why the Legion and the Movement take pains to offer a careful intellectual formation to their priests and lay people. Marcel Clement, a French intellectual who directs the paper *L'homme nouveau*, wrote:

> During their period of formation and afterwards, Legionaries form teams comprising various nationalities. From here springs the necessity of speaking several lan-

---

[9] Bishop Roger J. Foys D.D., bishop of Covington. Letter to Álvaro Corchera LC (27 September 2002)
[10] Paul VI (2 January 1974)

guages and getting accustomed to discovering the most diverse aspects of cultures within the Universal Church in every instant. . . . I have witnessed the harmony of their specifically religious and priestly formation, and seen how attuned to non-clerical culture it is.[11]

After teaching a course at the Legion's Regina Apostolorum Pontifical University in Rome, Father Richard John Neuhaus observed:

There were about sixty students in the course, almost all priests or seminarians, and I have never encountered anywhere a group of students more eager, articulate or intellectually astute. And yes, they are orthodox and excited by the truth of the Church's teaching. Critics who depict Legionaries as pious brainwashed zombies walking in lockstep under an authoritarian regime are, in my experience, preposterously wrong.[12]

"A sower went out to sow . . . "

Pope John Paul II has also shown his appreciation for the quality of formation that Legionaries and Regnum Christi members receive in countless ways. He esteems the self-sacrificing work to which the founder has dedicated the greater part of his life.

In October 1990, the Pope invited Father Maciel to participate in the Eighth General Assembly of the Synod of Bishops dealing with the topic of *Priestly Formation in Current Circumstances.* John Paul II opened the session in the Synod Hall on October 1. During the Synod, Marcial had the chance to read and study the "Instrumentum Laboris" (the synod's working paper), assist at the daily Synod sessions, and carefully prepare his talk for the general assembly and contributions to the smaller study groups. On October 12, in the 18th general

---

[11] Marcel Clement, "Une espérance pour l'évangélisation," in *L'homme nouveau,* (20 January 1991)
[12] Richard John Neuhaus, "Feathers of scandal" in *First Things,* March 2002, p. 76

session, Father Maciel spoke to the Synod participants about the priest's *forma Christi* (the form of Christ). Throughout the month of October, he sought to share his experience with the other Synod Fathers, and learn from them in a cordial exchange of ideas and initiatives.

Father Maciel had just finished editing a book on the theme of priestly formation entitled *Integral Formation of Catholic Priests*.[13] Several days before the concelebrated Mass with the Pope in St. Peter's Basilica to conclude the Synod on October 28, he presented a copy to all the Synod Fathers. In a book review, Father Álvaro Huerga OP commented:

> It is common to say that what is most needed in our confused times are clear ideas. M. Maciel's book is full of "clear", resplendent ideas. They are contagious ideas as well, one of the characteristics of the "lively, encouraging" message of this Mexican priest: patriarch of a large family that bears a stamp of combativeness and generous service to sow seeds of evangelization.[14]

Analyzing the book's content, Father Vittorio Marcozzi SJ explained how Father Maciel had perceived

> that love is the fundamental motivation of priestly formation. However, for it to be able to take deep root, it is necessary to know human nature as fully as possible: [a nature] that is fundamentally good, but with limits that must be recognized, taking into account the effective help that grace can give. Jesus gives us the most luminous example of anthropological and pedagogical realism. Important, too, his observations dealing with the characteristic features of today's man.[15]

---

[13] The first edition was printed by the Legion of Christ in Rome in June 1990. The book was published by the Spanish-language publishing house *Biblioteca de Autores Cristianos* (B.A.C.) several months later (December, 1990).

[14] Álvaro Huerga OP, *Book Review* (1990)

[15] Vittorio Marcozzi SJ, *Book Review* (1990)

Several months later, the Holy Father offered numerous signs of spiritual closeness, support, and affection to Father Maciel, the Legionaries and Regnum Christi members as they celebrated the Legion of Christ's 50th Anniversary. On 3 January 1991, in an unprecedented gesture, John Paul II ordained 60 Legionaries of Christ. They were accompanied by thousands of Legionaries, diocesan priests, and lay people—members and friends of the Regnum Christi Movement—who prayed the Litany of the Saints during the ordination Mass in St. Peter's Basilica to invoke their protection over the soon-to-be-ordained seminarians.

In his homily, the Pope exhorted them to draw close to Jesus . . .

> Jesus loves you as friends; he has given his life for you, he has shown his love to the extreme, his affection which knows no limits, because no one has greater love than he who lays down his life for his friends (*Jn* 15:13). The priesthood, which from today on is your legacy and part of our Lord's inheritance, is an initiative of the love of Christ who has chosen you and constituted you in the ministry: "I have chosen you and appointed you to bear fruit" (*Jn* 15:16).[16]

. . . and to be aware of their mission:

> Place your trust in God, dear new priests. Consider that you have been called by God in a particularly important moment. The Church, in fact, is set to begin the third Christian Millennium; Latin America is preparing to commemorate the 5th Centenary of the New World's evangelization. You are called, therefore, to be evangelizers of a new stage of hope for the Church and the world.[17]

---

[16] John Paul II (3 January 1991)
[17] *ibid*

In the evening of 4 January 1991, during the concluding event of the 50th Anniversary celebrations, Father Maciel summed up the profound meaning of everything he had experienced since the foundation and all the occurrences that were still to come with a simple declaration: "At the end of our lives, nothing will remain but what we have done for God and for mankind, our brothers and sisters."[18]

Father Maciel had to return to Rome from Mexico unexpectedly on 1 April 1992, having been informed by the Vatican that the Holy Father wanted him to participate in the Press Conference on April 7 to present the apostolic exhortation *Pastores Dabo Vobis* ("I will give you shepherds"), a document the Pope was offering the Church as the result of the Synod on priestly formation. Over the next several days, Marcial attended several meetings in the Vatican to prepare his presentation on "Latin America and the Post-Synodal Exhortation *Pastores Dabo Vobis.*"

In October 1992 the Holy Father invited Father Maciel to participate in the fourth Conference of the Latin American Episcopacy in Santo Domingo, dedicated to the theme *New Evangelization, Human Betterment, and Christian Culture.* Two other Legionaries took part as well: Father Arturo Gutiérrez, as the Conference's official spokesman to the Press, and Father Javier García, as an expert for the Holy See. Father Maciel worked in commission seven, dedicated to the theme of religious life.

Evangelizing Europe

An important appointment for the history of the congregation awaited Father Maciel when he returned to Rome from the Conference in Santo Domingo: the Legion of Christ's second ordinary General Chapter (November—December 1992). The aim of the first General Chapter had been to institutionalize, consolidate and expand the Legion and Regnum Christi.

---

[18] Marcial Maciel LC (4 January 1991)

The aim of the second General Chapter was to spur on the Movement's apostolic activity.

In the '90s, the Legion and the Movement widened their radius of action to four continents, with a special emphasis on Europe. On 18 December 1992 the Legionary priests taking part in the Chapter attended a private audience with the Pope. The next day, in his homily during the Mass of thanksgiving to conclude the General Chapter, Father Maciel explained that the Legion had just received a new task: "There was something that could be called new in the Pope's words . . . After [his discourse], he spoke to me about Europe: briefly, just a few words. . . . And he told us to prepare ourselves to re-evangelize Europe."[19]

Without neglecting the other continents, the Legion of Christ and priests and lay members of Regnum Christi have made a decided effort to establish a presence in Europe as a response to the Holy Father's watchword. They were already present in Spain, Italy, and Ireland. In the decade following the second Chapter, they expanded their ministry to countries in Eastern Europe such as the Czech Republic, Hungary, Poland and Slovakia, as well as central European countries like Austria, Belgium, France, Germany, Holland and Switzerland. The founding steps were small, but the Legion of Christ opened two novitiates on European soil (Germany and Italy) and two minor seminaries (France and Italy) during this period.

A wide variety of apostolic projects got started: schools, cultural foundations (such as the Guilé Foundation,[20] with headquarters in Boncourt, Switzerland) and works of Christian charity such as the *Villaggio dei Ragazzi.*

---

[19] Marcial Maciel LC (18 December 1992)

[20] The Guilé Foundation was brought into existence through the initiative of a Swiss industrialist, Mr. Charles Burrus, and his wife. Its main goal is to promote values rooted in the dignity of the human person, part of the legacy of the Judeo-Christian tradition. These values belong to the universal patrimony of the human race, independent of religious or cultural origin. The Burrus family, the bishop of Basil, and the Legionaries of Christ (as spiritual and doctrinal assessors) began the Guilé Foundation in 1997.

The *Villaggio dei Ragazzi* (Boys' Village) in Maddaloni, one of the poorer areas of the Italy, offers education, food, housing, and religious and human formation to 1,200 students. More than 500 of these are on scholarships. The majority of them come from broken homes or low-income households.

Villaggio dei Ragazzi came into being in the aftermath of World War II. An Italian priest, Father Salvatore D'Angelo, seeing so many children and youth left homeless in the area around Caserta, just north of Naples, was inspired to gather the street children together and offer them a place to stay, an education and a future.

Father D'Angelo saw that the Legion of Christ could guarantee the continuity of the work, and entrusted it to their care. The *Villaggio dei Ragazzi* currently has a pre-school, a primary and secondary school, a technical institute for industrial arts and another for aeronautics, a bachelor's program in linguistics and a Higher Institute for interpreters and translators.

Two universities were opened on European soil during the 1990s: Francisco de Vitoria University (Madrid), and the Pontifical Regina Apostolorum University (Rome).

As so often before in the Legion's history, the permission to establish a pontifical university came through the special intercession of Mary. Father Maciel writes:

> I remember that when I was in Brazil, they sent me a memo informing me that it would be practically impossible to obtain the Athenaeum's establishment before year's end. At the bottom of the page, by way of reply, I had just written: "I have the moral certainty that the Blessed Virgin will resolve this problem on time" when I unexpectedly received news that permission had been granted. God had acted. The Blessed Virgin, at whose feet I had laid this apostolic initiative, had once again kept watch over our footsteps.[21]

---

[21] Marcial Maciel LC, *Letter to the Rector, Deans, and Professors of Regina Apostolorum Athenaeum*, (Rome, 15 November 1993)

> She, our good Mother, revealed her boundless love
> once again . . . [She] wanted the decree of establishment
> to be signed by the Prefect of the Congregation for
> Catholic Education, his Eminence Cardinal Pio Laghi,
> on September 15: the Solemnity of our Lady of Sorrows,
> Patroness of the Legion.[22]

Regina Apostolorum was established by the Congregation
for Catholic Education on 15 September 1993. His Holiness
Pope John Paul II granted it Pontifical status on 11 July 1998.
From the very start, Cardinal Angelo Sodano, Vatican Secretary of State, offered decisive support to obtain the ecclesial
permissions and approval for the university's construction. He
laid the cornerstone as work began and on 31 December 2000
blessed the facilities of the new building.

Besides Faculties of Philosophy and Theology, the Pontifical Regina Apostolorum University opened the world's first
Bioethics Faculty.[23] Students are also offered specialties in Psychology and Counseling, Environmental Sciences and "Science
and Faith." There is an Informatics Center for Human Sciences,
a Center for Seminary Formators, and an Institute for Higher
Studies on Woman.

The university's Institute for Religious Sciences offers
yearly specialization courses.[24] The topics range from vocational ministry and the direction of religious communities to
the pedagogy of consecrated life. These courses are especially
directed towards formers and superiors of female religious congregations or institutes. The university makes the most of modern technology and provides classes via video-conferencing to
seminaries and affiliated extensions on other continents.

The Italian Environmental Minister, Altero Matteoli, inaugurated Regina Apostolorum's "Specialization in Environ-

---

[22] Marcial Maciel LC, *Letter to all Legionaries of Christ and consecrated members of Regnum Christi*, (Madrid, 29 September 1993)
[23] Established by the Congregation for Catholic Education in 2001.
[24] Established by the Congregation for Catholic Education in 1999.

mental Sciences" on 15 November 2002. In his discourse, Matteoli expressed why the Ministry of the Environment chose to establish the program with a Pontifical University:

> We want to develop an ecology that is founded on a more optimistic concept of mankind and its capabilities. Humanity has the cultural, political, scientific and technological resources to conserve nature. Humanity is not a sickness, but medicine for our planet. It doesn't impoverish, but enriches the world. The offspring of humanity generates hope, not despair . . . The culture we want to take as a starting point to reflect again on the relationship between humanity and nature is based on principles that have given life to Christian humanism . . . In fact, we share with the Catholic Church a vision of the material world centered on the human person.[25]

Walter Veltroni, Rome's mayor, visited the Athenaeum a month later. Greeting the academic community, he said:

> Life's richness consists in creating a community where everyone's diverse specialties can exist and flourish. You do it by studying, seeking, delving deeper, understanding better—illuminated by faith. The synthesis of these two things is like a kind of "positive virus" that breaks out in society. People you meet will be "infected" in a positive way either by the one aspect, that of faith, or the other, that of having a mind open to searching, doubting, understanding. So I am pleased to meet you, because I consider you to be among the most important portions of this city. And I want all of you, representing so many different countries, to feel this city's affection and warmth.[26]

Rome has benevolently welcomed this new educational institute. After only ten years of existence, Regina Apostolo-

---

[25] Altero Matteoli, Italian Minister of the Environment (15 November 2002)
[26] Walter Veltroni, Mayor of Rome (9 December 2002)

rum Pontifical University ranks third in student enrollment among the ecclesiastical universities of the Eternal City.

Handing on the charism

Father Maciel's is an active style of governing that fosters teamwork, creativity and a spirit of initiative where members consider the mission of responding to the Church's needs as their own, and commit themselves to it. He encourages and supports their initiatives: what is more, even at 84 years of age, he takes an active, hands-on approach to their work and teaches them to proceed in the same way. Above all, Marcial is capable of making his goals and loves "catch on" in the lives of others.

In 1993 Marcial published three "thematic" letters to Legionaries and Regnum Christi members. In the first, *Time and Eternity* (March 10), he invited them to sit next to him, as it were, on the rock where he contemplated the meaning of life as a youth on Calabazo hill in Cotija de la Paz. There he had learned how precious time is. Time is fleeting. It is a treasure and a priceless talent that must be put at the service of what cannot change nor decay: God. Several months later, he wrote *Gospel Charity* (October 22) and *Apostles of the New Evangelization* (November 21). He invited the readers to live the commandment of love just as his missionary uncle Blessed Rafael Guízar had done as bishop of Veracruz, transmitting the Faith and striving to bring Christ's redeeming love to all mankind.

Father Maciel's goal is to share and convey the Movement's special charism not only to his Legionaries, but also to the priestly and lay members of Regnum Christi. Just as a tree grows because sap flows from trunk to branches, and from branches to twigs, Father Maciel and his cofounders want to transmit the spirit of the founding by fostering the same dispositions, loving the same "loves"—love for Christ, for the Church, for others—and living the same evangelizing drive that will convert them into prayerful, active apostles. If Marcial is not alone in founding the Legion of Christ and Regnum Christi, it is because many men and women strive to put their faith into action. They see the Church's mission as their own, and try to spend their lives out of love for the Church and their fellow human beings.

Seeing how many people have experienced a crisis of values and of meaning in their lives—either individually or as couples and families—Father Maciel launched the first *Alpha Omega* clinic in 1976, with the aim of nurturing specifically human values, offering personal and family counseling services, and providing them with psychological, medical, and spiritual assistance. Each clinic would have a team consisting of at least one priest, one psychologist, one psychiatrist, and a general practitioner.[27]

In September 1999, twenty-three years after this first initiative in the field of psychology, a Regnum Christi member, Dr. Gladys Sweeney, opened the *Institute for Psychological Sciences* (IPS) in Washington DC, an institute of higher education to promote a Christian vision of the human person in psychology.[28] Dr. Sweeney, founder and current director, says:

> The creation and development of the Institute for the Psychological Sciences quickly blossomed as the spontaneous result of my serving the Church within Regnum Christi's charism, when I saw there was a need to bring gospel values to the world of psychology. I thought that as a Christian, I could offer a response. God asked it of me, and I threw myself into it.[29]

She explains that the Institute's mission is two-fold:

> It includes the development of a psychology based on the Christian vision of the human being, created in

---

[27] *Alpha Omega* centers help people find meaning in their lives and draw up a personal project in accord with their human dignity, working to prevent certain mental health problems. The ultimate aim is to help them discover God as the source of every human value and consequently as the root of all true personal, familial, spiritual and social happiness.

[28] The Institute offers Masters and Doctorate programs in Clinical Psychology.

[29] Gladys Sweeney, dean of the *Institute for the Psychological Sciences, Written testimony* (20 November 2002)

God's image. It also involves the formation of a generation of psychologists who understand the genuine
meaning of human freedom, based on the truth of who
we are in front of God.

God has blessed the apostolate . . . [30]

The Movement's charism—contemplation linked to action—stimulates lay people to take leadership in building up a
civilization of justice and love: going out to meet the most
urgent needs of the Church, and offering concrete responses.

Many Mexicans were left homeless after severe earthquakes hit Mexico City in 1985. Students of the Anáhuac University got together to construct CIDECO, the *Centro Integral
de Desarrollo Comunitario* ("Integral Center of Community
Development") in Lerma, Mexico, a whole neighborhood of
200 houses for 1,000 people, complete with social services.[31]
CIDECO-Anáhuac and Gente Nueva created four additional
clinics to serve the indigenous Mexican communities in the
rural zones of Acapulco, Lerma, Sierra Mazahua and Temascal-
cingo, attending 5,000 patients each month. When Hurricane
Paulina battered the coasts of Guerrero, Plácido Domingo, who
had helped with the first CIDECO project after the earthquakes
in Mexico City, again offered his generous assistance, and the
Anáhuac social foundation built CIDECO-Acapulco: a complex consisting of a health center and 450 houses.

Regnum Christi members put a new housing project—an
entire village—on its feet in Santiago Nonualco after earthquakes shook El Salvador in 2001.

The mass media constitute a vast, fertile field of apostо-
late. Their social and cultural influence is immense; immense,
too, is their evangelizing potential when placed at the service

---

[30] Gladys Sweeney (20 November 2002)
[31] The clinic averages 2,500 monthly consultations and some 36,000 people have
received medical attention since its inception. More than 16,000 children and
young people have benefited from the educational center.

of the Church. The Legion of Christ and the Regnum Christi movement have also started to work in the media: magazines, internet portals, publishing houses, movies, news outlets and Catholic radio and television programming for every kind of audience.

The Los Angeles-based Catholic multimedia center *Hombre Nuevo* produces radio and television programming to spread the Faith and strengthen human values. Its programs are currently transmitted on 14 radio stations in the United States and 30 in Central America and the Caribbean. Father Juan Rivas LC, *Hombre Nuevo*'s director, explains the purpose of his work:

> When you ring church bells, you expect a reaction from the people. You don't ring the bells so that people will say how nice they sound or how lovely they are. You ring the bells hoping that people will stand up and come to church. The objective of Hombre Nuevo is to have no passive "listeners" but rather an audience that becomes "radio-active."[32]
>
> Our program is a summons," Father Rivas continues.
>
> We want Catholics who have left the Church to come back, those who are already in the Church to increase their knowledge of the Faith, and those who already know the Faith to become apostles, ardently announcing the Good News.[33]

In Los Angeles alone, more than 10,000 people are "radio-active" in the *Hombre Nuevo* apostolate:

> Some people help with music, others with fundraising or economic activities, others organize missions, others promote Christian Life Groups, others go door-to-door

---

[32] Juan Rivas LC, *En la onda de Cristo* (www.regnumchristi.org, Spanish language edition, 29 April 2001)
[33] *ibid*

distributing the Catholic pamphlets that we also produce. Others help with advertisements or offer to read
personal letters on the radio.[34]

Nevertheless, it is not organizational efficiency that produces results for *Hombre Nuevo*. Father Rivas underlines that
they owe their success to the multimedia center's consecration
to the Blessed Virgin Mary and to the doctrinal fidelity of their
sound Catholic catechetical content.

Supporting bishops

Father Maciel keeps certain apostolic undertakings of the
Legion of Christ especially close to his heart. He plans them,
activates their growth and follows their development with particular passion and hope. They are projects that stem from his
love for the Church and his desire to serve her by serving her
shepherds: the Pope, bishops, and priests.

In 1985, Father Maciel supervised the creation of the
Centrum pro Educatoribus Seminariorum ("Center for Seminary
Formers")[35] to assist the world's bishops by organizing and promoting on-going formation activities for the formation personnel of their diocesan seminaries. Some years later, the Pope
expressed deep concern over the situation of seminaries in
many parts of the world. He asked for help, and Father Maciel
established a seminary in Rome under the Legionaries of
Christ's care, putting it at the disposal of bishops to offer diocesan seminarians an integral priestly formation.

This seminary, called the International Pontifical College
"Maria Mater Ecclesiae," began the 1991–1992 school year with
a group of 16 seminarians at Via Aurelia 677, on the premises
of the Legion's general directorate.[36] It would later move to
Castel di Guido on the outskirts of Rome, where it remained
until November 1999.

---

[34] Juan Rivas LC, *En la onda de Cristo* (www.regnumchristi.org, Spanish language
edition, 29 April 2001)
[35] By 2003, more than 22,000 seminarians the world over had benefited from the
formation program offered by this Center
[36] There were 2 from Ecuador, 4 from Brazil, and 10 from Mexico

When he perceived Maria Mater Ecclesiae's rapid growth, Marcial put the Legion of Christ's own Center for Higher Studies at the disposal of diocesan bishops. A large college with room for three hundred seminarians, it was still new, having only been inaugurated eight years earlier. This became the International College's definitive home. In January 2001 the seminarians numbered over 200; by 2001 there were more than 250 seminarians from 82 dioceses and 21 countries; it currently houses approximately 300 seminarians from some 25 countries. Seminarians from Armenia, the Czech Republic, Croatia, Poland and the Ukraine study alongside seminarians from other far-distant corners of the world. Over the past several years, Mater Ecclesiae has offered special support to the bishops of Eastern Europe so that their seminarians can come to study and prepare themselves in Rome, and then return to build up the seminaries in their own countries, many of which are still getting on their feet again after the ravages of communism. The majority of the seminarians at the International Pontifical College are enrolled in the Philosophy and Theology Faculties of the Pontifical Regina Apostolorum University.[37]

Bishop Jorge Ardila Serrano of Girardot, Colombia, has sent a number of seminarians from his diocese to prepare themselves in Maria Mater Ecclesiae. In a letter to the rector he wrote:

> I have to admit that I am 100% satisfied with the way they are responding to their vocation under your apt direction and guidance: those who will be finishing [their studies] this year, and those who will be continuing. I have been clear when telling this to my brother bishops as well. I have told the Holy Father. I said the same thing last May in various departments of the Holy See on the occasion of my Ad Limina visit to Rome. The

---

[37] In 1998 a group of 31 Brazilian bishops under the guidance of the President of their Episcopal Conference, Cardinal Lucas Moreira Neves, asked Father Maciel for assistance in preparing seminarians who could eventually become seminary formers in their own dioceses. The Legion's formation center in Arujá (Brazil) opened its doors to a group of diocesan seminarians in February 2000. It currently offers formation to over 100 Brazilian seminarians.

Holy Father, in concrete, encouraged me very explicitly to take advantage of such an excellent way of preparing formation personnel. Accept, therefore, dear Father Juan Manuel, these expressions of my most heartfelt gratitude for all you've done for the deacons who now leave your College, and for everything you will continue to do . . . [38]

The Holy Father acknowledged Father Maciel's efforts in founding the International Pontifical College "Maria Mater Ecclesiae" out of love for the Church in a letter of gratitude written to the founder on the occasion of his 50th anniversary of priestly ordination:

To Father Marcial Maciel Degollado
General Director of the Legionaries of Christ,

On the occasion of your Golden priestly anniversary, I spiritually unite myself to you on such a solemn celebration, giving full thanks to the heavenly Father from whom every perfect gift descends (cf. *Jam* 1:7) for this half-century of generous self-surrender to the service of the Church as a priest. Still young, you felt a strong call to the priesthood, welcomed it within your heart, and a short time later, in times that were quite tragic for Mexico, you founded the religious institute of the Legionaries of Christ and the Regnum Christi Movement, consecrated to establishing his Kingdom, a Kingdom of peace and justice, love and solidarity among all men and women. Now, looking back over fifty years, you can repeat with the Psalmist: "But I will sing of your might; I will sing aloud of your steadfast love in the morning. For you have been a fortress for me and a refuge in the day of my distress. O my strength, I will sing praises to you, for you, O God, are my fortress, the God who shows me steadfast love" (*Ps* 59:16–17).

---

[38] Jorge Ardila Serrano, Bishop of Girardot, *Letter to Father Juan Manuel Dueñas LC* (30 August 1996)

In the apostolic exhortation "Pastores Dabo Vobis" I wrote that "the internal principle, the force which animates and guides the spiritual life of the priest inasmuch as he is configured to Christ the head and shepherd, is pastoral charity, as a participation in Jesus Christ's own pastoral charity, a gift freely bestowed by the Holy Spirit and likewise a task and a call which demand a free and committed response on the part of the priest" (*Pastores Dabo Vobis*, 23). From the day of your priestly ordination, you have wanted to set Christ, the New Man who reveals the Father's infinite love to mankind in need of redemption, as the criterion, center, and model of your whole life and priestly work, and that of those who have followed you ever since 1941. They have found in you an approachable spiritual father and an effective guide in the passionate adventure of total self-donation to God in the priesthood. Moved by a fond love for the Church and profound pastoral charity, you have also created numerous apostolic works directed by Legionary of Christ priests and lay members of Regnum Christi, currently present in sixteen countries on five continents.

Among these endeavors there are educational institutions at the service of children and youth; an ample gamut of organizations to promote human and Christian values in the family; centers to form catechists and missionaries; and initiatives whose aim is the integral betterment of the most vulnerable social groups. The Pontifical Athenaeum Regina Apostolorum and the "Maria Mater Ecclesia" College in Rome are of particular importance vis-à-vis the challenge of the new evangelization. They are dedicated to preparing, together with their bishops, future formers of diocesan seminaries.

Inviting you to intone the canticle of the "Magnificat" united to Mary Most Holy—who has always accompanied your steps, from your infancy to this moment of your priestly anniversary—I wish to assure you, dear Father Maciel, that I impart upon you and all the members of the Legion of Christ and the Regnum Christi Movement a special Apostolic Blessing, with affection and benevolence.

Vatican, November 15, 1994.
Ioannes Paulus PP II[39]

Filial Love for the Church's Shepherds

Father Maciel writes a thematic letter to Regnum Christi members each year for the Solemnity of Christ the King. In 1996, as the Pope's priestly jubilee was drawing near, Father Maciel wrote about the Vicar of Christ. He invited Regnum Christi members to contemplate the Holy Father's stature as a witness to Christ: "a man who knows how to transmit the Faith without fear or hesitation."

> If we . . . want to reach the deepest root that can explain his life, we find that the Holy Father is a man who is sure of his Faith. For him, faith is not a fancy, a dream or the fantasy of an infantile spirit. For him, believing is not desisting in the use of reason so as to penetrate some irrational darkness. Nor is it abandoning oneself to the blindness of the mind. For him believing is meeting a living person, Jesus Christ, in a mysterious but no less real way.[40]

Marcial Maciel doesn't spin theories when he speaks about love: he, too, contemplates a person. His love is real, tangible, personal affection. When he speaks about Christ, Mary or the Pope, he talks about a one-on-one relationship with them. For Marcial, to be in love with someone and to forge a true friendship means identifying yourself with the one you love, wanting the best for them, and striving to imitate their

---

[39] John Paul II, *Letter to Father Marcial Maciel LC* (Vatican, 15 November 1994). Father Maciel celebrated the 50th anniversary of his priestly ordination on 26 November 1994.

[40] Marcial Maciel LC, *Letter to Regnum Christi members* (Termini, Italy, 19 August 1996)

goodness. It means becoming more like them—drawn by affection, by admiration, or, as it were, by a type of osmosis. It means living alongside them, even if only in a spiritual way. To love the Pope means being devoted to "this" Pope: because of who he is as Christ's Vicar and because of who he is as a person, with all of his virtues, aspirations and dreams, and all of his projects for the good of the Church. This is how Marcial works, and this is what he transmits to his followers.

In July 2001, Cardinal Giovanni Battista Re, Prefect of the Congregation for Bishops, spoke to the Legionaries at their Center for Higher Studies in Rome. "Thank you indeed for your *sensus ecclesiae*,[41] for being in union with the Holy Father, and for your desire to help bishops in any part of the world," he said. "Legionaries of Christ, a heart-felt thanks."[42]

Marcial and the Legionaries of Christ are moved by their love for the Pope and for the shepherds of the Church. So are lay members of Regnum Christi. Not all lay people can undertake apostolates that let them share first-hand in the many sorrows and joys of their bishops, or partake in his pastoral service to the diocese in a direct way. Arturo González, however, a 40-year old from Monterrey, has had the chance to do both.

Arturo moved to Chiapas, Mexico, in 1994, when he began his work as a full-time catechist. A program that the Legion of Christ began in 1989 out of their "School of the Faith" in Mexico, *Evangelizadores a Tiempo Completo* ("Full-time Evangelizers") has a wide radius of apostolic action, and aims at strengthening and supporting the local Church by providing lay people who dedicate themselves full-time to the work of evangelization under the direction of their parish priests and bishops. Arturo González explains:

> During the summer of 1994, a priest friend of mine invited me to start up something that—although I didn't

---

[41] *Sensus ecclesiae* could be rendered as "Church-sense": an affinity that makes it connatural to think and act according to the Church's heart and mind.
[42] Giovanni Battista Cardinal Re (6 July 2001)

know it at the time—would change my life (and my family's life) forever. When I got home, I spoke to my wife about it, hoping deep down inside that she would say that it was crazy, [or ask] "how could they invite a man with a family to dedicate himself full-time to evangelization?" . . . Her answer surprised me even more than the original invitation had. She simply said: "Yes." . . .

One the most marvelous things that has happened . . . has been, without a doubt, the opportunity to work so closely alongside a number of Mexico's bishops.

Sometimes it is in an informal way, serving them as a driver or helping to prepare their house to receive fellow bishops. Other times they extend a direct invitation to work at their side to carry out a given project in the diocese or for a commission of the Mexican Bishops' Conference. I have seen them work into the small hours of the morning to draw up certain documents. I have seen them work with various groups and commissions on a diocesan or regional level. I have seen them spend long moments in front of the Blessed Sacrament, perhaps entrusting their diocesan tasks to God, aware that the work entrusted to them surpasses their abilities.

I have seen their joy when meeting with their priests or with the diocese' pastoral ministers; or with simple people who are capable of discovering in the bishop someone who guides them with a sure hand, by example and word, to meet Jesus Christ. . . . I have been able to count on their friendship –I consider this a great gift. But the greatest thing of all is that I have been able to pray for them. I constantly entrust them to God so that the Lord will be their strength.[43]

The full-time catechists have local headquarters and centers in 48 dioceses, and serve their respective bishops in El Salvador, Guatamala, Mexico, and Venezuela.

---

[43] Arturo González Mogas helps to form full-time catechists. *Written testimony* (27 November 2003)

By December 2002 there were 900 "Evangelizers" at work in 547 parishes, helping priests to visit 5,358 rural communities. The full-time catechists, in turn, formed over 16,000 local catechists and nurtured almost 75 priestly or religious vocations. During 2002, full-time catechists visited some 65,500 homes and entered into contact with a million people. The number of full-time catechists has since grown to more than 1,000.

In the Heart of the Church

On 19 March 1998, the Holy Father paid a brief visit to the Legion of Christ's Center for Higher Studies in Rome.

The Legionary religious lined the entire driveway as the Pope's car arrived, and greeted him with applause. Father Maciel, Father Luis Garza Medina (the Legion's general vicar), and Father Álvaro Corcuera (rector of the Center for Higher Studies) awaited the Holy Father in the vestibule.

Before going into the chapel, the Pope stopped for a moment before a model of the building complex that would eventually house the new Center for Higher Studies and the future Pontifical Regina Apostolorum University. At the time, the buildings were still little more than bricks and blueprints.

"And this one?" asked the Pope, tapping the floor on which he was standing with his cane.

"Holy Father," said Father Maciel, "this will be the new campus of the International College Maria Mater Ecclesiae, the seminary to serve bishops who want to send their seminarians to receive formation in Rome."

The Pope was visibly pleased to hear it.

In the chapel, the Legionaries prayed with the Vicar of Christ. With one voice they recited their "Prayer for the Pope," a prayer they say together each day after receiving Holy Communion. As they were getting arranged for a group photo with the Pope at the front of the chapel, John Paul II murmured: *se ve, se siente* ["you can see it, you can hear it"].[44] The Pope joined

---

[44] The Legionaries of Christ and Regnum Christi members generally cheer the Pope in large international papal gatherings using an expression coined in

them in the dining room for lunch and a few musical pieces offered to him by the Legion's seminary band.

Two months after this cordial, family-like get-together, another ecclesial gathering took place in Rome. It was much larger, but the family spirit was no less intense. Under a bright, late-afternoon sun on 30 May 1998, Saint Peter's Square and Via della Conciliazione, the road that leads up to it, were bursting with Catholic faithful, awash in a sea of colored handkerchiefs.

The Pontifical Council for the Laity had organized an event with the Pope for Movements and other new ecclesial realities, whose origin and courage inspired the theme of the get-together: "Gift of the Spirit, hope for humanity." There gathering had three fundamental objectives: (1) to bear witness to their communion with the Vicar of Christ, the point of unity for a wide range of charisms in the Church, (2) to thank the Holy Spirit for what he had done and would continue to do in the lives of individuals, in the world, and in the Church through these new ecclesial entities, and (3) to renew, on the threshold of the third millennium, their own missionary commitment.

Four founders spoke: Kiko Argüello of the *Neocatechumenal Way* (who moments before the Pope's arrival had led the multitude in singing one of his most well-known compositions, entitled *Resucitó*), Chiara Lubich of Mary's Work, *Focolare*, Monsignor Luigi Giussani, founder of Comunione e Liberazione, and Jean Vanier, of the *L'Arche* communities and *Faith and Light.* Other founders were also present: Eduardo Bonnin (*Cursillos de Cristiandad*), Carmen Hernández (cofounder, with Kiko Argüello, of the Neocatechumenal Way), Andrea Riccardi (Community of St. Egidio), don Oreste Benzi (Community of John XXIII). Many other groups participated in the event, such as the Charismatic Renewal (with Charles Whitehead, President of the *International Charismatic Catholic Renewal Service*),

Mexico during Pope John Paul II's first visit: *¡se ve, se siente, el Papa está presente!* ["You can see it, you can hear it; the Pope is here!] On more than one occasion the Pope has responded with *¡se ve, se siente,* Regnum Christi *está presente!* or *Legionarios están presentes!* [Legionaries are here!].

the Christian Life Movement, the Emmanuel Community, Marriage Encounter and World-Wide Marriage Encounter. Father Maciel also took part, accompanied by thousands of Regnum Christi members.

Almost half a million "living stones" of the Church were united in prayer on the eve of Pentecost, men and women from every part of the world, awaiting the coming of the Holy Spirit as the apostles had in the Upper Room twenty centuries earlier. "You can see it, you can feel it . . . ": the Pope was present. He said:

> Today the Church rejoices, seeing fulfilled once again the words of the prophet Joel that we just heard: "I will pour out my Holy Spirit on every person . . . " (*Acts* 2:17). All of you present here are tangible proofs of this "effusion" of the Spirit. Each Movement differs from the rest, but all are united in the same communion and for the same mission.[45]

In a recent thematic letter, *Vocation to Love,* Father Maciel wrote:

> Many of you were present in Rome when, in May 1998, the Holy Father convoked all the Church Movements, and witnessed the family spirit and sense of charity that we lived because of this encounter. In the third millennium of the Church's history, the new communities raised up by the Spirit of Pentecost should do their best so that the Spirit of Love will characterize their entire lives and their relations with each other and all the members of the Church.
>
> As individuals and as a Movement, our response must always be the practice of Christian charity in thought, word and works, far removed from criticism, back-biting, division and most especially from calumny. In this way Regnum Christi, together with the other

---

[45] John Paul II, *Discourse to Movements and new ecclesial communities,* Pentecost Vigil (30 May 1998)

Movements and associations, will be able to help the Church with a new flowering of Christ's love, living it exactly as the Church's first-century Christians did. It awoke even the admiration of the pagans to the point that they exclaimed: "See how they love one another!"[46]

A Founder's Dream

Father Maciel had had a dream: to build a shrine to Mary before he died. In 1958, Our Lady of Guadalupe parish opened in Rome.

He treasured another dream as well: to build a medical clinic in Cotija de la Paz to look after the poor and sick and care for them just as his mother, grandmother, and great-grandmother had done. Many residents of Cotija and the surrounding ranches did not have enough money to buy themselves an aspirin, let alone pay for operations, doctors or more costly medicine.

This dream, too, became a reality. His older brother Francisco had given him a property in Cotija called "The Sawmill," and Marcial set it aside for the clinic. He sat down and with genuine enthusiasm drew up the list of things that would be needed: an operating room, an room for X-rays, a lab, consulting rooms, an office for psychological attention, lodgings for the resident doctors, a chapel, and so on. He studied the clinic's lay-out, and his experience allowed him to select the building materials to be used and to carefully revise the blueprints with the architects.

The Center is designed as a hub from which medical services can be provided to Cotija's 82 neighboring communities. The idea was not only to cure illnesses and ease pain, but also to prevent sickness and offer comprehensive health education. Specialists from the Anáhuac University's School of Medicine offer diagnosis via satellite using an advanced "TeleMedicine"

---

[46] Marcial Maciel LC, *Letter to the participants in the 3rd International Youth and Family Encounter* (Rome, 29 December 2000–6 January 2001). This Encounter was part of the 60th Anniversary celebrations of the founding of the Legion of Christ and Regnum Christi.

system. The center hopes to provide more than 10,000 consultations per year, offering primary health care and treating complex conditions that imply diverse specialties.

Archbishop Giuseppe Bertello, the Pope's nuncio in Mexico, went to Cotija de la Paz to bless the clinic and preside at its inauguration on 2 February 2003. The faith of Cotija was just as enthusiastic and fresh as ever: the town lavished attention on the Holy Father's representative. There were balloons, ribbons, and welcome-posters in the streets, confetti and streamers, cheers and applause. Many residents gave the nuncio gifts typical of the area: cheeses and bread, creamy sweets, paintings and embroidery. He was accompanied by Bishop Carlos Suárez Cázares of Zamora and Bishop Jorge Bernal LC of the Chetumal-Cancún prelature. The State of Michoacán, Mexico, and the *Counsel of Cooperation for Development* of the autonomous community of Valencia, Spain, were the center's chief financers, so Mrs. Pilar Mateo[47] and Lázaro Cárdenas Batel, the governor of the state of Michoacán, were also in attendance.

Marcial decided to name the new complex the "Divine Providence Health Center." At the insistence of several Legionaries, a subtitle was added. It is now called the "Divine Providence Health Center" . . . of *Maura Degollado de Maciel*.[48]

---

[47] Vice-President of the *Generalitat Valenciana* and director of the institute from Valencia, Spain, that financed the clinic's construction.

[48] Mamá Maurita cared for her husband Francisco Maciel with love and exemplary dedication until his death on 20 December 1950 after a long and painful illness. Surrounded by the affection of her children and grandchildren, Maurita continued to offer them an example of Christian love. On 16 July 1976, in a ceremony presided by her son Father Maciel, she consecrated her life to God in the Regnum Christi Movement. After a life of tending to the sick and needy, she died on 25 December 1977. The cause of her beatification is underway in Rome.

XV

"Cast Out in the Deep"

Eyes of Faith

When Jesus Christ the Redeemer took flesh, he began a revolution: the revolution of Christian love. The Incarnation of the Son of God and his New Commandment are—to paraphrase an expression of Father Maciel—the watershed of human history.

The Church has offered men and women of all ages the fruits of redemption, won by Christ on the Cross. In the Church, as in any institution composed of human beings, there have been failures, errors, and sin. But as an institution founded by the Son of God and constantly assisted by the Holy Spirit, the Church has borne untold fruits of goodness, holiness, and Christian love.

On 4 January 2001, Pope John Paul II addressed the following words to several thousand Legionaries of Christ, Regnum Christi members and friends present in St. Peter's Square for the Legion of Christ's 60th Anniversary:

> One of the important spiritual traits of your service in the Church is your commitment to the spirit of authentic evangelical charity. . . . May the Lord preserve you in this spirit, helping you to bear witness in every way to that Christian charity which St Paul so masterfully described in the famous hymn to love found in his First Letter to the Corinthians (1 Cor 13:4–8) . . .
>
> Know that the Pope is close to you and is praying for you, so that you will be faithful to your Christian vocation and your specific charism.[1]

---

[1] John Paul II, *Words addressed to the Legionaries of Christ* . . . (Vatican, 4 January 2001)

God's plan of salvation has continued to unfold amidst, and often despite, the ups and downs of human history. He inspires new works within the Church when he deems the time is right. He brings new projects into existence, but has chosen to do so through certain concrete individuals. With men like Benedict he brought forth the monastic orders. Bernard, the son of a knight, reformed the Cistercian order; Francis, a merchant's son, founded one of the Church's first mendicant orders; Theresa, a noblewoman, reformed the Carmelites. It is easy to follow the tracks of an Ignatius of Loyola or a Dominic, a Francis de Sales or a Vincent de Paul, a John Bosco or a Joseph Cottolengo, a man like John-Baptist de la Salle or a woman like Theresa of Calcutta.

One by one, God beckons to particular men and women and, after allowing them to experience his love in a special way, places in their hands a mission to help strengthen his Church. Thus the Holy Spirit continues to act so that Christ's birth, death and resurrection bring to bear on every new generation. He reveals new facets of Jesus Christ's personality to them, and extracts the treasure of grace from the Gospel's untold richness and from its message of love.

To 6,000 young people who had come to Rome to celebrate the 60th Anniversary of the foundation, Marcial said:

> As soon as I was old enough to understand, I marveled a great deal over the fact that Christ—being God—would have become a man to save me and all people from sin. To think about the mystery of the Incarnation of the Divine Word; to consider that our whole full-sized God would have assumed human nature to teach me the way to heaven, really made me realize just how much Christ loved me, and loved all men and women. . . . "To love" means giving. And Jesus Christ showed me that he loved me with genuine love, with immense love . . .
>
> He suffered an atrocious agony, a frightening death, to pay for my sins, to open the way to heaven, to lead me to his Father. He died on the cross in the midst of the

most terrible and distressing torments. He rose, after dying, to open the gates of heaven . . . That was when I felt the challenge of this love. "I have to love Christ just as he has loved me!" . . .

I wanted to give myself to Christ, to preaching his Kingdom, to taking part, at his side, in the saving of souls for as long as he chose to give me life, so that the greatest possible number of men and women on earth would know, love, and follow him, and so find the road to eternal life, and so join him in heaven after their death.[2]

The Legion of Christ and Regnum Christi are only comprehensible in this context, as one link in the chain of divine initiatives that constitutes the history of salvation, as another work in the Church raised up by the Holy Spirit to bring about God's plan for the good of all.

"The Movement is not a human invention," explained Father Maciel in 1989, "but the result of a divine initiative that, once again in the history of salvation, makes use of poor, limited instruments to bring about his saving work."[3]

In September and October 2001, the founder granted several interviews to speak about the history of the Congregation, and one day, as he contemplated the past, the following words escaped him. In their simplicity, they open a window onto the mystery of his inner, personal response to the calling to be a founder.

From the day God inspired me to establish the Legion, I believe the whole journey has been a steady course of events that unveil the mystery of God's plan. One day I'm told that I have to go to a certain place and I set out along the road. I walk. I travel along. I know that I am bringing the project about, and I continually discover . . .

---

[2] Marcial Maciel LC (1 January 2001)
[3] Marcial Maciel LC (21 May 1989)

all kinds of surprises: some pleasant, some extremely costly, some painless, some heartbreaking and some that cause happiness. It is a journey where you continually contemplate God's project. . . . That is how I think of it. Really, how great, how good, how marvelous God is! ...

I started the journey when I was 16, 15 going on 16. Now I'm 82. I still haven't finished the journey, and, as I said, it has been a truly marvelous road . . . a continual miracle of God's providence.[4]

On Father Maciel's 80th birthday, Cardinal Darío Castrillón contemplated Marcial's vocation and summarized the trajectory of the mission that began so many years earlier, on that chilly evening at the Tingüindín train station:

Your service is a priestly one that out of love, and for love alone, has succeeded in leaving the imprint of the priesthood on many young men. Inspired by your example and dedication, they have learned how to identify themselves with Christ, the Only, Eternal Priest, forming a large priestly family at the service for humanity.

This "service" has consumed your time . . . times of incomprehension and times of serenity, times of sadness and times of joy, times to sow and times to harvest.[5]

Eyes on the future

Looking at the development of the Legion and the Movement, Father Maciel speaks of "poor, limited instruments," and certainly there is no proportional relationship between the instruments God used and what was wrought through them. A young man with a sixth-grade education who set out from Cotija, a congregation that was founded in a borrowed basement, 32 adolescents who traveled to Spain in the hull of an

---

[4] Marcial Maciel LC (Fall 2001)
[5] Darío Cardinal Castrillón Hoyos, *Letter to Marcial Maciel LC* (March 7, 2000)

ocean-liner and ended up sleeping in a cowshed off the Cantabrian coast . . .

Time takes its toll of human suffering on everyone, and founders and their cofounders are not exempt from the limitations and imperfections of human nature. If every human life is sown with silent sacrifices, acts of virtue and gestures of love that are visible to God alone, there are also things that are visible to everyone. There was a sapling that has now grown into a tree: its fruits are tangible, and its continued growth can be surmised. The sap coursing through the branches of its spirituality is nothing but Christian charity. It is a tree that sinks its roots into the quick of the Gospel. It continues to develop energetically for the whole world to see, working within the Church to build up a civilization of justice and love.

Like all the men and women who have founded religious communities, when all is said and done Father Maciel believes in the transforming power of Love. Christian love—the essence of the Legion's charism and spirituality—is the aspiration that guides all of his efforts. It is the objective he proposes to Legionaries of Christ and Regnum Christi members: to bring this Gospel message and spirituality to the farthest reaches of the world, preaching Jesus Christ's love, helping men and women to discover it at work in their own lives, and urging them to live the virtue of charity in all of its depth and beauty.

In his review of Father Maciel's book-length interview, Bishop Antonio Santarsiero OSJ wrote:

> Vatican II stressed the call to holiness. In previous generations, it was assumed (it certainly was not Church teaching) that lay people fulfilled their religious obligation by going to Mass on Sundays and Holy Days, whereas the day-to-day task of growing in holiness fell to priests and religious. The Council, however, affirmed: "Thus it is evident to everyone, that all the faithful of Christ of whatever rank or status, are called to the fullness of the Christian life and to the perfection of charity" (*Lumen Gentium*, 40). . . .

When I finished reading the book, I thought to myself: perhaps the new millennium is the appointed "hour" spoken of by St. John the Evangelist (12:27), when the Church will harvest ripened wheat from the seeds that were so well-sown in the blood of the twentieth century's saints and martyrs.[6]

Together with the whole Church, Legionaries of Christ and Regnum Christi members share this desire. They find encouragement in the words that the Holy Father John Paul II chose to conclude his 2001 apostolic letter *Novo Millennio Ineunte,* under the heading *Duc in Altum,* "Put out into the deep." He says:

Let us go forward in hope!

A new millennium is opening before the Church like a vast ocean upon which we shall venture, relying on the help of Christ. The Son of God, who became incarnate two thousand years ago out of love for humanity, is at work even today: we need discerning eyes to see this and, above all, a generous heart to become the instruments of his work. . . .

Now, the Christ whom we have contemplated and loved bids us to set out once more on our journey: "Go therefore and make disciples of all nations, baptizing them in the name of the Father, and of the Son and of the Holy Spirit" (*Mt* 28:19). The missionary mandate accompanies us into the Third Millennium and urges us to share the enthusiasm of the very first Christians: we can count on the power of the same Spirit who was poured out at Pentecost and who impels us still today to start out anew, sustained by the hope "which does not disappoint" (*Rom* 5:5).[7]

---

[6] Antonio Santarsiero, OSJ, bishop of Huari, *Book Review* (March–April 2004)
[7] John Paul II, Apostolic Letter *Novo Millennio Ineunte* "At the Beginning of the New Millennium," Vatican, 6 January 2001, 58

Upon the waters of this immense ocean of the third millennium, the Lord's words resound with renewed vigor in the Legion of Christ and the Regnum Christi movement, just as they ring out in the entire Church: *Duc in altum!* "Put out into the deep, and lower your nets for a catch!"[8]

---

[8] cf. *Lk* 5:4

Father Marcial Maciel LC presides over a Thanksgiving Mass in the Basilica of St. Paul Outside the Walls in Rome on 4 January 1991, to mark the 50th anniversary of the Legion of Christ and the Regnum Christi Movement.

I don't know how many days, months or years
you still . . . have planned for me to follow this path.
I don't know where the end will be,
when we will finally meet face-to-face.
I don't know where the end will be,
when I will finally be able to embrace you
with the eternal embrace I have longed for
throughout the whole journey.
You know.
Let me be faithful to the end.
I cannot doubt your fidelity and love.
The task and road that you chose for me have been costly:
   undoubtedly.
But how beautiful they have also been: how full of wonder!

Marcial Maciel, 10 March 1998

Chronology

1920

March 10   Marcial Maciel Degollado is born in Cotija de la
                  Paz, Michoacán, México.

1926

Final months   The Cristero war breaks out in Cotija and other
                  states of the Mexican Republic.

1928

February 10   José Sánchez del Río is killed in Sahuayo,
                  Michoacán.

1929

Summer   Cristero war ends.

1935

May   Marcial discovers that God is calling him to be a
                  priest.

1936

January 3   Marcial leaves home for the seminary.

January 6   Marcial enters Veracruz' minor seminary in Mexico
                  City.

June 19   Marcial receives the call to be a founder in the
                  chapel of Veracruz' minor seminary (Atzcapotzalco
                  neighborhood, Mexico City).

1937

Feb.–March   On vacation, seminarian Marcial Maciel actively
                  participates in the definitive re-opening of the
                  churches in several towns and cities of Veracruz.

After vacation   Marcial is transferred to another house of the semi-
                  nary of Veracruz, in Mixcoac, Mexico City. First

attempt at founding with a group of fellow seminarians.

1938

June 6 — Rafael Guízar Valencia, bishop of Veracruz and Marcial's great-uncle, dies.

September 2 — Marcial enters Montezuma seminary (New Mexico, USA) to continue his studies. Second attempt at founding.

1940 — Marcial departs from Montezuma and begins studying in Mexico City under Francisco González Arias, bishop of Cuernavaca.

October — Cotija de la Paz: Marcial's third attempt. He founds the "Immaculate Conception Apostolic School" in his hometown with a group of adolescents who want to be priests.

1941

January 3 — Founding of the Missionary Apostolic School of the Missionaries of the Sacred Heart in the borrowed basement of a house at 39 Turín Street, Mexico City. The Legionaries of Christ consider this their foundation date.

Early May — The nascent congregation moves to a newly-bought house, their first, at 21 Victoria Street, Tlalpan, Mexico City.

1944 — Move to a new house at 12 Madero Street, Tlalpan, Mexico City.

November 26 — Marcial Maciel is ordained a priest in the old Our Lady of Guadalupe basilica on Tepeyac hill, Mexico City.

1946

March 25 — The novitiate is founded in a new house next door to the apostolic school, at 10 Madero Street.

June 12 — Rome: Father Maciel's first audience with Pope Pius XII.

September — The first group of future Legionaries goes to Spain to begin studies at the Pontifical University of Comillas.

1948

May 25	The Holy See grants canonical approval to the congregation with the *nihil obstat*.
June 13	Canonical establishment of the Missionaries of the Sacred Heart and the Virgin of Sorrows (Legionaries of Christ) by Alfonso Espino y Silva, bishop of Cuernavaca.

1950

Fall	Inauguration of the Legion of Christ's major seminary (*Colegio Mayor*) in Rome, currently the general directorate of the Legionaries of Christ and the Regnum Christi Movement.

1954

February	The Cumbres school, the Legion of Christ's first work of apostolate, opens in Mexico City.

1956

Fall	The "Great Blessing" begins.

1958

September 5	Inauguration of the building for the Legion of Christ's novitiate in Salamanca, Spain.
December 12	Our Lady of Guadalupe church inaugurated in Rome.

1959

February 6	The "Great Blessing" ends.
	Father Maciel begins to establish the apostolic movement called Regnum Christi.

1964	The Anáhuac University opens in Mexico City.

1965

February 6	The Legion is granted definitive approval by the Holy See upon receiving its "Decree of Praise" (*Decretum Laudis*).

1966

June	Opening of the first "Mano Amiga" school in Mexico City, offering subsidized education to those most in need.

1970	Pope Paul VI entrusts a vast mission territory to the Legionaries of Christ on the Mayan coast of Quintana Roo.
Final months	Beginning of ECYD, an international organization for Catholic adolescents.
1983	
June 29	Definitive approval of the Legion of Christ's Constitutions.
1990	First Spanish edition of Father Maciel's *Integral Formation of Catholic Priests*.
1991	
January 3	Pope John Paul II ordains 60 Legionaries of Christ in St. Peter's Basilica in the Vatican on the 50th Anniversary of their founding.
	The International Pontifical College *Maria Mater Ecclesiae* is founded to help bishops form their diocesan priests.
1993	
September 15	The Athenaeum *Regina Apostolorum* is established in Rome. Pope John Paul II would later grant it the title of "Pontifical."
2001	
January 4	In an audience in St. Peter's Square, Pope John Paul II welcomes the Legionaries of Christ and Regnum Christi members who had come to Rome to commemorate the 60th anniversary of the Legion's founding.

Source Notes and Bibliography

1. Oral Sources

Abbreviation: "GS-LC" General Secretariat of the Legion of Christ (Rome)
One-source multiple listings have been arranged in chronological order.

Aguilar Ramos, Guadalupe, Testimony (Orizaba, c. 1970), in Audio-cassette Collection: GS-LC (Rome) - no date
Cited in footnotes as: Guadalupe Aguilar (c. 1970)

Antoniutti, Ildebrando, Words addressed to the Legionaries of Christ (Rome: Center for Higher Studies of the Legionaries of Christ, 7 February 1965) in Audio-cassette Collection: GS-LC (Rome) - 1965
Cited in footnotes as: Ildebrando Cardinal Antoniutti (7 February 1965)

Arumí Blancafort, Rafael, Testimony (Rome: Center for Higher Studies of the Legionaries of Christ, 1 January 1998), in Audio-cassette Collection: GS-LC (Rome)
Cited in footnotes as: Rafael Arumí LC (1 January 1998)

Barragán Lagrange, Flora, Testimony (1986) in Audio-cassette Collection: GS-LC (Rome) - *unspecified date*
Cited in footnotes as: Flora Barragán (1986)

Bizzarri, Luigi (director), Documentary Video *Pio XII, il Principe di Dio*, ["Pius XII, The Prince of God"] transmitted by Italian Television RAI 3, in the series *La grande storia* (Friday 3 June 2003)
Cited in footnotes as: Luigi Bizzarri, Pio XII, il Principe di Dio

Cortés Ávila, Jorge, Testimony (Rome: Center for Higher Studies of the Legionaries of Christ, 31 December 1997), in Video-cassette Collection: GS-LC (Rome) - 1997
Cited in footnotes as: Jorge Cortés LC (31 December 1997)

Degollado Guízar, Rafael, Testimony - interviewed by Fr. Rafael Moreno LC (Mexico City, 21 November 2001), in Audio-cassette Collection: GS-LC (Rome) - 2001
Cited in footnotes as: Rafael Degollado (21 November 2001)

Hernández Jiménez, Clemente, Testimony - interviewed by Fr. Evaristo Sada Derby LC (Mariano Escobedo, Veracruz, 1997), in Video-cassette Collection: GS-LC (Rome) - 1997
Cited in footnotes as: Clemente Hernández (1997)

Iglesias Valdizán, Elías, Testimony - interviewed by Fr. Evaristo Sada Derby LC (Comillas, Santander, 26 September 2001), in Video-cassette Collection: GS-LC (Rome) - 2001
Cited in footnotes as: Elías Iglesias (26 September 2001)

John Paul II, Words addressed to the Legionaries of Christ - Rome community (Rome: Center for Higher Studies of the Legionaries of Christ, 27 January 1980) in Video-cassette Collection: GS-LC (Rome)
Cited in footnotes as: John Paul II (27 January 1980)

— Homily: *On the priestly ordination of 60 Legionaries of Christ on the 50th Anniversary of the Legion of Christ and Regnum Christi* (Vatican, St. Peter's Basilica, 3 January 1991) in Video-cassette Collection: GS-LC (Rome) - 1991
Cited in footnotes as: John Paul II (3 January 1991)

Lemus, Samuel Bernardo, Conference addressed to the Legionaries of Christ in period of formation (Rome: Center for Higher Studies of the Legionaries of Christ, 14 October 2003), in Video-cassette Collection: GS-LC (Rome)
Cited in footnotes as: Father Samuel Lemus (14 October 2003)

— Testimony - interviewed by Ángeles Conde (Rome: Center for Higher Studies of the Legionaries of Christ, 17 October 2003), in Video-cassette Collection: GS-LC (Rome) - 2003
Cited in footnotes as: Father Samuel Lemus (17 October 2003)

López García, Gregorio, Testimony (Rome: Center for Higher Studies of the Legionaries of Christ, 31 December 1997), in Video-cassette Collection: GS-LC (Rome) - 1997
Cited in footnotes as: Gregorio López LC (31 December 1997)

— Question and Answer Session: consecrated women of *Regnum Christi* (Monterrey, Nuevo León: formation and study center *Domus Mariae de Las Encinas*, January 2003), in Video-cassette Collection: *Domus Mariae de las Encinas* center (Monterrey).
Cited in footnotes as: Gregorio López LC (January 2003)

Maciel Degollado, Marcial, Conference addressed to Legionary of Christ novices (Dublin: Novitiate of the Legionaries of Christ, 3 March 1965), in Audio-cassette Collection: GS-LC (Rome) - 1965
Cited in footnotes as: Marcial Maciel LC (3 March 1965)

— Conference on the *Decretum Laudis* addressed to the Legionaries of Christ - Rome community (Rome: Center for Higher Studies of the Legionaries of Christ, 1966) in Audio-cassette Collection: GS-LC (Rome) - 1966
Cited in footnotes as: Marcial Maciel LC (1966)

— Conference addressed to a group of Legionaries of Christ (Monticchio, Naples Italy, between July and September 1971), in Audio-cassette Collection: GS-LC (Rome) - 1971
Cited in footnotes as: Marcial Maciel LC (Summer 1971)

— Narrative of selected foundation experiences (Rome: Center for Higher Studies of the Legionaries of Christ, 1980s), in Audio-cassette Collection: GS-LC (Rome) – no date (1980s).
Cited in footnotes as: Marcial Maciel LC (1980s)

— Question and Answer Session: Legionary of Christ novices (Salamanca, Spain: Novitiate of the Legionaries of Christ, 1981), in Audio-cassette Collection: GS-LC (Rome) - 1981
Cited in footnotes as: Marcial Maciel LC (1981)

— Conference addressed to a group of Legionaries of Christ (Cotija de la Paz, Michoacán, September 1986), in Audio-cassette Collection: GS-LC (Rome) - 1986
Cited in footnotes as: Marcial Maciel LC (September 1986)

— Conference addressed to a group of Legionaries of Christ (Cotija de la Paz, Michoacán, 13 September 1986), in Audio-cassette Collection: GS-LC (Rome) - 1986
Cited in footnotes as: Marcial Maciel LC (13 September 1986)

— Conference addressed to the Legionaries of Christ: Rome community (Rome: Center for Higher Studies of the Legionaries of Christ, 21 May 1989, Solemnity of the Blessed Trinity) in Video-cassette Collection: GS-LC (Rome) - 1989
Cited in footnotes as: Marcial Maciel LC (21 May 1989)

— Words addressed to Legionaries of Christ and Regnum Christi members and friends: closing event of the Legion of Christ's 50th Anniversary (Vatican: Paul VI Audience Hall, 4 January 1991) in Audio-cassette Collection: GS-LC (Rome) - 1991
Cited in footnotes as: Marcial Maciel LC (4 January 1991)

— Conference on the founding (Rome: Center for Higher Studies of the Legionaries of Christ, January 1992), in Video-cassette Collection: GS-LC (Rome) - 1992
Cited in footnotes as: Marcial Maciel LC (January 1992)

— Marcial Maciel, Homily (Rome: Center for Higher Studies of the Legionaries of Christ, 18 December 1992) in Video-cassette Collection: GS-LC (Rome) - 1992
Cited in footnotes as: Marcial Maciel LC (18 December 1992)

— Conference addressed to Legionary of Christ novices (Cheshire, Connecticut, 10 March 1993), in Audio-cassette Collection: GS-LC (Rome) - 1993
Cited in footnotes as: Marcial Maciel LC (10 March 1993)

— Conference addressed to consecrated women of *Regnum Christi* (Rome: Residence of the Assistant to the General Director, 11 February 1996), in Audio-cassette Collection: GS-LC (Rome) - 1996
Cited in footnotes as: Marcial Maciel LC (11 February 1996)

— Testimony (Rome: Center for Higher Studies of the Legionaries of Christ, 29 December 1997), in Video-cassette Collection: GS-LC (Rome) - 1997
Cited in footnotes as: Marcial Maciel LC (29 December 1997)

— Testimony (Rome: Center for Higher Studies of the Legionaries of Christ, 1 January 1998), in Video-cassette Collection: GS-LC (Rome) - 1998
Cited in footnotes as: Marcial Maciel LC (1 January 1998)

— Words of gratitude on the occasion of his birthday addressed to the Legionaries of Christ: Rome community (Rome: Center for Higher Studies of the Legionaries of Christ, 10 March 1998), in Audio-cassette Collection: GS-LC (Rome) - 1998
Cited in footnotes as: Marcial Maciel LC (10 March 1998)

— Testimony - interviewed by Fr. Evaristo Sada Derby LC (Cotija de la Paz, Michoacán, 1999), in Video-cassette Collection: GS-LC (Rome) - 1999.
Cited in footnotes as: Marcial Maciel LC (1999)

— Testimony - interviewed by Fr. Evaristo Sada Derby LC (Cotija de la Paz, Michoacán, 7 October 1999), in Audio-cassette Collection: GS-LC (Rome) - 1999
Cited in footnotes as: Marcial Maciel LC (7 October 1999)

— Testimony - interviewed by Fr. Evaristo Sada Derby LC (Cotija de la Paz, Michoacán 9 October 1999), in Audio-cassette Collection: GS-LC (Rome) - 1999
Cited in footnotes as: Marcial Maciel LC (9 October 1999)

— Testimony - interviewed by Fr. Evaristo Sada Derby LC   (Cotija de la Paz, Michoacán, 11 October 1999), in Audio-cassette Collection: GS-LC (Rome) - 1999
Cited in footnotes as: Marcial Maciel LC (11 October 1999)

— Words spoken at the Regnum Christi Youth Encounter: 60th Anniversary of the Legion of Christ and Regnum Christi (Rome 1 January 2001) in Video-cassette Collection: GS-LC (Rome) - 2001
Cited in footnotes as: Marcial Maciel LC (1 January 2001)

— Question and Answer Session: Legionary religious in period of formation (Termini, Naples Italy, 10 August 2001), in Audio-cassette Collection: GS-LC (Rome) - 2001
Cited in footnotes as: Marcial Maciel LC (10 August 2001)

— Conversation with a group of Legionaries of Christ (Termini, Naples Italy, 25 August 2001), in Audio-cassette Collection: GS-LC (Rome) - 2001
Cited in footnotes as: Marcial Maciel LC (25 August 2001)

— Testimony - interviewed by Fr. Evaristo Sada Derby LC (Comillas, Santander, September - October 2001), in Video-cassette Collection: GS-LC (Rome) - 2001
Cited in footnotes as: Marcial Maciel LC (Fall 2001)

— Testimony - interviewed by Fr. Evaristo Sada Derby LC (Comillas, Santander, 22 September 2001), in Video-cassette Collection: GS-LC (Rome) - 2001
Cited in footnotes as: Marcial Maciel LC (22 September 2001)

— Testimony - interviewed by Fr. Evaristo Sada Derby LC (Comillas, Santander, 23 September 2001), in Video-cassette Collection: GS-LC (Rome) - 2001
Cited in footnotes as: Marcial Maciel LC (23 September 2001)

— Testimony - interviewed by Fr. Evaristo Sada Derby LC (Comillas, Santander, 25 September 2001), in Video-cassette Collection: GS-LC (Rome) - 2001
Cited in footnotes as: Marcial Maciel LC (25 September 2001)

— Conference addressed to the Legionaries of Christ (Rome, 11 February 2002), in Video-cassette Collection: GS-LC (Rome) - 2002
Cited in footnotes as: Marcial Maciel LC (11 February 2002)

— Testimony - interviewed by Ángeles Conde (Termini, Naples Italy, 4 September 2002), in Video-cassette Collection: GS-LC (Rome) - 2002
Cited in footnotes as: Marcial Maciel LC (4 September 2002)

— Testimony - interviewed by Ángeles Conde (Rome: Center for Higher Studies of the Legionaries of Christ, 6 September 2002), in Video-cassette Collection: GS-LC (Rome) - 2002
Cited in footnotes as: Marcial Maciel LC (6 September 2002)

— Testimony - interviewed by Ángeles Conde (Rome: Center for Higher Studies of the Legionaries of Christ, 19 September 2002), in Video-cassette Collection: GS-LC (Rome) - 2002
Cited in footnotes as: Marcial Maciel LC (19 September 2002)

— Conversation with a group of Legionaries of Christ (Rome: General Directorate of the Legionaries of Christ, Rome, 24 September 2002) Personal notes of a Legionary religious: Archive of the General Secretariat of the Legionaries of Christ
Cited in footnotes as: Marcial Maciel LC (24 September 2002)

— Testimony - interviewed by Ángeles Conde (Rome: General Directorate of the Legionaries of Christ, 1 October 2002), in Video-cassette Collection: GS-LC (Rome) - 2002
Cited in footnotes as: Marcial Maciel LC (1 October 2002)

— Conversation with consecrated women of *Regnum Christi* in Rome (Rome: Residence of the Assistant to the General Director, 8 October 2002) in Audio-cassette Collection: Residence of the Assistant to the General Director
Cited in footnotes as: Marcial Maciel LC (8 October 2002)

— Testimony - interviewed by Ángeles Conde (Rome: General Directorate of the Legionaries of Christ, 28 November 2002), in Video-cassette Collection: GS-LC (Rome) - 2002
Cited in footnotes as: Marcial Maciel LC (28 November 2002)

— Testimony - interviewed by Ángeles Conde (Rome: General Directorate of the Legionaries of Christ, 11 January 2004), in Video-cassette Collection: GS-LC (Rome) - 2004
Cited in footnotes as: Marcial Maciel LC (11 January 2004)

Maciel Degollado, Maura, Testimony - interviewed by Fr. Evaristo Sada Derby LC (Rome: General Directorate of the Legionaries of Christ, 30 August 2001), in Audio-cassette Collection: GS-LC (Rome) - 2001
Cited in footnotes as: Maura Maciel (30 August 2001)

— Testimony - interviewed by Fr. Evaristo Sada Derby LC (Rome: General Directorate of the Legionaries of Christ, 1 September 2001), in Audio-cassette Collection: GS-LC (Rome) - 2001
Cited in footnotes as: Maura Maciel (1 September 2001)

Maciel Degollado, Olivia, Testimony - interviewed by David Murray (Guadalajara, Jal., 27 August 2001), in Audio-cassette Collection: GS-LC (Rome) - 2001
Cited in footnotes as: Olivia Maciel (27 August 2001)

Matteoli, Altero, Inaugural Discourse, *Masters of Environmental Sciences* (Rome: Pontifical University Regina Apostolorum, 15 November 2002) in Audio-cassette Collection: Pontifical University Regina Apostolorum.
Cited in footnotes as: Altero Matteoli (15 November 2002)

Mora Reyes, Carlos, Testimony (Rome: Center for Higher Studies of the Legionaries of Christ, 1 January 1998) in Video-cassette Collection: GS-LC (Rome) - 1998
Cited in footnotes as: Carlos Mora LC (1 January 1998)

Pablo VI, Words to newly ordained Legionary priests (Vatican, 2 January 1974) in Audio-cassette Collection: GS-LC (Rome)
Cited in footnotes as: Paul VI (2 January 1974)

Re, Giovanni Battista, Words of greeting to the Legionaries of Christ (Rome: Center for Higher Studies of the Legionaries of Christ, 6 July 2001), in Audio-cassette Collection: Center for Higher Studies of the Legionaries of Christ (Rome)
Cited in footnotes as: Giovanni Battista Cardinal Re (6 July 2001)

Rodríguez Hernández, José Refugio, Testimony - interviewed by Fr. Luis Laureán Cervantes LC (Fortín de las Flores, Veracruz, Mexico, 14 August 2003) in Video-cassette Collection: GS-LC (Rome) - 2003
Cited in footnotes as: Father José Refugio Rodríguez (14 August 2003)

Sada Derby, Evaristo, Conference addressed to consecrated women of *Regnum Christi* (Monterrey, Nuevo León: formation and study center *Domus Mariae de Las Encinas*, 19 January 1997), in Video-cassette Collection: *Domus Mariae de las Encinas* center (Monterrey)
Cited in footnotes as: Evaristo Sada LC (19 January 1997)

— Testimony - interviewed by Ángeles Conde (Rome: Residence of the Assistant to the General Director, 21 January 2002)
Cited in footnotes as: Evaristo Sada LC (21 January 2002)

Silva, Rosa, Testimony - interviewed by Fr. Javier García LC (Mexico City, 17 July 1982), in Audio-cassette Collection: GS-LC (Rome) - 1982
Cited in footnotes as: Rosa Silva (17 July 1982)

Tena Rojas, Javier, Testimony (Rome: Center for Higher Studies of the Legionaries of Christ, 29 December 1997), in Video-cassette Collection: GS-LC (Rome) - 1997
Cited in footnotes as: Javier Tena LC (29 December 1997)

Veltroni, Walter, Words of greeting to the academia community of the Pontifical University Regina Apostolorum (Rome: Pontifical University Regina Apostolorum, 9 December 2002) in Audio-cassette Collection: Pontifical University Regina Apostolorum
Cited in footnotes as: Walter Veltroni (9 December 2002)

2. Written Sources

2.1 Unpublished Documents

Abbreviation: GS-LC – General Secretariat of the Legion of Christ (Rome)

Multiple listings of the same author have been arranged in chronological order.

Contents of documents with personal testimonies are published with the express consent of their authors.

—, *Account of Leonor Sánchez López' Death*, in Civil Registry of Orizaba Township, Deaths, Book 412, 1937, volume I, section 133, pp. 71-72

—, *Diary of the Missionary Apostolic School of the Sacred Heart of Jesus* (1941), Archive: GS-LC (Rome)

—, *Diary of the Juniorate in Cóbreces* (1947-1951), Archive: GS-LC (Rome)

—, *Letter of 1162 residents of Jesús María, Veracruz, to the President of the Republic* (Jesús María, Veracruz, 31 December 1936), in General National Archive (Mexico City), Presidents, Documental Group LC, Folder 916, Exp. 547.4/43

Ardila Serrano, Jorge, *Letter to Father Juan Manuel Dueñas LC* (Girardot, Colombia, 30 August 1996), in possession of recipient

Baeza, Francisco Javier, *Letter to Father Goyeneche* (Comillas, Santander, 2 February 1948), Archive: GS-LC (Rome)

Bernal, Jorge, *Written Testimony* (Chetumal, Quintana Roo, no date), Archive: GS-LC (Rome)

Castrillón Hoyos, Darío, *Letter to Marcial Maciel* (Vatican, 7 March 2000), Archive: GS-LC (Rome)

Chomnycky, Paul, *Letter to Father Álvaro Corcuera LC* (28 September 2002), in possession of recipient

Condorelli, Luigi (5 October 1956), Medical certificate: Personal documents of Fr. Marcial Maciel LC

Corcuera, Álvaro, *Written Testimony* (Rome, 10 April 2000), Archive: GS-LC (Rome)

Corripio Ahumada, Ernesto, *Handwritten note* (Rome, 9 December 1962), in *Guest Book*, General Directorate of the Legionaries of Christ (Rome)

Del Valle, José, *Letter to Father Marcial Maciel LC* (Villahermosa, Tabasco, 25 February 1965), Archive: GS-LC (Rome)

de Rebat, Virginia, Lucía Fernández Gertz and another unidentified signer, *Letter to the President of the Republic* (Mexico City, 2 March 1937), in General National Archive (Mexico City), Presidents, Documental Group LC, Folder 915, Exp. 547.4/43, 1 sheet

Di Meglio, Giuseppe, *Letter to Cardinal Luigi Lavitrano* (Madrid, 8 February 1948), Archive: GS-LC (Rome)

— *Letter to Mr. Salvador Sada Gómez* (Vatican, 22 February 1959), Copy, Archive: GS-LC (Rome)

Espino y Silva, Alfonso, *Letter to the Sacred Congregation for Religious* (Cuernavaca, Mexico, 27 February 1948), Archive: GS-LC (Rome)

— *Decree of the Canonical Establishment of the congregation of the Missionaries of the Sacred Heart and the Virgin of Sorrows* (Cuernavaca, 12 June 1948), Archive: GS-LC (Rome)

— *Letter to Father* Marcial Maciel LC (Monterrey, Nuevo León, 8 March 1965), Archive: GS-LC (Rome)

Fernández, Cristóforo, *Written Testimony* (Rome, 9 January 2002), Archive: GS-LC (Rome)

Foys DD, Roger J., *Letter to Father Álvaro Corcuera LC* (27 September 2002), in possession of recipient

Galas Arce, Santiago and Edné, *Message to Father Marcial Maciel LC on the occasion of the* Decretum Laudis (Mexico City, 1965), Transcription, Archive: GS-LC (Rome).

Galas Arce, Santiago and Luis Barroso, *Letter to Giuseppe Cardinal Pizzardo* (Mexico City, 14 July 1957), Archive: GS-LC (Rome)

Galleazzi-Lisi, Riccardo (no date, [October 1956]), Medical certificate: Personal documents of Fr. Marcial Maciel LC

Galrão Leite de Almeida, Marco Eugenio, *Letter to Father Álvaro Corcuera LC* (2 October 2003), in possession of recipient

Gambini, Enrico, Medical certificate (Rome: *Villa Linda* clinic, 10 October 1956): Personal documents of Fr. Marcial Maciel LC

García, Javier, *Interview with Soledad Maldonado* (Salamanca: Novitiate of the Legionaries of Christ, 2 August 1965), transcription, Archive: GS-LC (Rome)

— *Interview with Father Antonio Maldonado and his sister Esther* (Salamanca: Novitiate of the Legionaries of Christ, 25 August 1965), transcription, Archive: GS-LC (Rome)

González Mogas, Arturo, *Written Testimony* (27 November 2003), Archive: GS-LC (Rome).

Guízar Valencia, Rafael, *Letter to Father José María Flores* (Tacuba, Mexico City, 8 February 1937), transcribed in *Proceso de Escritos - del Proceso de beatificación y canonización del S. D. Rafael Guízar Valencia*, (original type-written), I, pp. 128-129

Guízar Valencia, Rafael; Nicolás Corona; Jesús Villarreal y Fierro; Francisco Miranda and José Pérez, *Letter of the Bishops of Veracruz, Papantla and Tehuacán and the representatives of 72 Catholic commissions of the State of Veracruz to the President of the Republic, General D. Lázaro Cárdenas* (Mexico City, 6 March 1937), in General National Archive (Mexico City), Presidents, Documental Group LC, Archive 915, Exp. 547.4/43, 1 page.

Huerga, Álvaro, Book Review: *Integral Formation of Catholic Priests* by Marcial Maciel LC (1990), Archive: GS-LC (Rome)

Izquierdo, Gustavo, *Written Testimony* (no date), Archive: GS-LC (Rome)

John Paul II, *Letter to Father Marcial Maciel LC, founder and general director of the Legionaries of Christ, on occasion of his 50th Anniversary of priestly ordination* (Vatican, 15 November 1994), Archive: GS-LC (Rome)

— *Words addressed to the Legionaries of Christ and members of Regnum Christi*, Audience on the occasion of the 60th Anniversary of the Legion of Christ and Regnum Christi (Vatican: St. Peter's Square, 4 January 2001)

— *Letter to the Most Reverend Father Marcial Maciel Degollado, general director of the Congregation of the Legionaries of Christ* (Vatican, 2 March 2002), Archive: GS-LC (Rome)

Lehonor Arroyo, Ignacio, *Letter to Father Marcial Maciel LC* (Tuxpan, Veracruz, 17 March 1965), Archive: GS-LC (Rome)

Maciel, Marcial*

— *Annotations regarding the years 1939-1940*: Personal documents of Fr. Marcial Maciel LC

— *Telegram* (Rome, 25 May 1948), Archive: GS-LC (Rome)

— *Words of Farewell to the Rome community* (Rome: Center for Higher Studies of the Legionaries of Christ, 3 October 1956), from the personal notes of one of the Legionary religious present, Archive: GS-LC (Rome)

— *Conversation with a group of Legionaries of Christ* (Rome: General Directorate of the Legionaries of Christ, 24 September 2002), from the personal notes of one of the Legionary religious present, Archive: GS-LC (Rome)

Letter to Ángeles Cónde (Rome, 17 October 2003)

*Letters not listed here: "Letters of the Founder", Archive: GS-LC (Rome)

Marcozzi, Vittorio, Book Review: *Integral Formation of Catholic Priests* by Marcial Maciel LC (1990), Archive: GS-LC (Rome)

Martín Artajo, Alberto, *Letter to Father Marcial Maciel LC* (Madrid, 9 March 1965), Archive: GS-LC (Rome)

Martín Del Campo, Manuel, *Letter to Father Marcial Maciel LC* (León, Mexico, 26 February 1965), Archive: GS-LC (Rome)

Martínez Somalo, Eduardo, *Decree,* Congregation for Institutes of Consecrated Life and Societies of Apostolic Life (Prot. n. R. 111- 2/96), (Vatican City, 27 July 1996), Archive: GS-LC (Rome)

Micara, Clemente, *Decree of the Vicariate of Rome* (Rome, 17 October 1952), Copy, Archive: GS-LC (Rome)

— *Decree of the Vicariate of Rome* (Rome, 6 February 1959), Archive: GS-LC (Rome)

— *Letter to Father Marcial Maciel LC* (Rome, 11 February 1965), Archive: GS-LC (Rome)

Oñate, Ángel M., *Report to his Excellency Francisco González Arias, Bishop of Cuernavaca* (Mexico City, 8 October 1945), Archive: GS-LC (Rome)

Palma, Víctor Hugo, *Letter to Father Álvaro Corcuera LC* (25 September 2002), in possession of recipient

Pasetto, Luca Hermenegildo, *Letter to Bishop Francisco González Arias* (Vatican, 2 September 1946), Archive: GS-LC (Rome)

Pérez-Gil, Manuel, *Testimony* (Mexico City: Student's Center, Female Branch of Regnum Christi, 25 April 1990), in annotations from the *Diary of the Student's Center, 1988-1990*, Mexico City: Student's Center Archive

Pérez Teuffer, Alejandro and Teresa, *Letter to Father Evaristo Sada LC* (Mexico, 3 January 2003), in possession of recipient

Pironio, Eduardo, *Decree of the Definitive Approval of the Constitutions of the Legionaries of Christ* (Vatican, 29 June 1983), Archive: GS-LC (Rome)

Porras, Francisco, *Letter to Father Marcial Maciel LC* (30 January 1995), Archive: GS-LC (Rome).

Quintero Arce, Carlos, *Letter to Father Evaristo Sada LC* (Hermosillo, Sonora, 27 November 2003), Archive: GS-LC (Rome)

Raimondi, Luigi, *Letter to Polidoro Van Vlierberghe* (Mexico City, 17 September 1957), Copy, Archive: GS-LC (Rome)

Rodrigo, Lucio, *Report for Monsignor Luca Hermenegildo Pasetto* (Comillas, Santander, 2 February 1948), Archive: GS-LC (Rome)

Rodríguez Magro, Amadeo, *Letter to Father Álvaro Corcuera LC* (1 November 2003), in possession of recipient

Ruíz, Samuel, *Handwritten note* (Rome, 8 December 1962), in *Guest Book,* General Directorate of the Legionaries of Christ (Rome)

Sacred Congregation for Religious, *Resolution N.5458-52* (Vatican: 23 December 1952), Copy, Archive: GS-LC (Rome)

Sacred Congregation for Institutes of Consecrated Life and Societies of Apostolic Life, *Decree,* Prot. n. R. 111- 2/96 (Vatican, 27 July 1996), Archive: GS-LC (Rome)

Soto, Gabriel, *Written Testimony* (Zacatecas, Mexico, 17 January 2004), Archive: GS-LC (Rome)

Sweeney, Gladys, *Written Testimony* (Washington DC, 20 November 2002), Archive: GS-LC (Rome)

Tena, Javier, *Written Testimony* (Rome, 3 January 2004), Archive: GS-LC (Rome)

Torres Villanueva, Alfredo, Conference (Salamanca: Novitiate and Juniorate of the Legionaries of Christ,15 November 1989), transcription of excerpts, Archive: GS-LC (Rome)

Valeri, Valerio, *Letter naming Visitator Alfredo Bontempi* (Vatican, 10 July 1957), Copy, Archive: GS-LC (Rome)

Villanueva, Ignacio, *Letter to Father* Marcial Maciel LC (3 January 1996), Archive: GS-LC (Rome)

van Vlierberghe, Polidoro, *Letter to the apostolic delegate in Mexico, Luigi Raimondi* (1958), Archive: GS-LC (Rome)

— *Letter to Father Marcial Maciel LC* (Illapel, 16 February 1965), Archive: GS-LC (Rome)

Wright, John Joseph, *Handwritten note* (Rome, 6 February 1970), in *Guest Book,* General Directorate of the Legionaries of Christ (Rome)

2.2 Published Works

—, "Los Sucesos" Orizaba Newspaper (Orizaba, 12 February 1937), Orizaba Township Historical Archive, Orizaba, Veracruz

—, *ibid*, (Orizaba, 24 February 1937), Orizaba Township Historical Archive, Orizaba, Veracruz

Clement, Marcel, *Un espérance pour l'évangélisation*, in "L'homme nouveau" (20 January 1991)

Colina, Jesús, *Christ is My Life: Interview with the founder of the Legionaries of Christ and the Regnum Christi Movement*, Manchester (NH): Sophia Institute Press, 2003

Degollado Guízar, Jesús, *Memorias*, Mexico: Jus, 1957

— *Proclamation* (1929), in Alfonso Alcalá Alvarado (coord.), *Historia general de la Iglesia en América Latina*. V. Mexico, Mexico: Paulinas, 1984, p. 333

— *Report given to the vice-president of the National Religious Liberty Defense League, Miguel Palomar y Vizcarra, on 21 November 1953*, in Antonio Rius Facius, *Méjico cristero*, Mexico: Patria, 1966, pp. 390-391

Maciel, Marcial, *Integral Formation of Catholic Priests*, North Haven: Circle Press, 1998

— *Oraciones de corazón a Corazón*, Mexico: Contenidos de formación integral, 2001

—*Salterio de mis días*, Rome: Ediciones CES, 1991

Mondragón J., *Album gráfico-histórico de los sucesos del 7 February 1937 en la ciudad de Orizaba, Veracruz*, Orizaba: J. P. Talavera, no date

Neuhaus, Richard John, *Feathers of scandal*, in "First Things", March 2002

Paul VI, Discourse to open the 4th session of Vatican II, *Credidimus caritati – Caritas Christi urget nos* (September 14, 1965), in *Insegnamenti di Paolo VI*, vol. 3 (1965), Vatican City, 1966

Promoters of the Cause for Canonization, Informative Bulletin *El mártir de Sahuayo* (Sahuayo, Michoacán, June 1997): Knights of Colombus, Council 4637, Sahuayo, Michoacán, Mexico

Rivas, Juan, En la onda de Cristo (29 April 2001), Regnum Christi webpage (www.regnumchristi.org), Spanish edition

Santarsiero, Antonio, Book Review: *Mi vida es Cristo* (Jesús Colina), in "Sacerdos," Italian edition, March-April 2004

Photographs: Credits

All photographs published in this book kindly provided by the photographic archive of the Legion of Christ (Rome), with the exception of:

p. 36, top: *Reynaldo Degollado* Photo Archive (Cotija de la Paz, Michoacán); Antonio Degollado: 1929

p. 36, bottom: *Alfonso Torres Vargas* Photo Archive (Zamora, Michoacán), property of Gonzalo Torres Ochoa; Alfonso Torres: 1912

p. 38, top: cf. Mondragón J., *Album gráfico-histórico de los sucesos del 7 de febrero de 1937 en la ciudad de Orizaba, Veracruz*, Orizaba: J.P. Talavera, no date

p. 82, bottom: *S. Gómez Tagle* Photo Archive (Mexico City): 1945

p. 132, bottom: *J. Jesús Jiménez* Photo Archive (Mexico City): 1950

p. 133, top: *Sciamanna* Photo Archive (Rome): 1950

p. 133, bottom: *Felici* Photo Archive (Rome): 1950

p. 134, top: *Felici* Photo Archive (Rome): early 1950s

p. 134, bottom: *Ysunza Nieto* Photo Archive (Mexico City): 1954

p. 135, top: *Olivieri* Photo Archive (Rome): 1955

p. 175, top: *Felici* Photo Archive (Rome): 1969

p. 263, top: *L'Osservatore Romano* Photo Archive (Rome): 1991

p. 264, top: *L'Osservatore Romano* Photo Archive (Rome): 1997

Supplementary Bibliography

—, *Constitución Política de los Estados Unidos Mexicanos* (Querétaro, 31 January 1917)

Aguilar Muñoz, Carlos, *Un capítulo de la historia de Orizaba: Apertura de templos*, Mexico: - 1952

Alcalá Alvarado, Alfonso, (coord.) *Historia general de la Iglesia en América Latina. V. Mexico*, Mexico: Paulinas, 1984

Barradas, Celestino, *Historia de la Iglesia en Veracruz*, 3 volumes, Jalapa: Ediciones de San José, no date (c. 1990)

— *Seminario, trayectoria de un siglo y realidad presente*, Mexico: «Ut Sint Unum» Jalapa Seminary, 1966

— *Seminario, trayectoria y presencia, 1864-1999*, Jalapa: Ediciones San José, 2000

Barrajón Muñoz, Pedro, *Monseñor Rafael Guízar Valencia amigo de los pobres*, Mexico: Diana, 1995

Bru Alonso, Manuel María, *Testigos del Espíritu. Los nuevos líderes católicos: movimientos y comunidades*, Madrid: EDIBESA, 1998

de la Mora, Justino, *Apuntes biográficos del Beato Mons. Rafael Guízar Valencia*, Jalapa: Editorial Mons. Rafael Guízar y Valencia, 1994 (new edition)

González Fernández, José Antonio, José Francisco Ruiz Massieu y José Luis Soberanes Fernández, *Derecho eclesiástico mexicano*, Mexico: UNAM - American University of Acapulco - Porrúa, 1992

Greene, Graham, *The Lawless Roads*, Bodley Head, 1978

Gutiérrez Casillas, José, *Historia de la Iglesia en* Mexico, Mexico: Porrúa, 1974

John Paul II, Apostolic Letter, *Novo Millennio Ineunte* "At the Beginning of a new Millennium", Vatican: Holy See, 6 January 2001

— Discourse to movements and new ecclesial communities, Pentecost Vigil, Vatican: St. Peter's Square, 30 May 1998

— Homily: Pentecost Sunday, Vatican: St. Peter's Square, 31 May 1998

López Beltrán, Lauro, *Diócesis y Obispos de Cuernavaca, 1875-1978*, Mexico: Jus, 1978

— *La persecución religiosa en Mexico*, Mexico: Tradición, 1987

Macías, José, *Montezuma en sus exalumnos. 1937-1962. Bodas de plata*, Mexico: - 1962

Medina Ascensio, Luis, *Historia del Seminario de Montezuma. Sus precedentes, fundación y consolidación, 1910-1953*, Mexico: Jus, 1962

— (compiled by), *Montezuma Íntimo. Su escenario. Su gente. Su vida*, Mexico: Jus, 1962

Meyer, Jean, *La Cristiada*, 3 volumes, Mexico: Siglo XXI, 1973

— *La Cristiada*, (fotográfico), Mexico: Clío, 1997

— *La persecución religiosa en* Mexico, in "Ecclesia, Revista de cultura católica" XIV (2000) 2/3, Mérida-Rome: Mayab University, 2000

Moreno García, Heriberto, *Cotija* (Township Monographs of the State of Michoacán), Morelia: Government of Michoacán State, 1980

Paul VI, Encyclical Letter *Ecclesiam suam,* Vatican: Holy See, 6 August 1964

— Encyclical Letter *Humanae Vitae,* Vatican: Holy See, 25 July 1968

Peñalosa, Joaquín Antonio, *Rafael Guízar, a sus órdenes,* Jalapa, Veracruz: Editorial Mons. Rafael Guízar y Valencia, 1992 (new edition)

Poblett Miranda, Martha, (compiled by), *Cien viajeros en Veracruz. Crónicas y relatos*, IX. *1928-1983*, Veracruz: Government of the State of Veracruz, 1992

Pontifical Gregorian University, *Catalogus Professorum et Alumnorum Pontificia Universitas Gregoriana*, Rome: PUG -

— *Solemnis Premiorum Distributio in Pontificia Universitate Gregoriana*, Rome: PUG -

Rius Facius, Antonio, *Méjico cristero*, 2 volumes, Mexico: Asociación Pro-Cultura Occidental, 2002 (new edition)

Romero Vargas, José, *Cotija, cuna de trotamundos* (volume 1), Mexico: Progreso, 1973

— *Cotija, durante las revoluciones* (volume 2), Mexico: B. Costa – Amic Editor, 1978

Williman, John Baker, *La Iglesia y el Estado en Veracruz, 1840-1940,* Mexico: SepSetentas, 1976